project management techniques

– college edition –

This book explains the techniques used by the Project Management Software, PMBOK, APM bok, and the SAQA unit standards

email: rory@burkepublishing.com
web site: www.burkepublishing.com

Rory Burke

Project Management Techniques (college edition)

Rory Burke

ISBN-13: 978-0-9582-7334-3

ISBN-10: 0-9582 733-4-0

First published: 2007
Reprinted: 2007

Copyright ©:   Burke Publishing
                    Email: rory@burkepublishing.com
                    Website: www.burkepublishing.com (Instructor's Manual)

Distributors: UK: Marston Book Services, email: enquiries@marston.co.uk

                    USA: Partners Book Distributing, email: partnersbk@aol.com

                    South Africa: Blue Weaver Marketing, email: orders@blueweaver.co.za

                    Australia: Thames and Hudson, email: orders@thaust.com.au

                    Hong Kong: Publishers Associates (PAL): pal@netvigator.com

DTP: Sandra Burke
Cover Design: Simon Larkin
Sketches: Buddy Mendis, Michael Glasswell
Printer: Everbest, HK / China

Production notes: Page size (168 x 244 mm), Body Text (Minion Pro, 11 pt), Chapter Headings (Helvetica, bold, 60 pt), Subheadings (Helvetica, bold, 11 pt), Software InDesign, Photoshop, Illustrator, CorelDRAW, PC and Mac notebook computers.

ISBN-13: 978-0-9582-7334-3
ISBN-10: 0-9582 733-4-0

Dedicated ....to Linda, Dominique and Simon.... thank you for the experience with **'High Anxiety Safaris'**!

Content

Cosmic MBA Series

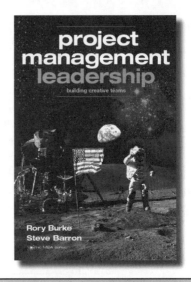

Introduction to Project Management	Project Management Leadership
ISBN 0-9582 733-3-2	ISBN 0-9582 733-5-9
Project Management BOK	Leadership Styles
Project Lifecycle	Team Creation
Feasibility Study	Team Development Phases
Scope Management	Team Dynamics
Estimating Techniques	Delegation
Risk Management	Problem Solving
CPM	Decision Making
Procurement Management	Creativity and Innovation
Resource Management	Negotiation
Project Control	Conflict Resolution
Communication / Meetings	Communication Theory
OBS / Matrix	Team Meetings
Project Management Office	OBS/Matrix
Event Management	Outdoor Team building

Cosmic MBA Series

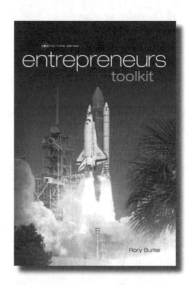

Project Management Entrepreneur
ISBN 0-9582 733-2-4

Entrepreneurs Toolkit
ISBN 0-9582 391-4-2

Levels of Entrepreneurship
Entrepreneur BOK
Small Business Management Skills
Product Lifecycle
Creating a New Venture
PM Entrepreneur Traits
Problem Solving
Risk Management
Networking
Business Plan
Gantt Charts
Procurement Management
Resource Management
Quality Control Plan
Project Teams

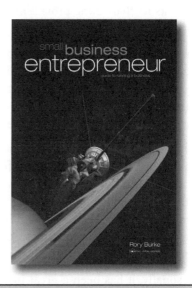

Small Business Entrepreneur
ISBN 0-9582 391-6-9

Foreword

Over the past few years Project Management education has become one of the most popular professional development programmes. This is a reflection of the need and value for these project management skills in the modern business environment.

When SAQA, the Services SETA, the Project Management Standard Generating Body (SGB), and the Project Management Institute worked together to register the Further Education and Training Certificate: Project Management (NQF 4, SAQA ID 50080) and the set of unit standards leading towards this qualification, they utilized locally and internationally recognized best practice and standards in project management. This qualification provides an entry point to further learning for NQF level 5 and above qualifications as well as a international qualification in Project or General Management.

New courses obviously meant new academic material, and during the tender process it was clear that the author destined to write the project management material was Rory Burke. Rory has designed this book to incorporate these SAQA unit standards (120373, 120375, 120383, 120374, 120377, 120379) and also to respond to market requests to change the project management syllabus to ensure that it is appropriate for the further education market.

This book is ideal to support the project management courses that are helping to fill the gap of project management skills so desperately needed in developing economies. Almost everything we do can be managed as a project, and governments are supporting this approach by also repacking their work as projects. Project management is definitely the management skill of the future.

It has been a journey full of 'lessons learnt' for all. Rory learnt our National Unit Standards by heart and I, learnt that authors can write excellent material in a short space of time, anywhere in the world! Project management application is about learning the tools and techniques for project management, and applying it to all project undertakings – such as a big and life changing project like sailing from 'Greenwich to the Dateline', medium and focus changing projects like curriculum development or small, but spiritually enhancing projects, such as planning that special occasion.

Personally, it has been a great privilege and honour to work with Rory during the development of this book, and I hope that each learner will understand and share his passion and dedication for Project Management.

Annemie Willemse
BA Hons, Information Science

Foreword

I must say I was rather chuffed when Rory asked me to write the foreword for his book - then I had second thoughts. I realised that as Rory is my cousin he could get me much cheaper than Bush, Blair, or even Charlize Theron. Also I am a broadcaster by profession - speech comes easily, but writing is a chore to me. The odds were moving towards a sneaky opt-out on my part when I was struck by a remarkable coincidence - now you'll have to pay attention to this.

Rory's father was my first cousin on my mother's side. My father had a first cousin called James who also wrote books - so here I am - the exact fulcrum in the balance between **James Joyce** and Rory Burke. Such a unique literary position is not granted to many!

Now there are of course differences between the two authors. Rory's work for instance has never been banned. Perhaps if he were to adopt a racier style this accolade might come his way. On a scale of incomprehensibility I would rate Rory's work somewhere between Ulysses and Finnegan's Wake, but then Project Management is a subject in which I am blissfully innocent. I saw the film of Ulysses before I took up the book and will look forward to seeing the video version of Rory's book - and if there is a part in it for Arnold Schwarzenegger as Project Manager so much the better.

Even though I have not read this book I must strongly urge you to buy a copy. You see Rory has promised to buy me dinner at the Royal Irish Yacht Club the next time he sails into Dun Laoghaire, but only when the first 250,000 copies are sold - and I'm getting hungry.

Val Joyce

Blackrock, Dublin

Author's Note

There is a silent revolution happening in the field of project management education - up to now all the project management courses have been loosely structured around the PMBOK. But now SAQA have introduced a number of unit standards which have given project management its first academic foot hold.

Project Management Techniques – college edition, has been written as a project management tools and techniques book which focuses on the tools and techniques used by the PMBOK, the APM bok, the competency standards, the unit standards and the planning software.

These standards are ideal for learners who may be involved in technical projects, business projects or developmental projects which cut across a range of economic sectors. These standards will also add value to learners who are running their own business and recognise that project management forms an integral component of their business.

The project management software has revolutionized how information is processed, communicated and stored. Common data bases have integrated departmental information, and the software has greatly increased the planning and control processing power. This book will explain with theory and examples how the software calculates and crunches the numbers. The limiting element with project management computing is not the software or hardware, but how the tools and techniques are applied.

As the use of projects becomes more pervasive, so more managers are entering the field of project management. Their success will be helped by their ability to develop and apply a comprehensive toolkit of planning and control techniques - as a mechanic works with a bag of tools, so the project manager works with a computer producing organisation charts, work breakdown structures, Gantt charts, resource histograms and cashflow statements.

This book is structured inline with the PMBOK's nine knowledge areas, the APM bok, the Australian competency standards, and the SAQA unit standards for project management (numbers 120373, 120375, 120383, 120374, 120377, 120379). The text also explains the planning and control techniques used by the project management software. These standards form the corner stones of project management and will help you ringfence what you need to know. An Instructor's Manual is available for lecturers and can be downloaded from **www.burkepublishing.com**.

After completing another around the world lecturing tour of universities, I was asked to put back some of the project management techniques I had taken out in a previous edition. So I am pleased to say worked examples for PERT, line of balance and crashing are back in the text.

I wish to thank Ken Irwin, Peiter Steyn, Bruce Rodrigues, Mark Massyn and Steve Barron for discussing the finer aspects of project management. I also wish to thank Beryl Liebetrau, Jan Hamon and Ollie Logan for proofing reading, Sandra Burke for setting up the book, and Annemie Willemse and Val Joyce for writing inspirational forewords.

Rory Burke

Director of Burke Publishing
(Cape Town, Oxford, Chicago, Melbourne, Hong Kong)

Interview at the BBC

1

Introduction to Project Management

Learning Outcomes

After reading this chapter, you should be able to;

Understand the definition of a project and the definition of project management

Explain the process of management-by-projects

Outline the project management standards

Project management offers a structured approach to managing projects. The purpose of this book is to outline the latest planning and control techniques used by industry, commerce, sport and domestic projects. It also covers the techniques referred to in the body of knowledge (**APM** and **PMBOK**), and particularly the techniques used by the **project planning software.**

As the use of projects becomes more pervasive so more managers are entering the field of project management. Their success will be helped by their ability to develop a fully integrated information and control system to plan, instruct, monitor and control large amounts of data, quickly and accurately to facilitate the problem-solving and decision-making process. To achieve these goals the project manager needs a comprehensive **toolkit** - just as a plumber works with a bag of tools, so the project manager works with a computer producing organisation charts, work breakdown structures, barcharts, resource histograms and cashflow statements.

1. What is a Project?

The PMBOK defines a project as: '.... *a temporary endeavour undertaken to create a unique product or service. Temporary means that every project has a definite end. Unique means that the product or service is different in some distinguishing way from all similar products or services.*'

Traditionally work in the construction industry and defence procurement were seen as projects, but in recent years most proactive companies are structuring their work as projects (management-by-projects) and using project management techniques to ensure successful completion.

Projects range in size, scope, cost and time from mega international projects costing millions of dollars over many years - to small domestic projects with a low budget taking just a few hours to complete. Consider the following projects:

- Career development (education and training courses).
- Designing and constructing a building, a house or a yacht.
- Designing and testing a new prototype (a car or a washing machine).
- The launch of a new product (advertising and marketing project).
- Implementing a new computer system (IT project, or upgrade).
- Designing and implementing a new organisational structure (HR project).
- Planning and conducting an audit (quality management project).
- Disaster recovery (limiting the damage of fires, floods etc.).
- Olympics, or Springboks' tour of New Zealand (a sports project).
- Rolling Stones' world tour (an entertainment project).
- Moving house or going on holiday (a domestic project).

Other distinctive features of a project include:

- A **start and finish** (sometimes difficult to define - the start may have crystallised over a period of time and the end may be a slow phase out).
- A **lifecycle** (a beginning and an end, with a number of distinct phases in between).
- A **budget** with an associated cashflow.
- Activities that are essentially unique and **non-repetitive**.
- Use of **resources** from different departments which need co-ordinating.
- A **single point of responsibility** (i.e. the project manager).
- **Fast tracking** - getting your product to market before your competitors.
- **Team roles** and relationships that are subject to change and need to be developed, defined and established (team building).

Within the context of this book a project may be defined as a beneficial change which uses the special project management techniques to plan and control the scope of work in order to deliver a product to satisfy the client's and stakeholders' needs and expectations.

2. Project Management

Project management is defined by the PMBOK as: '..... *the application of knowledge, skills, tools and techniques to project activities in order to meet stakeholder's needs and expectations from a project.'* In other words the project manager must do whatever is required to **make the project happen** - one could not have a wider all encompassing job description!

This definition clearly identifies that the purpose of the project is to meet the stakeholders needs and expectations. It is, therefore, a fundamental requirement for the project manager to establish who are the stakeholders (besides the client) and analyse their needs and expectations to define, at the outset, the purpose of the project, its scope of work and objectives (this will be developed in the *Feasibility Study* chapter).

The discipline of project management can be described in terms of its component processes, conveniently defined by the PMBOK as nine knowledge areas:

- Scope
- Time
- Cost
- Quality
- HRM
- Communication
- Risk
- Procurement
- Integration

A brief description of the nine knowledge areas are discussed later in this chapter.

The APM bok defines project management as '...*the most efficient way of introducing change .... achieved by:*

- *Defining what has to be accomplished, generally in terms of time, cost, and various technical and quality performance parameters;*
- *Developing a plan to achieve these and then working this plan, ensuring that progress is maintained in line with these objectives;*
- *Using appropriate project management techniques and tools to plan, monitor and maintain progress;*
- *Employing persons skilled in project management - including normally a project manager - who are given* [single] *responsibility for introducing the change and are accountable for its successful accomplishment.'*

Companies performing projects will generally subdivide their projects into several phases or stages to provide better management control. Collectively these project phases are called the project lifecycle. Along with the project lifecycle some of the other special project management techniques that form part of the project management integrative process are:

- Work breakdown structure (WBS)
- Critical path method (CPM)
- Resource smoothing
- Earned value
- Configuration control.

3. Management-by-Projects

Many organisations are changing in nature as more of them are accomplishing their business through projects. This management-by-projects approach has been used in engineering, construction, aerospace and defence for many years, and now we see other organisations buying into the process; pharmaceutical, medical, telecommunications, software development, systems development, energy, manufacturing, educational and service organisations. The management-by-projects approach encourages:

- organisation flexibility
- decentralised management responsibility
- holistic view of problems
- goal-orientated problem solution processes.

Time Magazine identifies these profound changes happening in the job market. *'Full-time, full-year workers are no longer as dominant as they were. There is more self-employment, more part-time employment and the beginnings of what might be called task employment.'* I would call this project employment. Therefore, for employer and employee to make the most of the new employment patterns a working understanding of *management-by-projects* and project team dynamics is essential.

Oracle: *'The business world is moving increasingly towards projects orientation operation to measure the true costs and perfectibility of any business endeavour.'* It is very difficult, if not impossible, to quantify costs if they are grouped together and shared - the only way would be a sharing percentage.

Programme Management: Where the project management office (PMO) is managing a large capital project (e.g. new Airbus), it may be subdivided into a number of smaller related projects to achieve a single common goal, for example, the body, the wings, the engines and the electronics.

Portfolio Management: Defines a project management office (PMO) that is running a number of unrelated projects. For example, this could be managing the repairs and maintenance of a large telecom type company, a power station or a water utility.

Small Projects: Managing small projects has its own unique problems. Although small projects may appear to be simple, they are often associated with a lack of definition (no drawings, no specifications and no contract), instructions are given verbally, and minimum standards are not established. There are no arbitration mechanisms, no exit strategies, and as small projects often have a short duration this does not allow time to establish a management system.

General Management: Although this book is about project management, the successful project manager must also be competent in a wide range of general management skills in addition to the nine knowledge areas. These would include:

- recruiting and personnel
- economics
- computer systems
- legal contracts
- personnel and human resources
- sales and marketing
- accounting and salaries.

The project manager would obviously not be expected to be an expert in all these fields, but for a project to be successful all these topics may need to be addressed at one time or another. And, as the single point of responsibility, the project manager will be responsible for either performing the work, or delegating it (see figure 1.1).

Production Management: Although projects are deemed to be unique, in reality they usually consist of groups of repetitive tasks. Henry Ford emphatically showed years ago that production lines are the quickest, and most cost effective way to manufacture thousands of cars. The same rule applies to projects, if there are repetitive tasks, then setting up a production line to carry them out would be more efficient and cost effective.

Technical Management: The technical aspects of the project also need to be managed. On smaller projects the project manager may be expected to be the technical expert as well as the manager. In fact, early on in ones career a young person will probably only be appointed as project manager if they are a technical expert.

There is usually a certain amount of skills overlap between project management, general management and technical management. This can be simply presented as intersecting circles (figure 1.1).

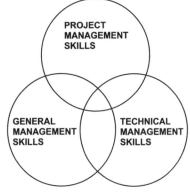

Figure 1.1: Intersecting Management Skills - shows the overlap between the different management skills

Project Management Environment: The project environment directly impacts the project and how it should be managed. Projects are not carried out in a vacuum, they are influenced by a wide range of stakeholders and issues. Consider the following:

- Stakeholders (all interested parties)
- Client / sponsor's requirements
- A company's organisation structure
- Market requirements
- Competitors
- New technology
- Rules and regulations (Health and Safety)
- Politics (both internal and external)
- Cultural, social and religious backgrounds
- Economic cycle.

The project environment consists of the numerous stakeholders and players that have an input or are impacted by the project. All must be managed as any one person could derail the project (see stakeholder analysis in the *Feasibility Study* chapter). For project managers to be effective they must have a thorough understanding of the project environment which may well be changing and the goal posts continually shifting.

4. Project Management Software

Today, powerful but inexpensive project management software is readily available for the personal computer. This has essentially moved project management computing away from the data processing department to the project manager's desk. This represents a major shift in the management of information.

Whilst project planning software will certainly help the project manager plan and control their projects, its application will only be effective if the planning and control techniques are clearly understood. The purpose of this text is, therefore, to develop these techniques through manual exercises, but with the assumption that computer systems will be used later.

ONE COMPUTER

MANY DISCIPLINES

5. Project Management Associations

A number of project management associations and institutions have formed chapters around the world to encourage the development of project management as a profession. These project management chapters organise regular meetings and newsletters to keep their members informed about project management issues, such as:

- Body of knowledge
- Certification of project managers (PMP)
- Unit standards
- Ethics
- Global forum.

Body of Knowledge: Over the past fifty years a considerable body of knowledge has built up around project management tools, skills and techniques. This database of information has been developed into the following:

- The APM's bok - Association of Project Managers (UK)
- The PMI's PMBOK - Project Management Institute (USA)
- The IPMA's BOK - International Association of Project Managers (formerly called INTERNET)
- The AIPM's Competency Standards for Project Management (Australia)
- ISO 10006 *'Guideline to Quality in Project Management'* - to assist clients evaluating the effectiveness of the project management system
- South African unit standards.

The purpose of a body of knowledge is to identify and describe best practices that are applicable to most projects most of the time, and for which there is widespread consensus about their value and usefulness of the best practices. The body of knowledge is also intended to provide a common lexicon and terminology within the profession of project management - locally and internationally. As a relatively young international profession there is still a need to converge on a common set of terms. The PMBOK describes project management under the following nine knowledge areas:

- **Project Scope Management:** Is the processes required to ensure that the project includes all the work required, and only the work required, to complete the project successfully. It is primarily concerned with defining and controlling what is or is not included in the project, to meet the clients's and stakeholders' goals and objectives. It consists of authorisation, scope planning, scope definition, scope change management and scope verification.
- **Project Time Management:** Includes the process required to ensure timely performance of the project. It consists of activity definition, activity sequencing, duration estimating, schedule development and time control.

- **Project Cost Management:** Includes the process required to ensure that the project is completed within the approved budget. It consists of resource planning, cost estimating, cost budgeting, cashflow and cost control.
- **Project Quality Management:** Includes the process required to ensure that the project will satisfy the needs for which it was undertaken. It consists of determining the required condition, quality planning, assurance and control.
- **Project Human Resource Management:** Includes the process required to make the most effective use of the people involved with the project. It consists of organisation planning, staff acquisition and team development.
- **Project Communications Management:** Includes the process required to ensure proper collection and dissemination of project information. It consists of communication planning, information distribution, project meetings, progress reporting and administrative closure.
- **Project Risk Management:** Includes the process concerned with identifying, quantifying, and responding to project risk. It consists of controlling the risk management plan and being prepared for disaster recovery.
- **Project Procurement Management:** Includes the process required to acquire goods and services from outside the company. It consists of procurement planning, solicitation, source selection, contract administration and contract closeout.
- **Project Integration:** Integrates the three main project management processes of planning, execution and control - where inputs from several knowledge areas are brought together.

The body of knowledge can be subdivided into four core elements which determine the **deliverable** objectives of the project:

- Scope
- Time
- Cost
- Quality

The other knowledge areas provide the **means of achieving** the deliverable objectives, namely:

- Integration
- Human resources
- Communication
- Risk
- Procurement and contract.

APM bok: The APM bok takes a much broader approach than the PMBOK, by subdividing project management into 55 knowledge areas. It incorporates not only inward focused project management topics (such as planning and control techniques), but also broader topics in which the project is being managed (such as social and ecological environment), as well as specific areas (such as technology, economics, finance, organisation, procurement and people, as well as general management). The topics are described at an outline level, leaving the details to recommended texts (on their book list) to explain the working of the knowledge areas (see www.apm.org.uk).

Certification of Project Managers (PMP): The certification process offers a means for experienced project managers to gain a formal qualification in project management. There is a trend away from the knowledge based examinations which assess a person's knowledge, towards competence based examinations which assess a person's ability to perform. The PMI's certification is called the Project Management Professional (PMP). There is an increasing recognition of certification and for some projects it is being made a mandatory pre-qualification.

Competency is a mixture of explicit knowledge derived from formal education, tacit (implied) knowledge and skills derived from experience. For young professionals, explicit knowledge is more important, but the other competencies will become increasingly important as they progress in their careers. The PMI's (PMP) is a single level certificate programme, which measures explicit knowledge directly through a multi-choice test, and tacit knowledge and skill indirectly by assessing the candidate's work experience. It is therefore aimed at an early to mid-career professional.

The IPMA and AIPM (Australia), on the other hand, have developed a multi-stage programme. At the first stage explicit knowledge is measured directly through a multi-question test. This is aimed at the professional managers starting their careers. At the second stage tacit (implied) knowledge and skill are measured directly. This is early to mid stage certification, equivalent to PMP. At the third stage, the programme measures performance of senior project managers directly. And IPMA has a fourth stage to measure the performance of project directors.

Global Project Management Forum: Some of the key topics discussed at the global project management forum included:

- What industries or types of projects are the main users of modern project management in your country?
- What industries or areas of application in your country have the greatest need for more or better project management?
- What industries or organisations offer the greatest opportunities for growth of professional project management in your country?

The answers to these and other questions relating to standards, certification, a global PMBOK and advancing the project management profession see the PMI's publication, *The Global Status of the Project Management Profession*.

6. Benefits of Project Management

The benefits of using a project management approach, obviously follows on from addressing the needs of the project. The project manager is responsible for developing a plan through which the project can be tracked and controlled to ensure the project meets preset objectives. To do this effectively the project manager requires accurate and timely information. This information should be supplied by the planning and control system, which outlines the scope of work and measures performance against the original plan.

Although the planning and control systems will incur additional management costs (project team), it should be appreciated that lack of information could be even more expensive if it leads to poor management decisions, mistakes, rework and overrun. Listed below are some of the main benefits associated with a fully integrated project planning and control system:

- **Client:** The project manager is the project's *single point of responsibility* and the company's representative to the client (and other stakeholders). During meetings with the client the planning and control system will provide information about every aspect of the project.

- **Single Point of Responsibility:** With the project manager responsible for the complete project, this should limit scope overlap and scope underlap.

- **Estimating:** The estimate forms the basis of the project plan. If you cannot estimate and measure it, how can you manage it?

- **CPM:** The critical path method calculates all the activities start dates, finish dates and floats. Activities with zero float form the critical path which determines the duration of the project - delaying a critical activity will delay the project.

- **Fast Track:** Brings a new product to the market quickly before the competitors.

- **Schedule Gantt Chart:** Communicates the what, where, when and who.

- **Project Integration:** Co-ordinates and integrates the contribution of all the project participants.

- **Reporting Interfaces:** The planning and control system's database can be structured around the work breakdown structure (WBS) for project reporting and around the organisation breakdown structure (OBS) for corporate reporting. Without an integrated system the two reporting requirements would have to be processed separately.

- **Response Time:** Timely response on project performance is essential for effective project control. The project planning and control system can adjust the content and frequency of the feedback to address the needs of the project, while the corporate systems may be less flexible.

- **Trends:** Projects are best controlled by monitoring the progress trends of time, cost and performance. This information may not be available to the project manager if the trend parameters are derived from a number of different functional sources and not communicated.

- **Procedures:** The planning and control system enables the project manager to develop procedures and work instructions which are tailored to the specific needs of the project.

- **Project Management Office (PMO):** Offers a centre for project management excellence.

Although there are many benefits from using project management techniques, senior management should tread carefully if the project management culture is not already established within the company, as a resistance to change could derail the project.

7. Role of the Project Manager

It is appropriate to conclude this chapter with a few words on the role of the project manager. Experience has shown that the selection of the project manager is a key appointment which can influence the success or failure of the project. As the *single point of responsibility*, it is the project manager who integrates and co-ordinates all the contributions, and guides them to successfully complete the project.

The role of the project manager should be outlined in the **project charter** (see *Scope Management* chapter) along with the purpose of the project. The successful project manager should be able to:

- Select and develop an operational team from a standing start
- Lead the project team and manage information
- Anticipate problems, solve problems and make decisions
- Integrate and network with project stakeholders
- Be operationally flexible and be able to spot entrepreneurial opportunities
- Plan, expedite and get things done
- Gain power through negotiation and persuasion
- Understand the environment within which the project is being managed
- Review, monitor, assess performance and apply control
- Administer the contract, the scope of work and scope changes
- Manage within an environment of constant change
- Create a positive working environment
- Keep the client happy.

We are witnessing a silent revolution - the transition from conventional functional management to project management. I hope you are on-board!

Case Study and Exercises:

You have been appointed by the CEO of an international telecommunications company to make a short presentation to the board of directors about the benefit of using a *management-by-projects* approach on the company's next project. Your short presentation (written and/or verbal) should consider the following:

1. Explain what project management is, and why it is different to other forms of management.
2. Explain how project management can be applied to your company's projects.
3. Point out the trend towards professional project management and your local project management society / association who are supporting certification.
4. Outline the role of the project manager.
5. Suggest a small pilot project on which you can develop your project management systems.

"...I've got all the tools now where's the project?..."

2

History
of Project
Management

The history of project management is often associated with the construction of the massive Egyptian Pyramids and the Great Wall of China. They were certainly large complex structures, built to high standards, that have stood the test of time and must have required an enormous workforce. But with no documented evidence the management techniques used can only be based on conjecture. Although archeologists are starting to suggest that the construction of the pyramids were the largest fill-in job the world has ever seen - when the River Nile flooded annually the workforce would move off the land to work on the pyramids. They were not slaves as Hollywood suggests, but willing workers who were probably paid. And when the annual floods subsided they would return to their farms.

Modern day project management is associated with Henry Gantt's development of the barchart (early 1900s), and project management techniques which were specifically developed for the military and aerospace projects of the 1950s and 1960s in America and Britain. It is these special distinctive project management tools and techniques which are referred to in the body of knowledge, used by the planning software and developed in this book.

Today, rapidly changing technology, fierce competitive markets and a powerful environmental lobby have all encouraged companies to change their management systems - in this sink or swim, adopt or die environment, project management and management-by-projects are offering a real solution.

1. Gantt Chart - 1900s

The history of the barchart can be traced back to World War 1 when an American, **Henry Gantt** (1861 - 1919), designed the barchart as a visual aid for planning and controlling his shipbuilding projects. In recognition, planning barcharts are often called after his name - **Gantt charts**. The Handbook of Industrial Engineers (1982, p.11) acknowledges the Gantt chart for significantly reducing the time to build cargo ships during World War 1.

Figure 2.1 indicates the format of a Gantt chart, where the top line is a calendar time-scale in days [1] and the activities [2] are listed on the left hand column. The scheduling of each activity is represented by a horizontal line [3], from the activity's start to finish date. The length of the activity line is therefore, proportional to its estimated duration.

Gantt further used this barchart to track progress by drawing a second line alongside the planned schedule to indicate work done [4]. The relative position of the progress line to the planned line indicates percentage complete and remaining duration, while the relative position between the progress line and Timenow [5] indicates actual progress against planned progress.

Figure 2.1: Gantt Chart - shows the key features of the Gantt chart

The Gantt chart has stood the test of time and is widely acknowledged today as the most effective method of communicating planning information - people find them easy to use and understand. A survey by Microsoft Project users found that 80% of managers preferred the Gantt chart to the network diagram for planning and controlling their projects.

Henri Fayol: In 1916 Fayol, a French industrialist, presented a management process that consisted of:

- Planning (forecasting)
- Organising (staffing)
- Commanding (motivation)
- Directing (co-ordinating)
- Controlling (monitoring).

Fayol's principles are fundamentally universal and apply to all types of management, whether ongoing or project, and if you add initiation and closing, then you have the key components of the planning and control cycle developed in chapter 7.

2. Project Management 1950s and 1960s

Nearly all of the special project management techniques we use today were developed during the 1950s and 1960s by the US defence-aerospace industry (DoD and NASA) - this includes program evaluation and review technique (PERT), earned value (EV), configuration management, value engineering and work breakdown structures (WBS). The construction industry also made its contribution to the development of the critical path method (CPM) using network diagrams and resource smoothing - the motivation for CPM was scheduling urgency and engineering management. During this period large scale projects were effectively shielded from the environment, society, and ecology issues. The Apollo space programme and the construction of nuclear power stations typified projects of this period. Some of the key achievements during this period are chronologically listed below:

1950s - Development of PERT and CPM.

1950s - Development of the concept of a **single point of responsibility** for multi-disciplined projects - one person is responsible for completing the project.

1960 - NASA experiments with **matrix** organisation structures.

1962 - NASA introduces a PERT type system that emphasised the need for cost control and the WBS.

1963 - Earned value adopted by the USAF.

1963 - Project lifecycle adopted by the USAF.

1963 - Polaris was the first British project on which the sub-contractors were required contractually to use advanced project management systems.

1964 - Configuration management adopted by NASA to review and document proposed changes.

1965 - DoD and NASA move from cost-plus contracts towards incentive type contracts such as firm fixed price or cost plus incentive fee.

1965 - The mid 1960s saw a dramatic rise in the number of projects in the construction industry that used modern project management techniques.

1965 - The TSR-2 (swing-wing bomber) highlighted the problems of **concurrency**, i.e. starting the development and production before the design was stable. Increasing the scope of work led to cost overrun and delays - eventually the project was scrapped.

1966 - A report in 1966 stated that not enough time was spent on front-end definition and preparation (of the project lifecycle); there were wide variations in standards of cost and schedule control; and inadequate control over design changes.

1967 - International Project Management Association (IPMA) founded (formerly called INTERNET). Grouping of over 20 international associations.

1969 - Project Management Institute (PMI) formed, certification and the PMBOK (1987, 1996, 2000) were to follow.

3. Network Diagrams

For a project plan to be effective it must equally address the parameters of activity time and activity logic. This logical relationship is required to model the impact schedule variance will have downstream in the project. As projects became larger and more complex, the Gantt chart was found to be lacking as a planning and control tool because it could not indicate the logical relationships between activities. Although the linked Gantt chart does show logical relationships, it soon becomes cluttered as the number of activities and logical relationships increase.

In the 1950s feedback from industry and commerce indicated that project cost and time overruns were all too common. It was suggested at the time that the project estimates were on the optimistic side in order to gain work, however a more important reason emerged which indicated that the planning and control techniques available to manage large complex projects were inadequate. This encouraged the development of scheduling methods which integrated project procurement, resources and costs.

With these shortcomings in mind, network planning techniques were developed by Flagle, the US Navy and Remington Rand Univac. Flagle wrote a paper in 1956 on *'Probability based tolerances in forecasting and planning'*. Although it was not published in the Journal of Industrial Engineers until April 1961, it was in a sense the forerunner of the US Navy's program evaluation and review technique (PERT). Both PERT and Remington Rand Univac's critical path method (CPM) used a similar network format, where the activities were presented in boxes and the sequence of the activities from left to right showed the logic of the project (see figure 2.2).

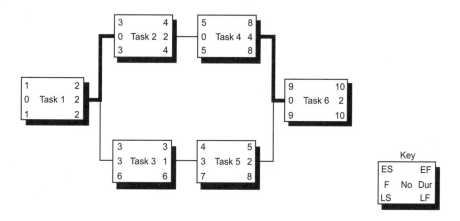

Figure 2.2: Network Diagram (showing logical relationships)

Network diagrams were also being developed in other countries. In France Professor Roy developed *Graphes et Ordonnacements* (networks and schedules). In Russia a technique which translates to 'Lattice Planning' was developed, and in the UK the CEGB developed a CPM system for a maintenance overhaul at Keadby Power Station.

4. Critical Path Method (CPM)

The main difference between CPM and PERT is how they addressed activity time duration. The accuracy of an activity's time estimate usually depends on the information available from previous projects. If an activity has been performed before, its duration can be reasonably accurately estimated. However, activities with a new scope of work, which are difficult to measure or dependent on other uncertain variables, may have a range of possible time duration.

CPM uses a deterministic approach, which suits a project where time duration can be accurately predicted, e.g. a construction project. While PERT on the other hand uses a probabilistic approach, which suits a project where time duration may vary over a range of possibilities, e.g. a research project.

The critical path method (CPM) also called critical path analysis (CPA) was developed around 1957 by Remington Rand Univac as a management tool to improve the planning and control of their turnaround time (production to sales) - the benefits were quickly recognised and they soon paid back their development costs.

CPM was initially setup to address the **time cost trade-off** dilemma (crashing) often presented to project managers, where there is a complex relationship between project *time-to-complete* and *cost-to-complete*. If the duration of the project is shortened, will the project cost more or less? Some time related costs will reduce (plant hire), while others will increase (workers overtime). On large complex projects you need a model like CPM to work out the overall impact of these types of changes.

The initial growth of CPM in the industrial market was slow. This was partially due to the lack of project management education and CPM training offered at the time by the universities and colleges. Also, as with the PERT application, the computer hardware and software facilities were limited compared with the personal computers of today. Further, the systems were not interactive. They required a batch card input through a hands-off data processing department, which often led to an inherently slow response.

5. Program Evaluation and Review Technique (PERT)

In the late 1950s the US Navy set up a development team under Admiral Red Raborn with the Lockheed Aircraft Corporation, and a management consultant Booz Allen & Hamilton - to design PERT as an integrated planning and control system to manage the hundreds of sub-contractors involved in the design, construction and testing of their Polaris Submarine missile system.

PERT was developed to apply a statistical treatment to the possible range of activity time duration. A three time probabilistic model was developed, using pessimistic (p), optimistic (o) and most likely (m) time duration (see figure 2.3). The three time durations were imposed on a normal distribution to calculate the activity's expected time.

T (expected) = (a + 4m + b) / 6

Example:
a = 6 days, m = 8 days, b = 13 days
T (expected) = (6 + [4x8] +13) / 6 = 8.5 days

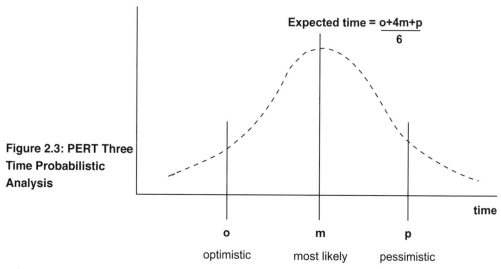

Figure 2.3: PERT Three Time Probabilistic Analysis

Expected time = $\dfrac{o+4m+p}{6}$

time

o   m   p

optimistic   most likely   pessimistic

Exercise:

a = 8 days
m = 12 days
b = 20 days

Solution: See end of chapter

In practice one would estimate the duration around the most likely time. The *optimistic* time would be slightly shorter, if everything went better than planned. While the *pessimistic* time would be extended if everything went worse than planned (late delivery, or a machine breakdown).

The success of the Polaris Submarine project helped to establish PERT in the 1960s as a planning tool within many large corporations. At the time PERT was believed to be the main reason the submarine project was so successful, meanwhile CPM was not receiving anywhere near as much recognition even though it also offered a resource allocation facility.

There were, however a number of basic problems which reduced PERT's effectiveness and eventually led to its fall from popularity. Besides the computer limitations previously mentioned, statistical analysis was not generally understood by project managers - they must have been pleased to see the end of standard deviations and confidence limits.

Other features of PERT, however, are seeing a renaissance as the benefits of **milestone** planning is becoming more widely used. By defining a series of milestones you can simplify the planning process at your level and make your sub-contractors responsible for achieving their key dates.

Even with the powerful planning software available today there is still a need to empower an increasingly educated workforce. The early differences between CPM and PERT have largely disappeared and it is now common to use the two terms interchangeably as a generic name to include the whole planning and control process.

6. Activity-on-Arrow / Activity-on-Node

Network diagrams were originally developed as both *activity-on-arrow* and *activity-on-node*. The *activity-on-arrow* wrote the activity details on the arrow, while the *activity-on-node* wrote the activity details in the node. *Activity-on-arrow* was initially preferred by engineers in the 1960s, but with the transition from manual calculations to computers so the preference changed to activity-on-node.

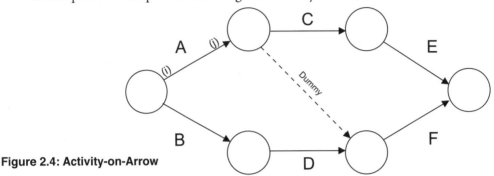

Figure 2.4: Activity-on-Arrow

The benefits of activity-on-arrow (AOA):

- The activity (i, j) identification indicates the preceding and succeeding activities, this is very useful when walking through a large network. However, it does mean that when an activity is inserted its neighbouring activities' numbers will have to change - not so on AON as inserting an activity only changes the logical links.

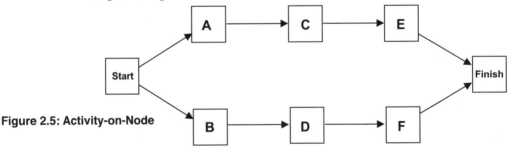

Figure 2.5: Activity-on-Node

The benefits of *activity-on-node*: (AON)

- AON offers a number of logical relationships between the activities, such as *start-to-start*, *finish-to-finish* and *lag*. This overcomes the AOA's need for dummy activities (see Lockyer, 1989).
- The AON also offers a professional presentation, which is generally known today as a *network diagram*.
- AOA uses a dummy activity to clarify the logic, but it is possible to have a double dummy that is illogical.

There are many other management tools that present information in a box; WBS, OBS and *flow charts*. After carrying out the activity calculations, both methods should produce exactly the same result.

7. Project Organisation Structures

Up to the mid 1950s projects tended to be run by companies using the traditional functional hierarchical organisation structure, where the project work would be passed from department to department. There were also examples of pure organisation structures where everyone worked on the same project (e.g. The Manhattan Project). But as projects became more complex (particularly the aerospace and military projects), meeting budgets became more important, delivering the project on time was more crucial and working with many disciplines, departments or companies became a fact of life - so out of necessity '*project focused*' organisation structures started to develop.

In the 1950s Bechtel was one of the first companies to use a project management organisation structure to manage their oil pipeline project in Canada where responsibility was assigned to an individual operating in a remote location with an autonomous team. This is a good example of an organisation structure with the project manager as the **single point of responsibility** with autonomous authority over a pool of resources. The norm during this time (and still is for many companies) would be for the head of department or functional manager to be responsible for the project as it passed through their department. The project approach is to assign responsibility to one person who would work on the project full-time through the project lifecycle from initiation to completion. In due course this person was called the **project manager**.

As the project responsibility shifted from the functional managers to the project managers so the functional departments were increasingly seen as a pool of company resources that could be used on any project. This new organisation structure where the project lines of responsibility and authority overlaid the functional lines of responsibility and authority became known as the matrix organisation structure (see the chapter on *Project Organisation Structures*). This enabled companies to work on many projects at the same time, share resources, address scope overlap and underlap, and most importantly have one person communicating with the client. Matrix organisation structures were soon to become synonymous with project management (see figure 2.6). The matrix structure answers the question - "*If the project manager is not co-ordinating the project who is???*".

Figure 2.6: Matrix Organisation Structure

8. Project Management in the 1970s

The Vietnam war, the OPEC oil embargoes and environmental pressure groups all featured in the 1970s to constrain projects across a wide range of industries and commerce. Environmental matters became a project issue impacting on: pollution (oil spills), nuclear waste, noise pollution (Concorde), and roads (impact on the countryside).

Project management continued to grow and develop into a multi-disciplined profession with its distinctive tools and techniques. High technology companies outside the defence and construction industries were starting to use project management systems effectively enabling them to design to cost.

This was a period of refinement as the problems of using the distinctive tools and techniques became apparent. During this period, public sector projects experienced a high failure rate. This could be attributed in part to poor project definition (scope management), poorly defined project organisation structure (matrix structure), and failure to consider the impact of external factors (stakeholders).

Project management associations in America (PMI) and Britain (APM) were establishing project management as a profession, as project experience was beginning to supersede ideas, project results were starting to reinforce concepts and the distinctive tools and techniques were being refined.

9. Project Management in the 1980s

In the 1980s there was a significant increase in the influence of external stakeholders, the green issue and CND - this put increasing pressure on designers to find acceptable solutions for all the stakeholders.

As project management tools and techniques proliferated in the 1960s, were refined in the 1970s, so they were integrated in the 1980s into accepted practices. The integration of time, cost and quality was initially presented as a triangle of balanced requirements - where a change in one parameter could affect the others (see figure 2.7). This was later joined by scope and the organisation breakdown structure (OBS) to indicate that the scope of work was performed through an organisation structure. There was also an increasing awareness of external issues, so the project environment was included (see figure 2.8).

Figure 2.7: Time, Cost and Quality Triangle (trade-off)

Project Lifecycle: In the 1960s and 1970s project management tools and techniques tended to focus on the **implementation phase** of the project lifecycle (see *Lifecycle* chapter). The implementation phase certainly accounted for the greatest level of effort where the majority

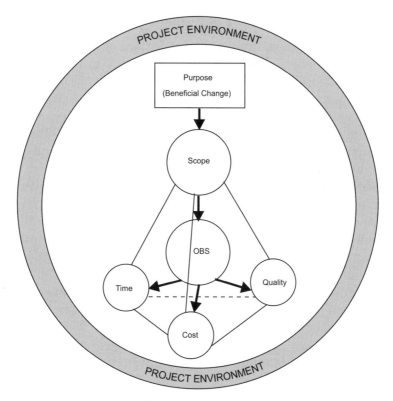

Figure 2.8: Project Environment Model (encourages project managers to look at the bigger picture and consider all the stakeholder's needs)

of the expenses were incurred, but in the 1980s the emphasis was beginning to shift and focus more on the front-end of the project that had the greatest opportunity to add value. This is where the stakeholder's needs were analysed, feasibility studies conducted, risk and uncertainty assessed and the product or facility designed. The front-end approach further emphasised that the cost of making any changes due to design errors or the client changing the scope were becoming increasingly more expensive as the project progressed.

The product lifecycle encouraged the designers to look at the bigger picture and consider the trade-off between construction costs and maintenance costs. They were also encouraged to consider how upgrades, expansions, half-life refits, decommissioning and disposal would be carried out (see *Project Lifecycle* chapter).

The 1980s saw a proliferation of personal computers and an explosion of software, both for business applications in general and project management specifically. The project manager with a computer, which began as the exception, soon became the norm. The pressure was now on for the project manager to become computer literate.

PMBOK: Professionalism was developed through ethics, standards and accreditation, which led to the first project management body of knowledge (PMBOK) in 1987. This offered an integrated and structured approach rather than an ad-hoc collection of tools and techniques.

10. Project Management 1990s and 2000s

In the 1990s fierce competition from the Far East encouraged leaner and meaner, flatter and more flexible organisation structures, together with a more efficient systems approach. Large companies found that by using a *management-by-projects* approach they could assign their work to many small project teams, which were able to quickly respond to innovation, new ideas and market competition and keep the spirit of the small entrepreneurial company alive even in large corporations. The nineties saw increasing deregulation, GATT agreements, reduced tariff barriers and expanding IT facilities communicating through the Internet.

Total quality management (TQM) emerged as a comprehensive project management technique, emphasising the importance of the client, continuous improvement, team work, and management through the project lifecycle. However, the adoption of TQM within project management initially proceeded relatively slowly, but with the introduction of ISO 9000 Quality Management System, TQM gained wider acceptance.

Another development of the 1990s was the **project management office** (PMO) not only to manage projects, but as a centre of excellence to develop a project management culture within the company.

11. History of Project Management Computing

The development of schedule Gantt charts, network diagrams and other distinctive project management tools were originally developed for manual calculation. These tools were gradually computerised during the 1960s and 1970s using mini and mainframe computers, but it was the introduction of the personal computer (PC) that ushered in a dramatic explosion and proliferation of project management software. Some of the key dates to note are:

1977 Launch of Apple 11, the first PC.

1979 Launch of VisiCalc, the first spreadsheet. Lotus and Excel were released a few years later.

1981 Launch of the IBM PC - this established the market standard.

1983 Launch of Harvard Project Manager, the first planning software package.

1990s Launch of Windows, networks, Internet and email

2000s Internet broadband, mobile communication for voice and data. Development of web site facilities; B2B (business-to-business) procurement, and real-time progress reporting.

The introduction of the PC in the late seventies (Apple 11) and the IBM PC (1981) in the early eighties with accompanying business software encouraged the growth of project planning software and the use of project management techniques.

The history of PC based project management computing dates back to 1983 with the launch of the **Harvard Project Manager** a planning software package. Although this may be an isolated event it does reflect the general development of a broad range of management software taking place at the time.

The sequence of dates indicates that project management techniques were developed first, followed by hardware and software. However, the situation has changed in recent years with the computer facilities now leading the development of the management techniques, for example, B2B is changing procurement management. The limiting factor now is project management education and training. This more than any other factor holds the key to successful implementation of the latest project management technology.

This concludes the chapter on the *History of Project Management* - the following chapter will introduce the *Project Lifecycle* which is widely used as a model to visualise the whole project from the cradle to the grave.

Key Points:

- Henry Gantt developed the barchart in the early 1900s.
- Most of the planning and control techniques used today were developed in the 1950s and 1960s on US defence and aerospace projects.
- The personal computer (PC) ushered in a dramatic explosion and proliferation of project management software.

PERT Solution: 12.6 days

Case Study and Exercises:

Project management techniques were originally developed to plan and control large capital military projects, particularly the US military projects in the 50s and 60s. Since then project management has expanded to all sectors of industry and commerce. Give a brief presentation (written or verbal) on:

1. How project management has been introduced into your industry and your company.
2. How project management computer systems have been introduced into your industry and your company.
3. Henry Gantt developed the barchart, and Henri Fayol developed a management process. Discuss how adoptions and improvements on these original systems are used on your projects.
4. The time, cost, quality trade-off clearly shows a relationship between the three parameters. Give examples how these trade-offs apply to your projects.
5. The project environment model encourages us to look at the bigger picture. Give examples of how external stakeholders have influenced your projects.

3

Project Lifecycle

Learning Outcomes

After reading this chapter, you should be able to;

Understand how a project can be subdivided into four phases

Appreciate the importance of front-end design and development

Relate the lifecycle phases to different types of contracts

The project lifecycle and the work breakdown structure (WBS) have come to the forefront in recent years as key frameworks or structures for subdividing the project's scope of work into manageable phases or work packages. Where the WBS is a hierarchical subdivision of the scope of work, the project lifecycle subdivides the scope of work into sequential project phases.

The PMBOK states; '... *because projects are unique and involve a certain degree of risk, companies performing projects will generally subdivide their projects into several project phases to provide better management control. Collectively these project phases are called the project lifecycle.*'

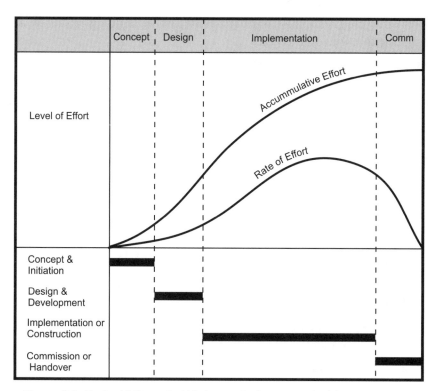

Figure 3.1: Project Lifecycle (this is a typical presentation showing the Gantt chart, project phases, level of effort and rate of expenditure)

1. Project Lifecycle (4 phases)

There is general agreement that most projects pass through a four phase lifecycle under the following headings (see figure 3.1):

- **Concept and Initiation Phase:** The first phase starts the project by establishing a need or opportunity for the product, facility or service. The feasibility of proceeding with the project is investigated, and on acceptance of the proposal, moves to the next phase.

- **Design and Development Phase:** The second phase uses the guidelines set by the feasibility study to design the product, outline the build-method and develop detailed schedules and plans for making or implementing the product.

- **Implementation or Construction Phase:** The third phase implements the project as per the baseline plan developed in the previous phase.

- **Commissioning and Handover Phase:** The forth phase confirms the project has been implemented or built to the design and terminates the project.

Project Lifecycle (example): Consider a simple house building project which passes through the following four phases:

Concept and Initiation Phase: The desire for a new house develops into a need Options and alternatives are considered; the feasibility of the best options are evaluated.

Design and Development Phase: The preferred option is now designed and developed in detail, together with all the associated planning of schedules, procurement, resources and budgets. The land and long lead items may be bought in this phase.

Implementation or Construction Phase: The contracts are let and the house is built to the detailed plans developed in the previous phase. Changes may be made to the original *baseline plan* as problems arise or better information is forthcoming.

Commissioning and Handover Phase: The building is inspected and approved. The house is now ready to be handed over to the owner.

Taking the project lifecycle model a step further, consider some other interesting characteristics:

- The project phases take their name from the **deliverables** of the phase, e.g. initiate, design, construct or handover.
- The sequence of the project phases generally involves some form of technology transfer or handover from one phase to the next phase, such as:
  - Project brief to design and development
  - Detailed design to manufacture
  - Construction to commissioning
  - Commissioning to operation.

This has also been called *over-the-wall* transfer if it is not accompanied with appropriate discussions and explanations.

- The end of a project phase is generally marked by a review of both the deliverables and performance in order to determine if the project should continue into the next phase.
- Each phase can be planned and controlled as a mini project.
- Each phase may be performed by different departments or contractors.
- As the project progresses through the phases, if the goals and objectives change, so the project management process should reflect these changes.

Some other characteristics of the project lifecycle that will be developed in the following sections include:

- Inputs, processes and outputs within each phase.
- Key activities, milestones, hold-points and approvals within each phase.
- Overlaps between phases (fast tracking).
- Plotting level of effort (labour or cashflow) against the project lifecycle.
- Plotting level of influence against the cost of changes (to show front-end importance).
- Project lifecycle costing.

2. Input, Process and Output Format

The project lifecycle subdivides the project into a number of definable project phases or stages and these phases in turn can be further subdivided into an input, process and output format. This is consistent with the body of knowledge's approach to describing the project management process in terms of input, output, tools and techniques (see figure 3.2).

Concept	Design	Implementation	Commission
Input	**Input**	**Input**	**Input**
Project Brief (problem / opportunity) Project Charter (initiation)	Approval	Approval	Certificate of completion
Process	**Process**	**Process**	**Process**
Feasibility Study	WBS, Estimate, Risk Analysis, CPM, Gantt chart, OBS	Award contracts, plan and control, scope change control.	Test, run-up equipment
Key Activities	**Key Activities**	**Key Activities**	**Key Activities**
Identify Stakeholders Cost Benefit Analysis	Model testing Prototype Testing	Plan and control	Quality testing
Hold Points	**Hold Points**	**Hold Points**	**Hold Points**
Market Research Approval	Design approval	Required by client Required by QC	Client witness
Output	**Output**	**Output**	**Output**
Project Proposal (solution)	Baseline plan	Certificate of completion	Closeout report
Decision	**Decision**	**Decision**	**Decision**
Proceed Yes or No	Proceed Yes or No	Ready to handover for commissioning	Project accepted. Handover for operation

Figure 3.2: Project Lifecycle Components (for a typical project, using this as a standard proforma relate the components to one of your projects)

3. Key Activities, Milestones, Hold-Points and Approvals

Within each phase there may be a number of key activities, milestones and hold-points which help to focus the project team and impose control. The following proforma would be a useful document for capturing and presenting this information (see figure 3.2 and 3.3).

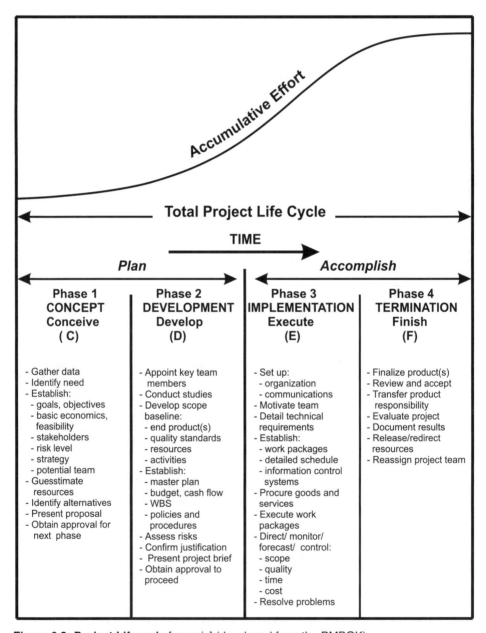

Figure 3.3: Project Lifecycle [generic] (developed from the PMBOK)

4. Overlap Between Phases (fast tracking)

The project phases are shown here in sequence, but in practice there may be some overlap between the phases. Deliverables from the preceding phase are generally approved before work starts on the next phase. However, if the deliverables are approved progressively and work begins on the following phases before the previous phases are totally complete, this practice would be called fast tracking. For example, on a ship building project the construction of the hull may start progressively as the drawings are available and similarly be commissioned progressively as the work is completed.

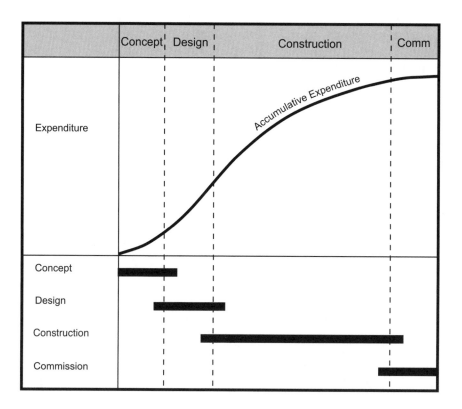

Figure 3.4: Project Lifecycle (showing the Gantt chart of the four main activities overlapping the project phases)

5. Level of Effort

The project lifecycle is often presented with its associated level of effort. This level of effort could be any parameter that flows through the project that can be measured, but it is most commonly expressed as manhours or costs. These parameters can be presented as a line graph of '*rate of expenditure*' and/or a line graph of '*accumulated expenditure*' (see figure 3.1).

The '*accumulated expenditure*' profile clearly shows a slow build-up of effort during the initial phases as the project is being designed and developed. The build-up of effort accelerates during the implementation phase to a maximum as the work faces are opened-up, before a sharp decline as the work is completed and commissioned and the project draws to a close.

From this curve one would naturally assume that as the greatest level of effort occurs during the implementation phase - this is after all where the product is made. Certainly the tools and techniques developed in the 1960s (PERT, CPM, WBS) were all focusing on this phase. But we need to consider the difference between efficiency and effectiveness - efficiency is doing activities right, while effectiveness is doing the right activity (see next section).

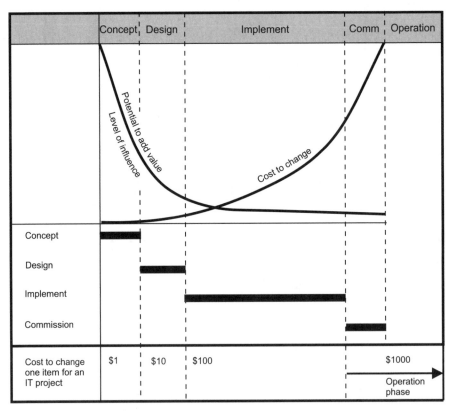

Figure 3.5: Potential to Add Value / Cost of Changes (showing typical cost of changes in the IT industry)

6. Level of Influence vs Cost of Changes (front-end importance)

In the 1960s and 1970s project management tools and techniques tended to focus on the implementation phase of the project lifecycle which certainly accounted for the greatest level of effort where the majority of the expenses were incurred, but in the 1980s the emphasis began to shift and focus more on the front-end of the project where the design and development decisions were made. This is where the stakeholder's needs are analysed, feasibility studies conducted, value management encouraged, project risk assessed and the product designed. Therefore, the initial phases offer the greatest potential to add value whereas the implementation phase, even though it has the greatest expenditure, should do no more than implement the product as designed. Further, the cost of making any changes due to design errors or the client changing the scope were recognised as becoming increasingly more expensive as the project progressed (see figure 3.5).

As projects become more involved and complex, together with time pressures to shorten the implementation phase (fast track to bring the product to market), so the need to get the design right from the outset becomes more important. Consider a shipbuilding project where the cost of changing the engine room arrangement at the concept and design phases would be the cost of design hours for reproducing a number of drawings. However, a change at the implementation phase would not only incur design costs but also the cost to remove machinery already fitted, together with the cost of new equipment, additional labour and maybe time penalties for late delivery. This cost profile encourages model testing and computer aided simulation where ideas and options can be developed and tested cost effectively before the implementation phase.

The stakeholders level of design influence or potential to add value to the project reduces as the project progresses. As the design develops design freezes must be imposed progressively for the design to progress. For example, if the foundations are changed after the building has been designed then all design figures must be recalculated.

This is clearly illustrated in figure 3.5 where the level of influence and cost of changes are plotted against the project lifecycle. At the outset of the project the potential for adding value and cost savings are at their highest, but steadily reduce as the project progresses - loosely mirroring this curve are the associated cost of any changes. **The financial encouragement is, therefore, to spend proportionally more time and effort during the initial phases to get the design right before implementation.**

In the IT industry a rule of thumb for the cost to make changes increases by a factor of ten. For example, if it costs $1 in the concept phase, it will be $10 in the design phase, $100 in the implementation phase, and a $1000 during operation (see figure 3.5).

The opportunities for improving performance and results on all types of projects are at the front-end. The ability to influence the project, to reduce project costs, build-in additional value, improve performance and increase flexibility is highest at the very early conceptual and design stages. But by the time the construction or implementation gets under way the ability to influence the costs has reduced considerably. It, therefore, follows that the project manager should be appointed during these early phases to ensure that the maximum advantage is taken to influence the project effectively.

7. Level of Detail

The project management philosophy of subdividing the scope of work into a number of smaller units to increase the level of detail and control can also be applied to the project lifecycle. Each phase can be subdivided into a further four phases and run as mini projects (see figure 3.6):

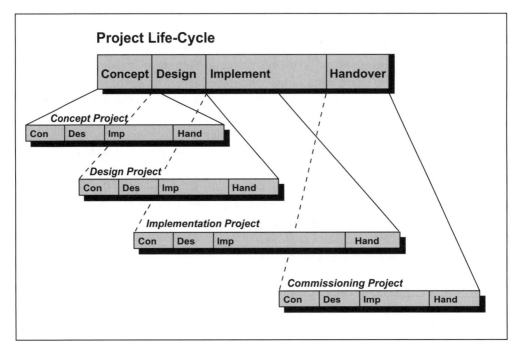

Figure 3.6: Project Lifecycle (showing how each phase can be subdivided into its own life-cycle of four phases)

The concept phase could be subdivided into a feasibility study project:

- **Concept:** should we carry out a feasibility study?
- **Design:** plan the feasibility study, select the team.
- **Implement:** carry out the feasibility study.
- **Commission:** closeout the feasibility study and present the report.

The same type of subdivision can be applied to the other three project phases and, if required, these sub-phases in turn can be further subdivided until an appropriate level of subdivision is achieved. The project lifecycle can also be subdivided along the lines of the stakeholders, designers, contractors and suppliers with each having their own four phase project lifecycle that integrates with the client's project lifecycle.

8. Product Lifecycle (8 phases)

The classic project lifecycle only considers the project from concept to handover. However, if the project is to build a facility, a factory, a computer system or sports stadium, for example, then (looking at the project from the client's perspective) the efficient operation of the facility and the return on investment should also be considered. To look at the wider picture we use what is termed the *'product lifecycle'*, which considers the facility from *the cradle to the grave* (figure 3.7).

This view highlights why decisions made during the initial phases can have a large impact during later phases even though they may be many years away and the facility might be operated by another company. It is important to look at the project as a whole from conception to disposal, to ensure that all the interrelated activities are identified. Seemingly simple decisions made during the initial phases of the project (equipment selection, for example) could have a major impact on future equipment maintenance and upgrading. By looking at the product lifecycle as a whole these issues can be highlighted.

Pre-Project Phase: Projects usually evolve from the work environment or market within which a company operates. There is usually some event which **triggers** the project. Consider the following:

- Your R&D generates new ideas, innovation and creativity
- Upgrade a system (computer system) to take advantage of new technology
- Market research identifies market changes
- Responding to your competitor's new product
- Expand your facilities to meet increased demand
- Output from quality circles, to improve efficiency and effectiveness
- Disaster recovery, accident, or cyclone damage.

Managing the pre-project environment is essential to a company's survival in a changing world.

Project Lifecycle: (four phases already discussed)

Operation Phase: Although the operation phase may be the whole purpose of the project, it usually falls outside the project manager's sphere of influence. However, the project manager would interface with the operation's manager with respect to:

- Handover
- Maintenance
- Upgrade and expansion
- Disposal

Maintenance Phase: The maintenance phase(s) are embedded in the operation phase to keep the facility functioning. Ease of maintenance and minimum impact on production are important design considerations.

Up-Grade, Expansion Phase: Also called *'half-life refit'*. At some point the facility will require a major upgrade, refit or expansion to keep it running efficiently and competitively. New technology, competition, market requirements, rules and regulations are all factors influencing this phase. Consider managing this change as a mini project

- these type of projects are characterised by tight time scales to get the facility up and running again with minimum disruption of their markets and clients.

Ease of upgrade or expansion is a consideration here - was it allowed for in the initial design? A good example of where expansion was incorporated in the design is the A34 dual-carriageway to Southampton (UK). Although only two lanes were initially built, the bridges were constructed to span four lanes, so that when they did build the additional two lanes they did not have to rebuild the bridges as well.

A good example where expansion was not planned for is the Auckland harbour bridge (NZ). Originally built with four lanes, but within ten years the volume of traffic demanded another four lanes. Fortunately, the bridge supports were over designed and could accommodate additional lanes *'clipped-on'* to the outside.

Any company working in a high technology environment will be well aware of the short lifecycle of their products. Upgrading and the ability to accommodate new technology are essential to extend the life of the computer system and stay competitive in the market place.

Your company's organisation structure will also change with time, particularly if the company has adopted a management-by-projects approach. The organisational structure should consider this at the design stage creating flexible; organisation structures, office space, computer facilities and car parking.

Decommission and Disposal: The final part of the product lifecycle is decommissioning and disposing of the facility. As people become more aware of the environment, so the impact of disposing of a facility needs to be considered at the design phase. A good example of where disposal would appear not to have been thought through is the decommissioning of nuclear power stations. It is reported that Britain has budgeted over £10 billion pounds to decommission their Magnox power stations. Another environmental issue is the decommissioning of offshore oil rigs. Recently an oil company had to abandon plans to dispose of an oil platform at sea after bowing to the environmental lobbing. The fashion industry knows exactly how to dispose of its products - have a sale!

Project Management Entrepreneur: Figure 3.7 shows the management skills required along the lifecycle. It is generally accepted that project management skills are required to implement a project, and general management and small business management skills are required to manage the facility on a day-to-day basis.

The top bar of figure 3.7 shows that entrepreneurial skills are also required, because it is the entrepreneurial skills of the client that initiates the project in the first place. Entrepreneurs are experts at spotting marketable opportunities and making them happen. During the project, the entrepreneurial project manager will naturally look for opportunities as the project goes forward. Project management entrepreneurs are not good at accepting design freezes. This will put added pressure on design control, but at least the project will end up with the latest technology.

Once the facility is complete the small business entrepreneur will not only be trying to improve the efficiency and productivity of the facility, but will also be monitoring the competition (product and pricing), advances in technology and market needs.

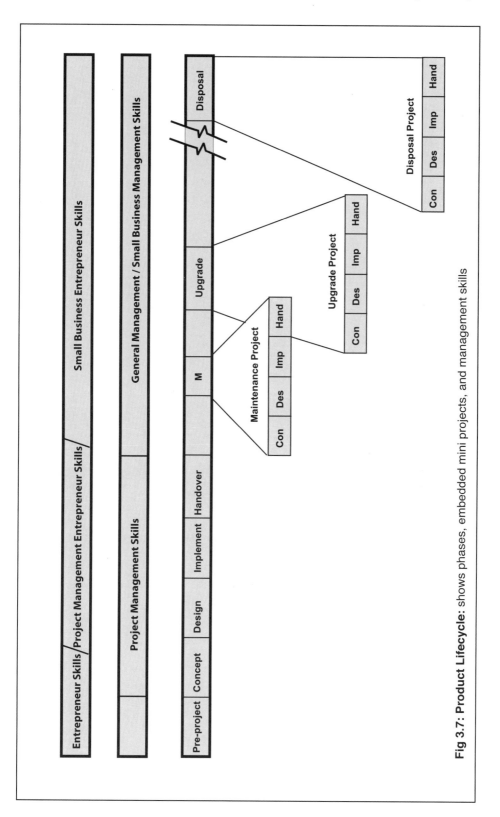

Fig 3.7: Product Lifecycle: shows phases, embedded mini projects, and management skills

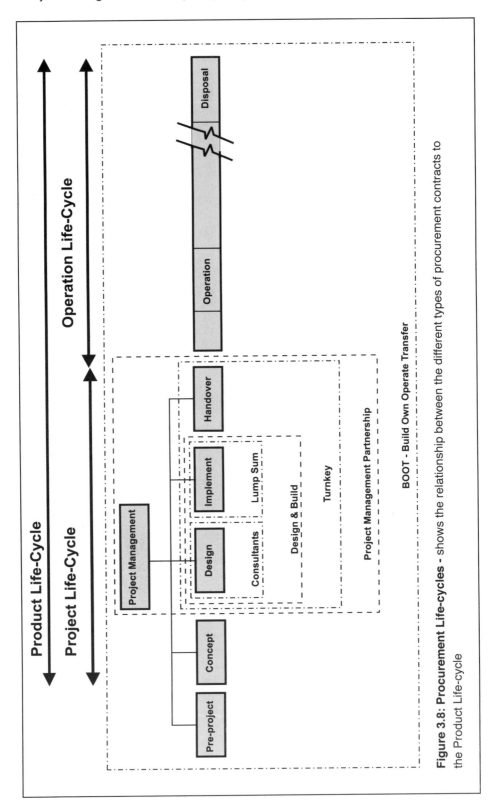

Figure 3.8: Procurement Life-cycles - shows the relationship between the different types of procurement contracts to the Product Life-cycle

9. Lifecycle Costing (procurement lifecycle)

Projects are often implemented to provide a facility or to produce a product that will give the client a return on their investment. By looking at the bigger picture the designers are able to trade-off the cost of the construction with the cost of maintenance, upgrading, expansion and disposal over the life of the facility. The extreme case would be a cheap construction which turned out to be expensive to operate and maintain, difficult to upgrade and expand, and an environmental disaster to dispose of.

One of the methods of addressing this problem is to make one company responsible for all aspects of the product lifecycle, thus eliminating any short term construction gains. These are often called **BOT** contacts (Build, Operate and Transfer), **BOOT** contracts (Build, Own, Operate and Transfer), **ROT** contracts (Refurbish, Operate and Transfer), **PPP** contract (Public Private Partnership), or **PFI** contract (Private Finance Initiative), where a company is given a licence to finance, build, operate and sell a product (see figure 3.8). Governments find these contracts attractive as they are seen to provide facilities without having an impact on their budget. The facility could be a power station, bridge or tunnel and the investors would receive a return by selling their product through electricity bills, or tolls.

Using the project lifecycle can be compared to how we drive a car, a learner driver looks no further than the car in front, but with maturity and experience a driver looks further afield and takes in the whole picture and makes decisions accordingly.

Case Study and Exercises:

The project lifecycle enables the project manager to look at the total picture (from the cradle to the grave). Prepare a short presentation (written or verbal) on how the project lifecycle can be applied to a book publishing project and/or your project. Consider the following:

1. The phases of the lifecycle, particularly if they are different to the classic four phase model.
2. The product lifecycle from concept to disposal. Outline how design considerations at the outset influence how upgrades and refits (new editions) happen down stream in the lifecycle.
3. As a design develops, design freezes have to be imposed to constrain the options and focus on an optimum solution.
4. The value / changes model indicates that the cost of changes increase as the project progresses.
5. Each phase of the project lifecycle can be subdivided into its own mini lifecycle and, further each phase of this lifecycle can also be subdivided, and so on. Give an example how this can be applied to your project as a method of subdivision leading to planning and control.

4

Feasibility Study

Learning Outcomes

After reading this chapter, you should be able to;

Conduct a feasibility study

Identify project stakeholders

Identify client needs and project constraints

Ideas, needs and problems crystallise into projects in different ways. The process of project formulation varies in different companies and on different types of projects. However, whichever way your projects develop there should at some point be a feasibility study to not only ensure the project is feasible, but also ensure it is making the best use of your company's resources.

The lead up to the feasibility study (from the client's perspective) is the formalising of the project with the project charter. The project charter outlines the purpose of the project and what it is meant to achieve. Likewise, the feasibility study should be formalised with requirements, boundaries and expected outcomes:

- Who is responsible?
- Project brief to be analysed
- Who should be involved?
- Level of detail
- Budget for the feasibility study
- Report back date.

At this point senior management have only made the decision to proceed with the feasibility study. The decision to proceed with the implementation of the project will be made later - presumably based on the feasibility study's recommendations.

It is a senior management responsibility to select the project manager for the feasibility study. It is then the project manager's responsibility to select the feasibility study team. It is most important that the team membership should include a representative of the future operators. This will encourage the operators to have an input into the design and a certain amount of control over their destiny. The company should make sure that the team members have sufficient time to develop the new product. This may mean releasing them from part or all of their present duties.

1. Stakeholder Analysis

The purpose of the needs analysis is to determine the needs and expectations of all the stakeholders. Project stakeholders are people and organisations (both internal and external) who are either actively involved in the project, or whose interests may be impacted by the project being implemented. It is the project manager's responsibility to identify all the stakeholders and determine their needs and expectations. These needs and expectations should then be managed, influenced and balanced, to ensure project success. The project manager should create an environment where the stakeholders are encouraged to contribute their skills and knowledge as this may influence the success of the project. Consider the following headings:

- **Originator:** The person who suggests the project.
- **Owner:** The person whose strategic plan creates the need for the project.
- **Sponsor:** The company or client who authorises expenditure on the project - this could also be an internal client or venture capitalists.
- **Project Champion:** The person who makes the project happen. Often a person with influence in high places.
- **Users:** The people who will operate the facility on behalf of the owner when the project is completed.
- **Customers:** The people who receive and pay for the benefit from the facility. For example, we are all customers for electricity, telephones and commercial travel facilities.
- **Project Team:** The team members who plan, organise, implement and control the work of the sub-contractors to deliver the facility within the constraints of time, cost and quality (also consider the impact on their families).
- **Senior Management:** Within your company who you **need** to support your project (mentor support and coaching).
- **Functional Managers:** Within your company who will be supplying the workforce for your project (matrix structure).
- **Boss:** Your boss, the person you report to, can play an important role in establishing your working environment.
- **Colleagues:** Although they may not be working on your project, indirectly they can supply useful information and offer moral peer support.
- **Sub-contractors:** The external companies or people offering specialist expertise to supplement the company's resources.
- **Suppliers and Vendors:** External companies or people who supply materials and equipment have a wealth of experience about their products.

- **Supporters:** The parties who provide goods and services to enable the facility to be built. For example, the suppliers of telephones, electricity, the postal service and even the corner shop.
- **Legal Requirements:** Rules and regulations both national and international that must be complied with.

There are other external stakeholders who, although they may not be directly involved with the project, can still influence the outcome:

- Regulatory authorities - health and safety
- Trade unions
- Special interest groups (environmentalists) who represent the society at large
- Lobby groups
- Government agencies and media outlets.

Some stakeholders are only interested in the outcomes of the project, while others are only interested in the project while it is being implemented. Stakeholders can be further classified into those who are *positively* impacted and those who are *negatively* impacted by the project. In this situation can the positively impacted compensate the negatively impacted parties? (See the dam project example in the Cost-Benefit Analysis section later in this chapter, to quantify the stakeholders risk tolerance as this will influence their reaction to the project). Where possible identify the key decision makers (those with power) and focus your attention on their needs. Any differences between the stakeholders should be resolved in favour of the client and customers, but not necessarily at the expense of the other stakeholders.

Some stakeholders will support the project, while others will oppose the project. It is important to address those who oppose the project and discuss their fears, because it is these stakeholders that could derail your project particularly if they have power and influence. Some of their concerns may be valid and with some flexibility could be accommodated. At the end of the day you may not be able to please all your stakeholders and in this conflict environment you will need to establish the **priority** of your stakeholders' needs and make your decisions accordingly (see table 4.1).

Stakeholder	Needs and Expectations	Priority

Table 4.1: Stakeholder, Needs, Expectations, and Priority (proforma)

It is the project manager's responsibility to build coalitions among the various stakeholders - this is a way of gaining power. The project manager must network and negotiate authority to move the project forward, so the success of the project may depend on the project manager's ability to build a strong team from the internal and external players.

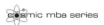

2. Define the Client's Needs

The starting point for a project is usually to address a problem, need, or business opportunity that may be internal or external to your company. The sponsor may start a project to implement a change, make a product, enter a new market or solve a problem. The evolution of needs from something quite vague to something tangible that serves as the basis of a project plan is the project manager's challenge. Some of the objectives may be stated as:

- The product must carry out a certain function at a predefined rate.
- The product must operate in a specific environment.
- The product must have a working life of so many years.
- The project's budget must not exceed $ x.
- The project must meet certain specifications and standards.
- The product must achieve reliability requirements - these may be quantified as mean time between failures (MTBF).
- The product must be energy efficient. A car would quantify this requirement as miles per gallon or kilometres per litre.
- The product must meet statutory health and safety regulations.
- The ergonomics must be consistent with the latest accepted practice.
- Ease of maintenance and repair must be incorporated into the design.
- A predetermined level of system redundancy and interchangeable parts.
- The operational requirements must achieve predetermined manpower levels and automation.
- The product must be manufactured with a predefined value of local content.
- The product must provide opportunities for future expansion.
- The project must be operational by a predefined date.
- The product must be manufactured by approved and accredited suppliers, if necessary pre-qualified by an audit.
- All suppliers must have implemented an approved quality system.
- All suppliers must have a good track record, supported by references.
- All suppliers must be flexible to accommodate any reasonable changes made by the sponsor during the manufacturing phase.
- All suppliers must be financially stable, supported by a bank reference.
- The end product must be marketable and profitable.

Many of the above items may be mutually exclusive, which means there will have to be a trade-off. For example, it is generally not possible to achieve both a minimum construction cost for a machine that also has maximum performance and minimum maintenance cost. These items of conflict need to be discussed and resolved during the early stages of the project, with all decisions recorded to form the basis of the design philosophy. This key document must be structured in such a way as to facilitate an audit trail of the decisions. If the field of the project is specialised the client may employ consultants and specialists to assist defining the scope - on small projects this task may fall to the contractor's project manager.

PMBOK / Lifecycle Matrix: Another way to identify the client's needs is to ask the client to specify their need with respect to each knowledge area as they pass through the project lifecycle.

	Concept	Design	Implement	Handover	Operation
Scope					
Time					
Cost					
Quality					
Procurement					
Risk					
Communication					
HR					
Integration					

Project Viability Check: The client may also need assistance checking the viability of the proposal. Will the product technically and commercially be fit for the purpose? Has the client kept away from wish lists and pipe dreams? These questions will form the basis of the client's feasibility study to which the contractor, as a practising specialist, can have a valuable input:

- Consider the impact location has on the project. For example, can the logistic requirements during the project and subsequent operation be met through existing roads and ports? Large infrastructure projects (power stations) often have to widen roads for their abnormal loads.
- Consider how the environment will impact the product, for example, a hotel in a hot country will require air-conditioning for a five star rating.
- Consider how the product will impact the environment. For example, will the product deplete the ozone layer, or increase global warming?
- Calculate the optimum size of the end product - economies of size are not always a straight line extrapolation, but pass through plateaus of optimum production.
- Are the aesthetics and style commensurate with current fashions? For example, modern office blocks and museums need to be stylish on the outside, to attract people to the inside.
- Define the target market. Who will buy the product? These questions can be quantified by market research.
- Assess the market supply and demand curve. What is the demand for the product now and forecast demand in the future?
- Assess the competition from other players in the market. How will an increase in your rate of production impact market share?

At the outset of the project it may not be possible to answer all of these questions. The unanswered questions will, however, indicate areas that need more research to gain a better understanding of the project and reduce risk.

3. Evaluate Constraints

Project constraints can be considered as internal or external restrictions that may impact the achievable scope of the project. These anticipated limitations can be quantified under three subheadings:

- Internal project constraints
- Internal corporate constraints
- External constraints

Internal Project Constraints: The internal project constraints relate directly to the scope of the project and ask basic questions about the product.

- Can the product be made? Can the company meet the specifications? Consider the delay to the Super Jumbo Airbus which cost the company dearly.
- Does the company have the technology? If not, can the technology be acquired through a **technology transfer**, and if so with whom? (South Africa took this approach to develop their offshore gas fields).
- Should we start the project now with the present technology or wait until new and better technology is available? (See figure 4.1).
- At what point in the development should a design freeze be imposed? This will impact the technology gap at the end of the project (see figure 4.1).
- Is the new technology component greater than 10%? Practitioners recommend the amount of innovation should be kept below 10% to reduce risk and uncertainty.
- Can the resources be trained up to the required level of ability, or should contractors be employed to meet the forecast skills requirement?
- Will the multi-project resource analysis consider the effect other projects will have on the supply of internal resources?
- Are there any special design requirements?

Figure 4.1: Technology Change Against Time (at some point you will have to implement a design freeze so you can build the product)

- Are special machines and equipment required? If yes, are they available?
- Are there special transport requirements? Can the product be transported to where it is required or does it need to be made piece-small and assembled on site?
- If new management systems are introduced will they be compatible with existing systems they need to interface with?
- Can the project be completed within the budget?
- What is the quality assurance requirement? For example, is accreditation to ISO 9000 required? Is the present quality management system sufficient?
- Are there company and project procedures in place? If not allow time to develop them.
- Is the project management office (PMO) established? Has the project manager been appointed, the project team selected, the office space allocated and are the equipment and information systems available?
- Can the project meet the client's completion date and any intermediate dates?
- Can the company accept the time penalties?
- Are the project risks and uncertainties acceptable?
- Can the company accept the terms and conditions outlined in the contract document?

All these questions relate directly to the project. The next section will show how the company itself can impose further constraints.

Internal Corporate Constraints: The company itself can impose further quasi constraints on the project. Corporate umbrella policy and strategy usually relate to long term issues that indirectly (and unintentionally) may impose limitations on the project.

- **Financial Objectives:** The project selection criteria may be based on a financial feasibility study quantified as, payback period, return on investment (ROI), net present value (NPV), internal rate of return (IRR) and a cost-benefit analysis.
  - The company may wish the project to maintain a positive cashflow.
  - The progress of the project may be encouraged or delayed to meet the company's annual budget.
  - The company's share price might impact on the project's ability to borrow.
- **Marketing:** The company may wish to diversify its products and enter new markets. Your project may be implementing the technology transfer for the company to operate in this market, or be a loss leader to enter a new market. The project must therefore accept subnormal profits to get a 'foot in the door'.
- **Estimating:** Due to a down turn in the economy, the company's main priority may be to keep the workforce intact. The lower the bid the greater the probability of being awarded the next contract. The lowest a company can bid is to cover direct costs, with the overheads being written-off. If this is the case, will the project's budget be based on the estimated cost or the sales price?
- **Partner:** The company may wish to take on a partner with previous experience in the field of the project (**technology transfer**) and also to spread the risk.

- **Industrial Relations:** Industrial unrest is often caused by conflict over pay and working conditions. The project manager may have little power to influence these conditions.
- **Training:** A project might become the training ground for new recruits, in which case the learning curve will be an expense to the project.
- **Exports:** The company could influence the quotation in an effort to acquire exports to enter new markets or take advantage of export incentives (buy work).

Where these company objectives are in conflict with project objectives the company objectives usually take preference. This could lead to increased project costs and delays that must be included in the baseline plan.

External Constraints: External constraints are imposed by parties outside the company and the project's sphere of influence. Many of these constraints may not be negotiable.

- National and international laws and regulations.
- Material and component delivery lead times.
- Unavailable resources, for example; after a flood or storm damage it could be difficult to find carpenters, or find welders while there are offshore projects, or computer programmers after a new software platform has been released. s
- Logistic constraints, availability of transportation.
- Availability of foreign currency and currency fluctuations.
- Environmental issues, Government legislation and pressure group activities, for example, Green Peace and CND. The nuclear, chemical, mining and transport industries have been particularly affected in the past.
- Climatic conditions, rain, wind, heat and humidity (El Nino).
- Market forces, supply and demand curve.
- Political unrest.
- Construction site in a residential area - there could be restrictions for working at night because of the noise pollution.
- Planning permission, licenses, permits, clearances, right of way, insurance.

These headings should not be seen as comprehensive, but as the forerunner of a company checklist that ensures all the appropriate questions are asked, which in turn should reduce the level of risk and uncertainty (see table 4.2).

WBS	Activity	Internal Project Constraints	Internal Corporate Constraints	External Constraints

Table 4.2: Table of Constraints (proforma to capture and present information)

4. Evaluate Alternatives and Options

The alternative analysis is the process of breaking down a complex product into its component parts before identifying different, and hopefully more effective methods of achieving the desired result. The process should start with a checklist to structure the thought process. This can be achieved through; the WBS (see *WBS* chapter), the project constraints (see table 4.2), or the project objectives (see table 4.3).

The technical definition should aid the direct comparison between alternatives. With a machine for example the capital costs should be compared with the operating and maintenance costs. Although this process should be ongoing during the project, the design freeze would usually signal the end of this phase. Once the manufacturing phase starts the emphasis would shift to consider manufacturing alternatives:

- **Time:** Can the project be completed quicker?
- **Cost:** Can the budget be reduced?
- **Quality:** Can the project be made to a more cost effective level of quality which would be acceptable to the client and quicker to produce?
- **Resources:** Will automation reduce the manpower requirement?
- **Technical:** Is there a simpler design configuration and simpler build method?
  - Can cheaper materials be used?
  - Has the latest technology been considered?
  - Has the use of different equipment and machines been considered?
  - Has the trade-off between cost, delivery schedule and technical performance been quantified?

5. Gather Information

Without the latest information on the product's technical and market issues the alternative analysis will be self-limiting (see table 4.3). Information is a prerequisite for effective problem-solving and decision-making. Information may be found in:

- Books and periodicals
- Technical reports
- Bureau specifications
- Sales and marketing brochures (product information)
- Market research (market trends and fashions)
- Internet (data base search)
- Stakeholders (interviews and questionnaires)
- Closeout reports.

WBS	Objectives	Alternatives and Options

Table 4.3: Table of Alternatives and Options (proforma)

Closeout Reports: Closeout reports from previous projects offer a valuable source of historical information. It cannot be over stressed how important it is for a company to learn from its previous experience - not only should the mistakes be noted, but also what went right, together with any recommendations for future projects (see *Scope Management* chapter).

The size of the company will influence how and where information will be available (or hidden)! In a small company, information may be collected by individual managers, while a large company may have a corporate library. The responsibility for setting up a data base of information should lie with either the project office or the company's general manager.

6. Value Management

Value Management is a structured, systematic and analytical process that seeks to achieve value for money by providing all the necessary functions at the lowest total cost, consistent with required levels of quality and performance. Underlying the value management theory is that there is always more than one way of achieving a function and that examination of alternatives should produce the most acceptable option. Value management looks at the project or product as a whole. It considers the relationship between function, cost and worth. Its purpose is to ensure value for money over the product lifecycle. Consider the following points:
- Identify unnecessary expenditure
- Challenge assumptions
- Generate alternative ideas

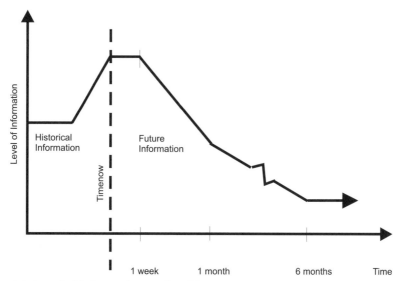

Figure 4.2: Level of Information against Time - shows how the level of accurate information varies with time. The highest level of information is required around timenow, with this requirement moving forward like a wave as the project progresses

- Promote innovation
- Optimize resources
- Save time, money and energy
- Simplify methods and procedures
- Eliminate redundant items
- Update standards, criteria and objectives.

Value management is about:
- Clarifying and satisfying customers' needs
- Creating ideas as to how a system can best do its job at appropriate levels of quality and performance
- Challenging assumptions and maximising returns on investment
- Participation by clients, end-users and stakeholders
- Seeing the purpose of the system itself
- Seeking the lowest total cost of providing the clients' needs - it is not about seeking the cheapest solution.

The process is one of participatory planning in which the project design team work closely with stakeholders in a workshop format seeking to identify those functions which the project must perform, consider:
- Identifying appropriate quality and performance criteria
- Creating alternative ways of performing these functions
- After analysis and evaluation, selecting the lowest total life-cycle cost option that satisfies those requirements.

During the value management workshop considerable advantage is gained by capitalising upon the synergy that is developed and upon the potential constructive overlap of expertise and knowledge within the project team. Team members are able to ask questions and generate ideas (brainstorming) about issues outside their specific area of expertise. Traditional design processes do not encourage overlap and rely upon specialists to work exclusively within their own areas.

7. Cost-Benefit Analysis

A cost-benefit analysis may be performed at this stage to establish the financial feasibility of the project. A cost-benefit analysis is generally based on the following economic principles:
- Pareto improvement criteria
- Hicks-Kaldor test
- Willingness-to-pay test

The basic concept is simply to express the costs and benefits in money terms. If the financial benefits exceed the costs, then the project passes the test. The **Pareto** improvement criteria is expressed as; *'The project should make some people better off without making anyone worse off'*. This situation may be difficult to achieve in reality.

The **Hicks-Kaldor** test seems more realistic. This states that; *'The aggregate gains should exceed aggregate losses.'* This framework will enable the people who gain, to compensate the people that lose. For example, a dam project may have many benefits to the community, but might cause the silting up of the river. If the financial benefits of having a dam exceed the costs of dredging the river, this project will satisfy the Hicks-Kaldor test.

The **willingness-to-pay** test is simply to determine how much your clients are prepared to pay for your product. The supply and demand curve (not shown here) explains how airlines manage to charge a range of air fares for the same seat.

With the presentation of the feasibility study to senior management, so ends this mini project. This concludes the *Feasibility Study* chapter, the following chapter will discuss *Project Selection*.

Key Points:

- Identify all your stakeholders - assess, quantify and prioritise their needs and expectations.
- Identify all the constraints, both internal and external.
- Consider alternative options to produce a better product.

Case Study and Exercises:

The feasibility study offers the project manager and management student a framework to assess the feasibility of a project against predefined parameters. Consider a Public Private Partnership (PPP), or BOOT (Build Own Operate and Transfer) project to (select a project):

- Refurbish and operate the London Underground.
- Build and operate a toll road or toll bridge.
- Build and operate a power station.

For your selected project structure your presentation (written or verbal) to include the following:

1. Identify the key stakeholders and determine their influence on the project.
2. Your client is the key stakeholder, identify their needs and how the project will fulfil their needs.
3. A key function of the feasibility study is to confirm that you can make the product or perform the service. Outline the build-method.
4. Identify any internal and external constraints that will impact your project.
5. The economists say if the '*aggregate gains exceed the aggregate losses*' then the project passes their test. How can this test be applied to your project?

5

Project Selection

Learning Outcomes

After reading this chapter, you should be able to;

Calculate the payback period

Use discounted cashflow selection techniques

Calculate the breakeven point

The selection of the right project for future investment is a crucial decision for the long-term survival of a company. The selection of the wrong project may well precipitate project failure leading to company liquidation. This chapter on project selection will outline a framework for evaluating and ranking prospective projects using numeric methods.

The project selection process is developed here as a separate chapter, but it should be recognised as a subsection of other knowledge areas, namely; scope management (scope initiation), project lifecycle (concept phase) and the feasibility study.

Project selection is making a commitment for the future. The execution of a project will tie up company resources and, as an opportunity cost, the selection of one project may preclude your company from pursuing another (perhaps more profitable) project. We live in a world of finite resources and, so cannot carry out all the projects we may want or need. Therefore, a process is required to select and rank projects on the basis of beneficial change to a company.

1. Project Selection Models

A numeric model is usually financially focused and quantifies the project in terms of time to repay the investment (payback) or return on investment. While non-numeric models look at a much wider view of the project considering items such as; market share, client retention, the move to a new field, or environmental issues.

The main purpose of these models is to aid decision-making leading to project selection. When choosing a selection model the points to consider are; realism, capability, ease of use, flexibility and cost effectiveness. Most importantly the model must evaluate projects by how well they meet a company's strategic goals and corporate mission. The following subheadings indicate the type of questions to ask:

- Will the project maximise profits?
- Will the project maximise the utilisation of the workforce?
- Will the project maintain market share, increase market share or consolidate market position?
- Will the project enable the company to enter new markets?
- Will the project maximise the utilisation of plant and equipment?
- Will the project improve the company's image?
- Will the project satisfy the needs of the stakeholders and their political aspirations.
- Is the project's risk and uncertainty acceptable?
- Is the project's scope consistent with company expertise?

This list can be developed further by weighting the evaluation items. The weighting indicates the value of the contribution to the company's strategic goals and objectives. With a numeric value for each project, the projects can be ranked in line with their contribution to the success of the organisation.

The relationship between a project's expected results and the company's strategic goals, needs to be established. In general the kind of information required can be quantified under the following headings (see Meredith):

- Production
- Marketing
- Financial
- Personnel
- Administration

Consider a project to introduce a new computerised information and control system. For this exercise the system is intended for both in-house use and a consultancy service.

Production Considerations (for new information and control system):

- Method of implementation
- Time to be up and running
- Other applications of the system
- Learning curve - time until the product is saleable
- Amount of double processing and waste
- Extent of outside consultants required
- Cost of power requirements
- Interfacing equipment required
- Period of disruption
- Safety of system

Marketing Considerations (for new information and control system):

- Number of potential users
- Market share
- Time to achieve proposed market share
- Impact on current system
- Ability to control quality of information
- Customer acceptance
- Estimated life of new system
- Spin-offs
- Enhanced image of company
- Extent of possible new markets.

Financial Considerations (for new information and control system):

- Cost of new system
- Impact on company cashflow
- Borrowing requirement
- Time to breakeven
- Payback period, NPV and IRR
- Size of investment required
- Cost of implementation
- Cost of training
- Cost of mistakes
- Level of financial risk.

Personnel Considerations (for new information and control system):

- Skills requirements and availability
- Training requirements (technology transfer)
- Employment requirements
- Level of resistance to change from current workforce
- Impact on working conditions
- Ergonomics, health and safety considerations
- Effect on internal communication
- Effect on job descriptions
- Effect on work unions
- Effect on morale.

Administration and other Considerations (for new information and control system):

- Compliance with national and international standards
- Reaction from shareholders and other stakeholders
- Cost of maintenance contract
- Disaster recovery planning
- Cost of upgrading the system to keep pace with new technology
- Vulnerability of using a single supplier
- Customer service
- Effect of centralised databases
- Extent of computer literacy
- Legal considerations.

This list is by no means complete, and you will notice that each heading has been conveniently subdivided into ten items, there could be more! The main **advantage** of this type of list is that it considers a wide range of factors which greatly helps to present a fuller picture of the project. However, the main **disadvantage** of the list approach is that all items are viewed with equal importance. Others are:

- Unknown level of error
- Different level of effect and importance
- Different level of risk and uncertainty
- Frequency of occurrence not known
- Threshold of rejection not quantified
- The list may contain redundant items
- Some items are intangible and therefore difficult to quantify
- The list could be incomplete.

Although the limitations seem to outnumber the benefits, the most important feature is that the checklist approach asks questions that encourage the managers to think about a wide range of possible problems.

2. Numeric Models

The numeric selection models presented here may be subdivided into financial models and scoring models. The financial models are:

- Payback period
- Return on investment (IOR)
- Net present value (NPV)
- Internal rate of return (IRR)

Companies tend to prefer financial models and often select solely on profitability. This may not be as drastic as it sounds because subconsciously the managers will be considering a wider scope of selection criteria.

In an investment appraisal only the incremental income and expenses attributed directly to the project under consideration should be included. Costs that have already been incurred (sunk costs) should be ignored as they are irrelevant to decisions effecting future projects. It should be noted that all the appraisal techniques discussed in this chapter have a limiting factor, they are based on a forecasted cashflow.

3. Payback Period

The payback period is the time taken to gain a financial return equal to the original investment. This period is usually expressed in years and months. For example, a company wishes to buy a new machine for a four year project (this example will be used extensively in this chapter). The manager has to choose between **machine A** or **machine B** - a mutually exclusive situation. Although both machines have the same initial cost ($35,000) their cashflows perform differently over the four year period due to different labour, material and maintenance costs. To calculate the payback period, simply work out how long it will take to recover the initial outlay (see table 5.1).

Years	Cash-Flow Machine A	Cash-Flow Machine B
0	($35,000)	($35,000)
1	$20,000	$10,000
2	**$15,000**	$10,000
3	$10,000	**$15,000**
4	$10,000	$20,000
Payback Period	2 Years	3 Years

Table 5.1: Payback Period (Machine A 2 years, Machine B 3 years)

Machine A will recover its outlay one year sooner than machine B. Where projects are ranked by the shortest payback period, machine A is selected in preference to machine B. The **advantages** of the payback method are that it:

- Is simple and easy to use.
- Uses readily available accounting data to determine cashflows.
- Reduces the project's exposure to risk by selecting the shortest payback period.
- Reduces the uncertainty of future cashflow.
- Is an appropriate technique to evaluate high technology projects where the technology is changing quickly.

The **disadvantages** of the payback period calculation are:-
- It does not consider the time value of money. The payback period is indifferent to the timing of the cashflow. The project with a high, early income (cash-inflow) would be ranked equally with a project that had a late income if the payback periods were the same (see figure 5.1).
- It is not a suitable technique to evaluate long term projects where the impacts of differential inflation and interest rates could significantly change the results.
- The figures are based on project cashflow only.
- Although the payback period would reduce the duration of the risk, it does not quantify the risk exposure.
- The payback period calculation does not look at the total project - what happens to the cashflow after the payback period is not considered. A project built up slowly to give excellent returns (**project F** in figure 5.2) would be rejected in favour of a shorter payback period (**project E** in figure 5.2).

The payback period is the most widely used project selection calculation, even if this is only an initial filter. Its main strength is that it is simple and quick.

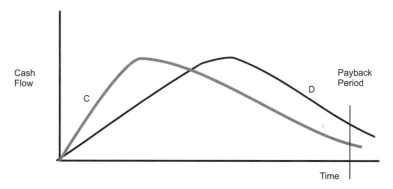

Figure 5.1: Payback Period (project C and project D have the same payback period even though their cashflows are different)

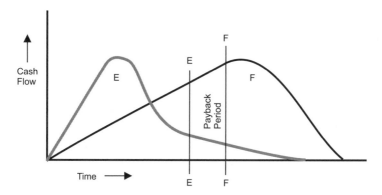

Figure 5.2: Payback Period (does not consider the cashflow after the payback period. In this case project F may be a better option even though project E has a shorter payback period)

4. Return on Investment (ROI)

Another popular investment appraisal technique that does look at the whole project is return on investment (ROI). This method first calculates the average annual profit, which is simply the project outlay deducted from the total gains, divided by the number of years the investment will run. The profit is then converted into a percentage of the total outlay using the following equations:

$$\text{Average Annual Profit} = \frac{\text{(Total gains) - (Total outlay)}}{\text{Number of years}}$$

$$\text{Return on investment} = \frac{\text{Average Annual Profit}}{\text{Original investment}} \times \frac{100}{1}$$

Using the machine selection project calculate the return on investment (see table 5.2).

Years	Cash-Flow Machine A	Cash-Flow Machine B
0	($35,000)	($35,000)
1	$20,000	$10,000
2	**$15,000**	$10,000
3	$10,000	**$15,000**
4	$10,000	$20,000
Total gains	$55,000	$55,000

Table 5.2: Return on Investment (ROI) Cash-Flow

Profit   (A & B)   = $55,000 - $35,000

Annual Profit   = $\frac{\$20,000}{4 \text{ yrs.}}$ = $5,000 per year (same for both machines)

Return on investment   = $\frac{\$5,000}{\$35,000} \times \frac{100}{1} = 14\%$

The return on investment method has the advantage of also being a simple technique like the payback period, but further, it considers the cashflow over the whole project. The total outcome of the investment is expressed as a profit and percentage return on investment, both parameters readily understood by management.

The main criticism of return on investment is that it averages out the profit over successive years. An investment with high initial profits would be ranked equally with a project with high profits later if the average profit was the same. Clearly the project with high initial profits should take preference.

This point is shown in the above example, where, although machine A and machine B have different cashflows, their profit and return on investment come out the same. To address this shortcoming of both return on investment and payback period, the time value of money must be considered using a discounted cashflow technique. This is particularly desirable where interest rates and inflation are high.

5. Discounted Cashflow (DCF)

The discounted cashflow (DCF) technique takes into consideration the time value of money, for example, a $100 today will **not** have the same worth or buying power as a $100 this time next year. Our subjective preference to $100 now is quite rational because we have seen the cost of goods rise with inflation. There are two basic DCF techniques that can model this effect, net present value (NPV) and internal rate of return (IRR).

These discounting techniques enable the project manager to compare two projects with different investment and cashflow profiles. There is, however, one major problem with DCF, besides being dependent on the accurate forecast of the cashflows, it also requires an accurate prediction of the interest rates.

6. Net Present Value (NPV)

To assist the understanding of NPV let us first look at compound interest which is commonly used in saving accounts. If we invest $100 at 20% interest, after one year it will be worth $120 and after two years compounded it will be worth $144. Now NPV is the reverse of compound interest.

If you were offered $120 one year from now and the inflation and interest rate was 20%, working backwards its value in today's terms would be $100. This is called the present value, and when the cashflow over a number of years is combined in this manner the total figure is called the net present value (NPV). This calculation is best set up in a tabular form using the following headings (see table 5.3).

Years	Project Cash-Flow	Discount Factor	Present Value
0			
1			
2			
3			
Total			NPV

Table 5.3: Net Present Value (NPV) (tabular format)

Where the cashflow timing is expressed in years from the start date of the project, the inflation impact is assumed to act at the end of the first year or beginning of the second year, therefore all cashflows in the first year are at present value.

Project cash-flow   = income - expenditure

Present value   = discount factor x cashflow

The discount factor is derived from the reciprocal of the compound interest formula.

Discount factor		=	$1 / (1 + i)^n$
where	i	=	the forecast interest rate
	n	=	the number of years from start date

The discount factor is usually read from a table, see table of discounting factors (table 5.4). Using the formula above, calculate a few of the discount factors to satisfy yourself of their origin. You can then forget the calculation and work straight from the tables.

Years	10%	11%	12%	13%	14%	15%	16%	17%
1	0.9091	0.9009	0.8929	0.8850	0.8772	0.8696	0.8621	0.8547
2	0.8264	0.8116	0.7972	0.7831	0.7695	0.7561	0.7432	0.7305
3	0.7513	0.7312	0.7118	0.6930	0.6750	0.6575	0.6407	0.6244
4	0.6830	0.6587	0.6355	0.6133	0.5921	0.5718	0.5523	0.5337
5	0.6209	0.5935	0.5674	0.5428	0.5194	0.4972	0.4761	0.4561

Years	18%	19%	20%	21%	22%	23%	24%	25%
1	0.8475	0.8403	0.8333	0.8264	0.8197	0.8130	0.8065	0.8000
2	0.7182	0.7062	0.6944	0.6830	0.6719	0.6610	0.6504	0.6400
3	0.6086	0.5934	0.5787	0.5645	0.5507	0.5374	0.5245	0.5120
4	0.5158	0.4987	0.4823	0.4665	0.4514	0.4369	0.4230	0.4096
5	0.4371	0.4190	0.4019	0.3855	0.3700	0.3552	0.3411	0.3277

Table 5.4: Table of Discounting Factors

The NPV is a measure of the value or worth added to the company by carrying out the project. If the NPV is positive the project merits further consideration. When ranking projects, preference should be given to the project with the highest NPV. Consider the machine selection example again, this time using NPV. Assume the discounting factor is 20%, set up the NPV format. The steps are as follows:

- Insert the cashflow
- Transfer the discounting factors from the table
- Calculate present value by multiplying cashflow by discount factor
- Aggregate the present values to give the NPV (see tables 5.5 and 5.6).

The NPV for machine A is $2692 and for machine B is ($1396). NPV analysis would select machine A in preference to machine B because it has a higher NPV. Machine B would be rejected in any case because it has a negative NPV. A negative NPV indicates the company would lose money by carrying out this project.

Column (1)	Column (2)	Column (3)	= (2) x (3)
Years	Project Cash-Flow	Discount Factor	Present Value
0	($35,000)	1	($35,000)
1	$20,000	0.8333	$16,666
2	$15,000	0.6944	$10,416
3	$10,000	0.5787	$5,787
4	$10,000	0.4823	$4,823
Total NPV			$2,692

Table 5.5: Machine A - Net Present Value Calculation (DF 20%)

Column (1)	Column (2)	Column (3)	= (2) x (3)
Years	Project Cash-Flow	Discount Factor	Present Value
0	($35,000)	1	($35,000)
1	$10,000	0.8333	$8,333
2	$10,000	0.6944	$6,944
3	$15,000	0.5787	$8,681
4	$20,000	0.4823	$9,646
Total NPV			($1,396)

Table 5.6: Machine B - Net Present Value Calculation (DF 20%)

The **advantages** of using NPV are:
- It introduces the time value of money.
- It expresses all future cashflows in **today's values**, which enables direct comparisons.
- It allows for inflation and escalation.
- It looks at the whole project from start to finish.
- It can simulate project what-if analysis using different values.
- It gives a more accurate profit and loss forecast than non DCF calculations.

The **disadvantages** are:-
- Its accuracy is limited by the accuracy of the predicted future cashflows and interest rates.
- It is biased towards short run projects.
- It excludes non financial data e.g. market potential.
- It uses a fixed interest rate over the duration of the project. The technique can, however, accommodate a varying interest rate, this will be explained later in this chapter.

Although NPV quantifies the profit this is expressed in absolute terms. Managers tend to prefer profitability expressed as a percentage. This can be addressed by using another DCF method called internal rate of return (IRR).

7. Internal Rate of Return (IRR)

The internal rate of return is also called DCF yield or DCF return on investment. The IRR is the value of the discount factor when the NPV is zero. The IRR is calculated by either a trial and error method or plotting NPV against IRR. It is assumed that the costs are committed at the end of the year and these are the only costs during the year. Consider the machine selection example again. Looking at machine A first, to reduce the NPV increase the discounting factor in small steps until NPV becomes negative.

Column (1)	Column (2)	Column (3)	= (2) x (3)
Years	Project Cash-Flow	Discount Factor 22%	Present Value
0	($35,000)	1	($35,000)
1	$20,000	0.8197	$16,394
2	$15,000	0.6719	$10,079
3	$10,000	0.5507	$5,507
4	$10,000	0.4514	$4,514
Total NPV			$1,494

Table 5.7: Machine A - Discount Factor 22% (The NPV is still positive, therefore increase the DF by 2%)

Column (1)	Column (2)	Column (3)	= (2) x (3)
Years	Project Cash-Flow	Discount Factor 24%	Present Value
0	($35,000)	1	($35,000)
1	$20,000	0.8065	$16,130
2	$15,000	0.6504	$9,756
3	$10,000	0.5245	$5,245
4	$10,000	0.4230	$4,230
Total NPV			$361

Table 5.8: Machine A - Discount Factor 24% (NPV still positive increase DF by a further 1%)

Column (1)	Column (2)	Column (3)	= (2) x (3)
Years	Project Cash-Flow	Discount Factor 25%	Present Value
0	($35,000)	1	($35,000)
1	$20,000	0.8000	$16,000
2	$15,000	0.6400	$9,600
3	$10,000	0.5120	$5,120
4	$10,000	0.4096	$4,096
Total NPV			($184)

Table 5.9: Machine A - Discount Factor 25% (NPV is now negative, therefore IRR must lie between 24% and 25%)

As the discount factor increases the NPV is reducing. The NPV becomes negative between 24% and 25%, therefore the IRR is between 24% and 25% for machine A. For machine B the NPV is already negative at 20%, so decrease the discounting factor until NPV becomes positive - try 18% to start with.

Column (1)	Column (2)	Column (3)	= (2) x (3)
Years	Project Cash-Flow	Discount Factor 18%	Present Value
0	($35,000)	1	($35,000)
1	$10,000	0.8475	$8,475
2	$10,000	0.7182	$7,182
3	$15,000	0.6086	$9,129
4	$20,000	0.5185	$10,316
Total NPV			$102

Table 5.10: Machine B - Discount Factor 18% (the NPV is now positive - try 19%)

Column (1)	Column (2)	Column (3)	= (2) x (3)
Years	Project Cash-Flow	Discount Factor 19%	Present Value
0	($35,000)	1	($35,000)
1	$10,000	0.8403	$8,403
2	$10,000	0.7062	$7,062
3	$15,000	0.5934	$8,901
4	$20,000	0.4987	$9,974
Total NPV			($660)

Table 5.11: Machine B - Discount Factor 19% (NPV is now negative again)

The IRR for machine B must lie between 18% and 19%. These values can now be presented in a tabular or graphic form.

Interest Rate	NPV Machine A	NPV Machine B
18%	-	$102
19%	-	($660)
20%	$2,692	($1,396)
21%	-	-
22%	$1,494	-
23%	-	-
24%	$361	-
25%	($184)	-

Table 5.12: Internal Rate of Return (IRR) (plot A and B against interest rate)

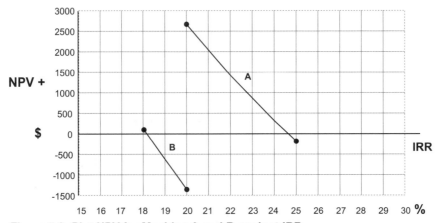

Figure 5.3: Plot NPV for Machine A and B against IRR

The IRR analysis is a measure of the return on investment, therefore, select the project with the highest IRR. This allows the manager to compare IRR with the current interest rates. One of the limitations with IRR is that it uses the same interest rate throughout the project, therefore as the project's duration extends this limitation will become more significant. This problem can be addressed, however, using a modified version of the DCF method which will be outlined in the next section.

8. Net Present Value (NPV) Using Variable Interest Rates

In the DCF examples discussed the discounting factor was kept constant for the duration of the project. This unfortunately is not a true reflection of the world markets which are quite volatile. Interest rates can fluctuate considerably over a two to three year period. Consider the following example which starts with $100, compound forward using different interest rates, then discount backwards using the same interest rates:

Year	Cash Flow	Interest Rate	Compound Interest	Discount Factor Yearly	Total Discount Factor	Present Value
1	100	10%	110	0.9091	0.9091	100
2		20%	132	0.8333	0.7576	100
3		15%	152	0.8696	0.6588	100

Table 5.13: Net Present Value (NPV) Using Variable Interest Rates

- The cashflow for the first year is $100.
- The forecast annual interest rates are 10%, 20% and 15% respectively.
- Using these annual interest rates the compound interest for the three years will be $110, $132 and $152 respectively.
- The annual discounting factor is taken straight from the discounting factor tables. Enter year 1 and the interest rate in each case.

- The total discount factor for the second year is the total for year 1 [0.9091] times the annual discounting factor for year 2 [0.8333], giving 0.7576. (This is the most complicated step, the rest is easy).
- The present value is the total discount factor times the compound interest value, for example, in year 3, the total discount factor is [0.6588] times the compound interest value [$152], giving, $100. This is what you would expect, each year should be discounted to $100.

Which DCF Method?: The text has outlined five financial selection acceptance models. Which method or methods should you employ? If the cashflow data can be set up on a computer spreadsheet there is no reason why you should not use all the methods outlined. Certainly payback period should be used as an initial filter, then two more calculations will give IRR.

For the DCF methods accountants suggest NPV should be used in preference to IRR, because NPV allows the user to vary the interest rate over the years whereas IRR employs one rate for all the cash-flows. NPV is a measure of profitability depending on the ingredients of a particular transaction, whereas IRR is dependent upon the opportunity cost of capital, which is a standard of profitability established by the capital markets.

In the absence of capital rationing, all projects that have an IRR above the opportunity cost should be considered and so should all projects that have a positive NPV. Whichever test is employed the same decision should be reached.

However, where capital shortages exist, the two approaches may indeed give conflicting results. In this situation NPV must be employed because the fundamental objective of financial analysis is not to measure profitability but to maximise the present value of the company's investment portfolio.

9. Scoring Models

The numeric models discussed so far all have a common limitation, they only look at the financial element of the project. In an attempt to broaden the selection criteria a scoring model called the factor model, which uses multiple criteria to evaluate the project, will be introduced.

The **factor model** simply lists a number of desirable factors on a project selection proforma along with columns for Selected and Not Selected. The following list shows a development of a rating sheet from Meredith.

A weighted column can be added to increase the score of important factors while reducing the scoring of the less important. The weighted column is calculated by first scoring each factor, then dividing each factor by the total score. The total of the weighted column should always add up to one. The factors can be weighted simply 1 to 5 to indicate; 1 "very poor", 2 "poor", 3 "fair", 4 "good" and 5 "very good". Three, seven and ten point scales can also be used.

Factors	Select	Do not select	Weighting
Profit > than 20%	x		
Enter new market		x	
Increase market share	x		
New equipment required		x	
Use equipment not being utilised	x		
No increase in energy requirements	x		
No new technical expertise required	x		
Use under utilised work force	x		
Manage with existing personnel		x	
No outside consultants required		x	
No impact on work for safety	x		
No impact on environmental issues		x	
Payback period < 2 years	x		
Consistent with current business	x		
Offer good customer service	x		
Total	**10**	**5**	

Table 5.14: Scoring Model

The **advantages** of using a scoring model are:
- It encourages objectivity in decision making.
- It uses multiple selection criteria to widen the range of evaluation.
- It uses a simple structure, therefore, easy to use.
- It uses selection factors structured by senior management. This implies that they reflect the company's goals and objectives.
- It makes it easy to change factors.
- It uses weighted scoring to reflect the factor's differential importance.
- It is not biased towards short run projects favoured by financial models.
- It has low weightings which can be removed from the list as they have little to no influence. This will reduce the number of questions.
- It is a weighted model which can also be used as a flag to improve projects by identifying the variance between the factor score and the maximum possible score.

The **disadvantages** of using a scoring model are:
- If the factors are not weighted they will all assume equal importance.
- A simple model may encourage the development of long lists that could introduce trivial factors and therefore waste management time.

10. Cost Breakeven Analysis

The cost breakeven analysis should not be confused with the cost-benefit analysis. The separation of costs into **fixed** and **variable** will be discussed in the *Project Estimating* chapter. This section on cost breakeven analysis will take this technique a step further to model how these costs change with increasing production and determine the breakeven point.

Example: A company makes a product which sells for $15 each. The variable cost per unit is $5, this covers labour and material, leaving $10 per unit as a contribution towards fixed costs. The fixed costs total is $75,000 per annum, which covers all the overhead costs. The breakeven point is reached when the contribution equals the fixed costs.

$$\text{Breakeven point} \quad = \quad \frac{\text{Fixed costs}}{\text{Contribution per unit}}$$

$$= \quad \frac{\$75,000}{\$10} \qquad = \qquad 7,500 \text{ units}$$

The breakeven point is 7,500 units, when sales income exactly balances the total cost of $112,500 (labour and material 7,500 x 5 = $37,500 + fixed costs $75,000). Output less than this amount would result in a loss, while greater output would make a profit. This profit or loss situation can be easily read off a graph, or calculated directly.

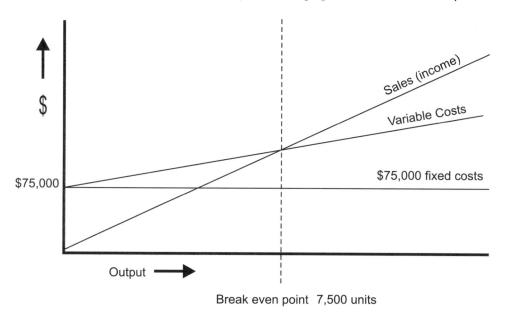

Break even point 7,500 units

Figure 5.4: Cost Breakeven Analysis

This technique allows the project manager to see at a glance how profit varies with change in volume. It can also be used to show the impact on the cost structure by switching from manual to automatic machinery.

Cost breakeven analysis can also be used to aid decision-making where two mutually exclusive projects present a different cost structure. Consider a project to install a heating system for an office block where project G has a high installation cost but low maintenance, while project H has a low installation cost but high maintenance costs. The cost breakeven analysis will indicate which system is the most cost effective for a given period of time.

11. Project Lifecycle Cashflow

Another way to model the project is to plot the cashflow and breakeven point against the project (or product) lifecycle. Initially the cashflow will be increasingly negative until the product goes into service and a return is achieved on your investment. In the long term you need to make allowances for a decline in income and profit, and not forget the cost to decommission and dispose of the facility.

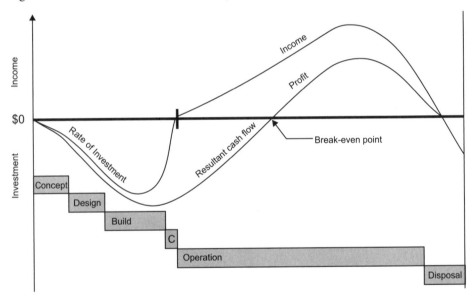

Figure 5.5: Project Lifecycle Cashflow (from the cradle to the grave)

This concludes the chapter on *Project Selection*. The following chapter will discuss *Project Estimating*.

Key Points:

- Selecting the 'right' project is crucial for your long term profitability.
- Payback period is the most commonly used selection technique
- The time value of money is addressed using discounted cashflow techniques.

Case Study and Exercises:

The selection of the right project may be the single most important consideration which determines success or failure. Outline how your company selects projects, and give an example of how the following are considered:

1. Departmental considerations.
2. Payback period (relate to project risk).
3. Discounted cashflow using the present forecast rate of interest.
4. Scoring models, considering as wide a net as possible.
5. Breakeven analysis.

"You don't think it's too flash?"

6

Project Estimating

Learning Outcomes

After reading this chapter, you should be able to;

Calculate a range of project costs

Use a range of estimating techniques

Collate estimates to produce a project budget

For the project manager to effectively plan and control a project, accurate estimating is essential. The estimator's task is to predict the project's parameters by building a model of the project on paper. The quality and accuracy of the estimate should be seen as the best approximation based on:

- Time available
- Information available
- Techniques employed
- Expertise and experience of the estimator

The quality and accuracy of the estimate can be continually improved as the project is progressively executed as more detailed and accurate information becomes available.

Unfortunately, the project manager may have to commit the company financially and contractually at the tender or quotation stage when the amount of data and information may be limited. For this reason alone, it is important to be able to provide accurate estimates based on incomplete information at the tender stage.

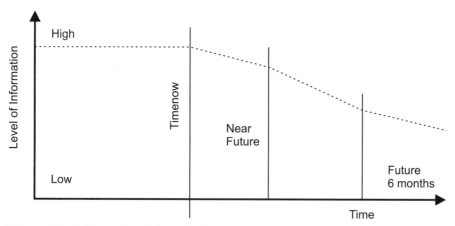

Figure: 6.1. Information Rolling Horizon

Although estimating usually focuses on the financial aspects of the project, it is important to remember that the costs cannot be accurately established until the other factors of scope, specifications, time, resources, materials, equipment and risks have been quantified.

Estimating is an integral part of the project management process, which should be based on past experience together with market norms and standards. Although the estimate will have an input into all areas of the project the investigation here will be restricted to **financial estimating**.

1. Estimating Terminology

In industry and commerce it is common to label the estimate according to its level of detail and accuracy. The following estimating terms; concept, feasibility, definitive and costing, relate quite closely to the project lifecycle phases. This classification depends on the quality of information available and the amount of effort put into compiling the estimate. The text will identify three types of estimate according to their purpose, scope of work, detail and level of accuracy.

1.1 Conceptual Estimate

Also called **order of magnitude, budget figure, ball-park figure** or **thumb suck**. The conceptual estimate addresses the needs of senior management who are presented with a number of possible projects. They need an initial filter to select those projects that warrant further investigation. This would occur in the concept and initiation phase.

The conceptual estimate will be based on a limited scope of work using scale factors or capacity estimates to give a low level of accuracy +/- 25%. A conceptual estimate would not be a legally binding document, however, professional competence could be questioned if the estimates were too far adrift. If the conceptual estimate looks promising, senior management will then allocate funds to finance a more detailed feasibility study.

1.2 Feasibility Study

Also called **preliminary estimate** or **comparative estimate**. Irrespective of how the project has evolved and crystallised the feasibility study investigates the feasibility of pursuing with the project within the defined boundaries and answers the question "*Should we go ahead with this project*?" (See *Feasibility Study* chapter).

The feasibility study should be managed as a highly structured mini project as set out in your company's procedure manual. It is essential at the outset to determine the needs and expectations of all the stakeholders. This can be achieved through a structured needs analysis to determine if the proposal (or alternatives) offer a real solution to address the project's brief. Although the feasibility study is characterised by information gathering, processing and reporting, the accuracy of the estimate may still be somewhat limited at about +/-10%.

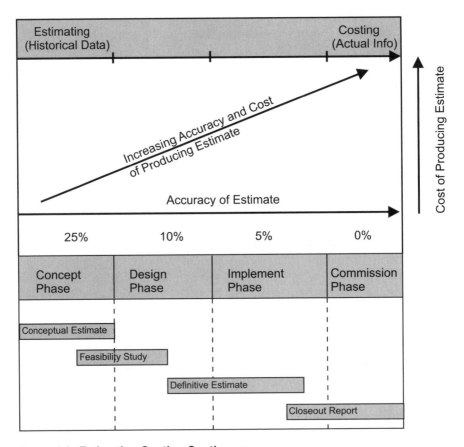

Figure 6.2: Estimating Costing Continuum

1.3 Definitive Estimate

Also called **detailed estimate**, **project control estimate, quotation** or **tender.** When the decision has been made to proceed to the next phase, the design and development phase, or planning phase, this will initiate another mini project to provide detailed designs and plans to build and manage the project.

The definitive estimate will be based on a considerable amount of data incorporating a developed scope of work, detailed WBS, detailed drawings, specifications, vendor quotations (that are now legally binding) and site surveys to give an improved accuracy of +/- 5%.

1.4 Costing

If estimating is defined as a quick method for pricing a project based on incomplete data, then costing may be defined as a detailed price based on a complete bill of materials (BOM) and parts lists. Costing requires the following items to be complete:

- Design and calculations
- Scope of work, bill of materials (BOM) and parts list
- Detailed planning
- Firm prices from subcontractors and suppliers, manhours and labour costs.

Almost every aspect of the project must be quantified, and with this high level of information and effort, accurate quotations of +/- 1% can be achieved. There is, however, a time and cost penalty, as costing is expensive and time consuming to produce.

1.5 Accuracy of Estimate

In figure 6.2 the level of accuracy is presented as a continuum from conceptual estimate at 25% to closeout report at 0%. As the graph moves from estimating to costing so the data moves from historical to actual information, and the level of accuracy increases, but so does the time to produce the estimate and the associated cost to produce the estimate.

Figure 6.2 shows the relationship between a higher level of accuracy and the increasing cost of producing it. Although it is not the project manager's function to set the company's profit margin, the project manager does need to know what the profit margin is, as this will influence the accuracy of the estimate and subsequent level of control. As a guide, the level of accuracy should be at least equal to, or greater than, the profit margin so that in the worst case a cost overrun would be accommodated by the profit margin.

Top-Down / Bottom-Up Estimating: Many projects can be estimated quickly using high level estimating techniques - this is called top-down. The converse (bottom-up) is when values are estimated at the work package level and rolled up. See *WBS* chapter for further discussion.

2. Project Costs

A project estimate can be subdivided into a number of different **costs**, consider the following:
- Direct costs
- Indirect costs
- Fixed and variable
- Time related costs
- Labour costs
- Material and equipment costs
- Transport costs
- Preliminary and general (P&G) costs
- Project office costs
- Project team costs.

2.1 Direct Costs

As the term implies, direct costs are those costs that can be specifically identified with an activity or project. The current trend is to assign as much as possible, if not all costs to direct costs, because direct costs can be budgeted, monitored and controlled far more effectively than indirect costs.
- Direct management costs refer to the project office running costs. Salaries for the project manager, project engineer, planner, accountant, secretary and QA.
- Direct labour costs refer to the people working on an activity, e.g. boilermakers, welders, fitters, computer programmers, etc.
- Direct material costs are for the materials, consumables, components which are used for completing an activity and an allowance for scrap and wastage.
- Direct equipment costs refers to machinery, plant and tools.
- Direct expenses include bought-in services that are specific to the project, for example, plant hire, surveyor, designer and subcontractor fees.

The distinctive nature of direct costs is that the total expense can be charged to an activity or project.

2.2 Indirect Costs

Indirect costs, also called **overheads**, are those costs that cannot be directly booked to an activity or project, but are required to keep the company operational.
- Indirect management costs refer to senior managers, the estimating department, sales and marketing, accounts, IT, general office staff, secretarial, administration and the personnel department.

- Indirect labour costs refer to the reception, maintenance, security and cleaners. Basically it includes all the employees who are required to keep the company functioning.
- Indirect materials include stationery, cleaning materials and maintenance parts.
- Indirect equipment includes computers, photocopiers and fax machines.
- Indirect expenses include training, insurance, depreciation, rent and rates.

Indirect costs are usually financed by an overhead recovery charge added to the earned man-hour rate and if not properly managed will eat away at the company profits. The acid test for the project's indirect costs and overheads, is to compare internal costs with the same services available outside the company.

2.3 Fixed and Variable Costs

Fixed and variable costs relate to how the costs change with the number of products being made. For example, costs such as, rent, labour and certain overheads are fixed (or so much per month), so are independent to the number of units made. But materials, equipment, transport and resource costs relate directly to the number of units made and are, therefore, a variable cost.

2.4 Time Related Costs

Critical path method (CPM) was originally developed to address the time / cost trade-off (crashing). If a project's duration is reduced or extended how will the costs change? To do this calculation you need to determine how costs are impacted by time. Consider the following:

- Rent increases with time.
- Running costs - water, electricity and gas would increase with time.
- If the project's duration is reduced, employee labour rate will increase if the workers have to work overtime.
- Contract labour on a fixed rate is not affected by time, but their productivity may reduce if they work long hours.
- Fixed price contracts may not be affected by time.

Simulating all the costs will give you the overall impact of time changes on project costs. This technique can also be used for project acceleration where you need to know the trade-off between the cost of accelerating a project to meet certain milestones compared with the penalties of failing to achieve them.

2.5 Labour Costs

This section will explain how to determine your labour charge-out rate. The labour costs considered here are for the project workforce and thus a direct cost. Although the salaries of a workforce may be clearly identified there are also a number of other associated costs which form part of the labour rate.

The labour rate is calculated by aggregating the various costs and dividing them by the number of manhours worked (in this case per month). This process is explained in the following worked example. Here the costs are subdivided into four main headings:

[1] Salary (see table 6.1)

[2] Associated labour costs (see table 6.1)

[3] Contribution to overheads

[4] Contribution to company profit.

		Cost per month	Days lost per month
1	Salary	$2,000	
2.1	Medical insurances	$50	
2.2	Sickness benefit		1
2.3	Annual holiday		1
2.4	Training courses	$30	1
2.5	Protective clothing	$20	
2.6	Car allowance	$250	
2.7	Housing allowance	$50	
2.8	Subsistence allowance	$100	
2.9	Pension	$100	
2.10	Tool allowance	$20	
2.11	Private jobs	$20	
2.12	Productivity bonus	$100	
2.13	Standing time		1
2.14	Inclement weather		1
	Total	$740	5 days

Table 6.1: Labour Cost

[3] **Contribution to overhead:** 30% of salary = $600

[4] **Company profit:** 25% of salary   = $500

Labour rate =   Total monthly costs
                 Total number of normal working hours per month

Where the total monthly costs are (salary + associated costs + contribution to overheads + company profit), and the working hours per month are (21 days less 5 days lost, times eight hours per day).

$$\text{Labour rate} = \frac{2000 + 740 + 600 + 500}{(21 - 5) \times 8}$$
$$= \$ 30/ \text{hr}.$$

Some of the above items may be difficult to quantify without access to statistical analysis, for example, days lost due to sickness and standing time. They should be recognised as potential costs and a figure assigned if only as a contribution to an unknown amount. The end product of this analysis should be a labour rate per hour.

Overtime: This brings us to an interesting question, based on the above calculations, how do you cost out overtime? If all the associated costs have been paid for by the contribution during normal working hours, can you assume they do not need to be paid for again? If yes, then you need only assign costs to the following headings:

- Labour wages overtime rate (time and a half or double time)
- Contribution to indirect variable costs
- Contribution to company profit.

You can also assume there will be no lost time, because you are either working overtime or not. In industry and commerce, however, the overtime rate to the client usually increases as a multiple of the employee overtime rate (time and a half, or double time).

2.6 Procurement Costs

This section will determine the procurement costs to acquire all the required bought-in goods and services. The simplest method is to add a percentage to the buying price to cover all the procurement costs. Consider the following (table 6.2):

Department	Scope of Work	Cost
Drawing Office	Bill of materials, specification	
Buying Office	Source of suppliers and vendors	
Quality Department	Prequalify suppliers	
Buying Office	Tender cycle, adjudication and selection	
Planning Office	Procurement schedule	
Buying Office	Place order, expedite	
Quality Department	Goods inwards inspection	
Warehouse	Material handling, inventory and stock control	
Accounts Department	Pay invoices	
Production	Scrap and waste	
Shareholders	Profit	
Total costs		

Table 6.2: Procurement Costs

$$\text{Procurement percentage} \quad = \quad \frac{\text{Procurement costs}}{\text{Total cost of materials}} \quad \text{x 100}$$

Many of the above costs may be covered by another budget, for example the inspection and pre-qualifying suppliers could fall under the QA budget, in which case they must not be included here (double accounting). The procurement costs would generally be developed at the company level and apply to all the company's projects. Typical percentages would be between 10% to 20%.

Old Stock: How does the estimator price material and equipment that has already been paid for on a previous project. What is the value of surplus material and equipment that has already been written-off? The estimator obviously has scope to price the old material and equipment from free issue to current market price. If the material is priced as free issue this will make your quotation more competitive. Company policy will determine stock rotation, which could be a mixture of:

LIFO - Last in first out
FIFO - First in first out

The material and equipment estimate usually allows the procurement manager the scope to save 5% to 10% on material and equipment costs through negotiation with the suppliers. In a competitive market this saving would significantly enhance the project's profit.

2.7 Transport Costs

It is important to appreciate the additional costs that may be incurred delivering the goods from the suppliers factory to the client's premises or site. Consider the following terms:

Ex-Works: It is the purchaser's responsibility to organise and pay for delivery, loading, transport and insurance from the factory gate.

FOB (Free on Board): The supplier will arrange for the goods to be loaded on board a ship, plane, train or truck at an agreed place. The supplier will pay for the port duties and export clearances, while the client is responsible for the transport, insurance and any import duties. It is important to clarify when the change of ownership and responsibility takes place. This is usually when the goods have been loaded.

CIF (Cost, Insurance and Freight): The supplier pays for the delivery of the goods to their final destination plus the insurance. The client pays for import duties.

DDP (Delivered Duty Paid): The goods will be delivered to the purchaser's front door. All the risks and costs relating to transport, insurance and duty will be the supplier's responsibility.

In order to compete successfully on the world market and convert quotations into orders it may not be sufficient to simply quote ex-works - at a minimum the quote should be 'per container load'. To quote in these terms will require the estimator to establish the weight and volume of the product needed to fill a container. A more useful quote to an international client would be FOB, for this it would be necessary to establish the cost of transport to the coast. But why not go further and quote CIF, or better still match other international exporters and quote DDP and delivery to the buyer's front door and quote in their own currency?

To offer these enhanced facilities will require the estimator to establish a data base of the 'total cost breakdown', so that they can respond quickly and accurately to an inquiry. DDP will also have the added benefit to the exporting country of earning additional foreign currency from the insurance and freight.

2.8 Project Management Office Costs (PMO)

The project management office (PMO) costs or **project management fee** are often separated out and might form a separate contract within the total project. The project management office costs not only include the management fee, but also many other associated costs. Many of the costs vary as the project passes through the project phases, there may be a number of part time team members either on contract or seconded from another department. Watch out for Parkinson's law (1957): "*Work expands so as to fill the time available for its completion.*" Once you have a data base of historical costs you may be able to relate this project management fee as a percentage of the project's value, about 6% to 10% would be typical.

Cost Breakdown Structure		Cost
Project Teams Salary	Project Manager	
	Project Engineer	
	Project Planner	
	Project Accountant	
	Procurement Manager	
	Quality Manager	
	Configuration Manager	
	Project Estimator	
	Project Secretary	
Project Office Costs	Rent, water, electricity	
	Office equipment	
	Stationary	
	Telephone, Internet	
Travel	Carpool	
	Accommodation, meals	
	Air flights	
Security	Reception, guards	
Training	Project Management, quality TQM, computer skills	
Marketing	Entertaining clients	
Total cost		

Table 6.3: Project Office Costs

2.9 Preliminary and General (P&G) Costs

If the project requires work on site, on location, or away from your office (virtual office), these costs are often separated out and called P&G's in the construction industry. A typical construction project would use the following headings: (Note, many of these headings have been identified already under indirect costs).

- Site establishment
- Site supervision
- Insurance and performance bonds
- Plant-hire, equipment, cranage, tools, vehicles and generators
- Site establishment, huts, toilets and fencing
- Site security, which would include the night watchman and guard dogs to protect the site from theft and vandalism
- Site services, which include telephone, electricity and water
- Temporary access roads and sign posts
- Scaffolding and ladders
- Temporary lights and power supply
- Accommodation for the workforce
- Special travelling expenses to site
- Special training and testing of tradesmen
- Material handling, which would include receiving inspection, off-loading, storage and inventory control
- Removal of rubbish, waste and scrap.

The costs assigned to these headings should include the normal recovery percentage for overhead costs and profit. Check that these costs are not being recovered elsewhere in the estimate, for example, site services and security may be provided by the client.

3. Estimating Methodology

This section will discuss some of the estimating techniques that can be used to predict the project's parameters and resource requirements quickly and accurately. The estimating techniques used by industry and commerce need to be agreed as the rules and procedures can vary tremendously from one company to another, consider the following:

- Jobbing
- Factoring
- Inflation
- Economies of scale
- Unit rates
- Day work.

The underlying assumptions of the estimate need to be explained and documented in an agreed format.

3.1 Jobbing

Also termed **job costing** or **operational estimating**. Jobbing is the process of including all the operations that go into executing an activity or task. Consider the following example (table 6.4) where the job is subdivided into its component parts. Once the activity has started, operational estimating enables the progress to be quantified:

- It provides a cost estimate for all the WBS work packages and activities.
- Progress can be measured as percentage complete or remaining duration.
- When the activity is complete the profit or loss can be calculated. This data can also be used to ensure that the estimating data base is kept up to-date.

Task	Description	Labour	Materials	Plant Hire	Transport	Total
100	Mark-out foundations	$1,000	$500			$1,500
200	Dig foundations	$5,000	$500	$1,000	$500	$7,000
300	Lay foundations	$3,000	$10,000	$3,000	$2,000	$18,000

Table 6.4: Operational Estimating Format

The operational estimating technique is a prerequisite for critical path method (CPM) planning and control. At the tender stage, however, there may not be sufficient time or need to produce an estimate with this level of detail. Certainly on award of contract, operational estimating must be carried out as it is part of the CPM process. We therefore need to look at other estimating techniques that are quicker to produce, but still provide a reasonably accurate estimate. The accuracy of the estimate can be improved by subdividing the WBS into more detailed work packages.

3.2 Factoring

Also called **component ratio** or **parametric method**. Factoring can be used when historical data from previous projects indicates that an item of the project can be expressed as a percentage of a known or calculated core cost (see table 6.5).

Management fee	5% of contract price
Quality assurance	1% of contract price
Engine beds	2% of engine costs
Pipe work	20% of generator costs
Consumables	10% of material costs
Profit	20% of construction price

Table 6.5: Factoring

Once the core costs have been established the associated ratios can be calculated very quickly. These ratios should be confirmed progressively as performance data becomes available.

3.3 Inflation

Also called **time based indices**. The project costs will change with time due to the non-reversible impact of inflation on the economy. If the current project is similar to a previous project completed a few years ago, the financial figures from the previous project can be used as the basis for the current estimate (see table 6.6).

	2010	2011		2012	
	Base cost	Inflation rate	New price	Inflation rate	New price
Labour	$500,000	10%	$550,000	8%	$594,000
Material	$400,000	15%	$460,000	5%	$483,000
Total	$900,000	12.2% average	$1,010,000	6.6% average	$1,077,000

Table 6.6: Inflation

The upward impact of inflation can be established using a Cost Price Index (CPI) and inflation indices. One of the problems with this method is that different commodities tend to escalate at different rates. This can however, be addressed by subdividing the project into its component costs by a CPI category, then applying an escalation factor to each, separately (see table 6.6).

3.4 Economies of Scale

Also called **cost capacity factor**. The cost capacity factor mathematically relates similar jobs of different sizes. If a job is twice as big as the previous job, will it cost twice as much? Usually not, for the following reasons:

Indivisibility: In a production process there may be certain indivisibilities, or fixed costs that are required just to be in business, but not related to output. For example, a firm may require a manager, a telephone and a secretary. These costs are indivisible because you cannot have half a manager merely because you want to operate at a lower output.

Specialisation: In a small business people have to be flexible and become a *Jack of all trades* to survive, but as companies grow in size so they are able to group work and assign repetitive tasks to one person. It is obviously more efficient (if not a little boring for the operator) to setup jigs to perform the same task repetitively.

Technical: Large scale production is often able to take advantage of automated machinery. The high capital expenditure can be written off over large production runs, thus reducing the unit cost, e.g. car production lines.

Scaling: There is not always a linear relationship between dimensions and volumes, e.g. on an oil tanker, the surface area increases at two-thirds the rate of the volume. Thus the tankers require proportionally less steel per cubic metre of cargo as they increase in volume. These economy of scale effects show that as projects get larger their unit cost reduces and the production becomes more efficient, however, there can be another side to the coin.

Diseconomy of Scale: As the output increases there are **diseconomies of scale** that are associated with the management function. When the organisation structure becomes large and bureaucratic the co-ordination between the management departments becomes increasingly more complex, costly and inefficient. Not only are the lines of communication longer, but inevitably there are more unproductive meetings.

These economies of scale which have a non-linear relationship can be quantified through a simple equation:

$$\$E = \$K \times (q1/q2)^p$$

where $\$E$ is the estimated cost
        $\$K$ is the known cost from a previous project
        $q1$ is the size of the new project
        $q2$ is the size of the old project
        p is the cost capacity factor raised to the power of p. The value of "p" is derived from empirical observations.

Consider a project to build a hotel with 1,000 rooms. If a similarly constructed hotel of 500 rooms was built for $10,000,000, what is the estimate for this 1,000 roomed hotel? (Assume $p = 0.8$)

$$\$E = 10,000,000 \times (1,000/500)^{0.8} = 17,411,011$$

This indicates that although the number of rooms doubles the estimated cost only increases by 74%.

3.5 Unit Rates

Also called **parameter costs**. Although a project tends to be a unique undertaking, much of the work may be repetitive. Parameter costs are developed from unit rates for common items of work based on previous projects. These unit rates need to be agreed with the client and any other relevant authority. This technique estimates a project's cost from an empirically developed book of unit rates. For example consider the following parameters (table 6.7):

Type of Rate	Scope of Work	Unit Rate
Per linear metre	Piping, wiring, welding, textiles	
Per square metre	Decorating, painting, house building	
Per cubic metre	Concrete, water supply	
Per tonne	Ship building, cargo freight	
Per HP or KW	Power, electrical supply, install a generator	
Per mile or KM	Transport	
Per day	Plant hire, car hire	
Per hour	Labour	
Per minute	Fashion garment construction	

Table 6.7: Unit Rates

Unit rates work well in a controlled work environment. However, many projects by virtue of their location and scope of work may involve other considerations:

- Unit rate estimating is appropriate for a contractor with a record of small jobs within a limited geographical area.
- As the contracts increase in size so the data base samples will tend to decrease in number.
- Costs are influenced by remote locations, logistics, travelling distances and the conditions of the roads.
- Weather conditions can be statistically predicted but what happens in practice may be very different (El Nino).
- Are there utilities available; Internet, mobile phone, water supply, power supply, accommodation, public transport, etc? Further considerations will be outlined in the estimating problem section later in this chapter.

Unit rates are probably the most commonly used estimating technique and will form the basis of most estimates. Unit rates are commonly used as they provide a simple contract to measure and budget. Even a fixed price contract usually contains a unit price clause for additional work.

4. Estimating Format

The final estimate will be a compilation of figures from many different sources. The challenge here is to present them all in one coherent summary document or budget which is agreed with the higher authority (and the client) in accordance with established standards and procedures. It is important to communicate estimates and budgets in a manner that ensures all relevant parties are clear of its content. Consider the following estimating formats (tables 6.8, 6.9 and 6.10):

WBS	Description	Budget
1.1		
1.2		
1.3		
1.4		
1.5		
Project management fee		
Sub-Total		
Profit		
Total		

Table 6.8: Estimating Format

In table 6.8 the WBS work packages form the main structure of the estimate and they can be subdivided further into CPM activities if a higher level of detail and accuracy is required.

WBS	Labour	Material	Machinery	Transport	Total
1.1					
1.2					
1.3					
1.4					
1.5					
Project office					
P&G's					
Sub-total					
Profit					
Total					

Table 6.9: Estimating Format

In table 6.9 the columns have been subdivided into the different types of costs (labour, material, machinery and transport) as discussed earlier in the chapter.

In table 6.10 the costs have been subdivided into the different estimating methods as discussed earlier in the chapter.

WBS	Jobbing	Factoring	Inflation	Economy of Scale	Unit Rates
1.1					
1.2					
1.3					
1.4					
1.5					
Project Office					
P&G's					
Sub-Total					
Profit					
Total					

Table 6.10: Estimating Format

It is essential to impose discipline and structure to the estimate so as to ensure that all parties are working to the same system. This can be achieved through company policies and standard procedures. These will obviously evolve and develop from the experience gained on previous projects. Using a standard estimating sheet for your type of work has many advantages:

- All the information can be rolled-up to one summary document or page.
- The structure of the estimating sheet is based on experience (learn from your achievements and mistakes).
- If the estimate is setup on a spreadsheet, you only need to input certain parameters as preset algorithms will calculate the rest and give you a professional looking quotation sheet.
- The estimating sheet's purpose is to calculate the work content - the schedule is developed from the CPM analysis.

5. Contingencies

So far the estimating has assumed that normal working conditions and practices will prevail. Unfortunately the real world does not work that way; allowances need to be made for risks and uncertainties. These allowances tend to get lumped together under the contingency heading which includes cover for the following non-recoverable items:

- Under estimating work content due to lack of scope definition.
- Delays in finalising designs due to client, designer and certifying authority.
- Additional work caused by design errors.
- Rework caused by production mistakes.
- Rework and replacement caused by material or component failure.
- Labour and equipment standing idle caused by import delays and inclement weather.
- Lost production caused by industrial action, strikes, work to rule or go slow.
- Limited supply of skilled labour locally.

The size of the contingency will depend on many factors:

- Type of project.
- General efficiency and competency of the company.
- Degree of risk and uncertainty.

The contingency allowance is usually added as a percentage to either, each work package or a blanket cover for the whole project, but not both. A blanket cover is obviously the easiest to apply, but this may unnecessarily increase your quotation. Adding a contingency at the work package level allows you to be more selective. Consider the following format (table 6.11):

WBS	Description	Budget	Contingency	Total
1.1				
1.2				
1.3				
1.4				
1.5				
Project Management fee				
Sub-total				
Contingency				
Profit				
Total				

Table 6.11: Contingencies (proforma)

You need to establish ground rules for managing the contingency;

- How should it be calculated?
- Who owns it?
- Who will manage it?
- How will it be allocated?
- Who will be advised of its existence?

6. Escalation

During periods of high inflation long term projects must consider the time value of money. The options are for the contractor to include an allowance in their quotation or for the client to escalate a base date tender. The mechanics of an escalation clause are:

- The client and contractor agree on which escalation index to use.
- The contractor quotes at **today's prices** with no contingency for inflation.
- Progress claims are escalated using published indices.

7. Bidders Dilemma

When tendering in a competitive market the contract price is one of the main selection criteria. The pricing dilemma facing senior management is the trade-off between reducing their profit and improving their chance of winning the contract, or increasing their profit, but reducing their chance of winning the contract.

Reducing the profit margin will improve the chances of your quotation being selected, but if the quotation is significantly lower than your competitors this will unnecessarily erode your profits. Therefore, before quoting a low price, first assess the market competition, your competitors' level of work, the client's budget and the state of the economy.

On the other hand, if the estimate is too high and the contract is awarded to your company, this will nicely increase your profits in the short term, but reduce the chances of further work if the same estimating data base is used on subsequent tendering.

If the quotation is reduced to secure the work what impact will this have on the original estimate? If the project manager requires 10,000 hours for a job and the quotation is reduced to 8,000 hours, then a project manager still requires 10,000 hours unless productivity is increased, production automated, or scope of work reduced.

8. Estimating Problems

The following list is a collection of points to be considered when estimating. Some of the common pitfalls to be aware of include:

- Keeping new technology under control - consider incrementally increasing technology, phased implementation and improving systems progressively. This is less risky than the big bang approach.
- Misinterpreting the scope of work and omissions.
- Risk and uncertainty are not considered.
- If work is priced out at the department average, regardless of who is doing the work, this simplifies the estimating, but the client may not be happy paying engineers' rates for an apprentice.
- The performance of individuals within a trade can vary considerably depending on their ability and commitment.
- Poorly defined or an overly optimistic schedule.
- Inflation on a long term project not considered.
- Lack of historical data, especially if this is a new type of project for the company.
- The main contractor will be at risk if they have to give a fixed price quotation to their client based on budget estimates from their subcontractors. However, the subcontractors may not be in a position to give a fixed quotation if the detailed drawings are not available.
- Make sure that costs are debited from the appropriate activity and not off-loaded to the activity with the fattest budget otherwise this will devalue your closeout report, and mislead future estimating.
- Consider your response to this reaction when requesting information, "*My people have no time to collect data, they are too busy doing the work.*"
- A NASA astronaut was asked what concerned him most about the flight? He replied, "*It's not sitting on a potential fuel bomb that concerns me most, but the 10,000 components that were made by the lowest bidder.*" (See the film Capricorn 1, which takes this problem to extreme possibilities).
- Terms and conditions of contract not quantified.
- Validity of the quotation not stated.
- Expenses often forgotten when estimating include:
  a) Commissioning and customer acceptance.
  b) Training of the client's technicians to use the installed equipment.
  c) Protective painting.
  d) Writing user manuals.

This concludes the chapter on *Project Estimating*. The following chapter will overview the *Planning and Control Cycle*.

Key Points:

- Estimating techniques and methods enable you to make quick and reasonably accurate quotations.
- Establish your cost structure (labour and materials) to simplify your estimating.
- Use estimating proformas to structure your estimates and quotations.

Case Study and Exercises:

Estimating techniques enable you to produce a reasonably accurate estimate quickly and efficiently. Although most companies set out to follow a tender schedule, when *'push comes to shove'*, many contracts are decided at the last minute, in which case it is essential to be able to respond quickly with an accurate estimate. Outline a number of estimating techniques you have developed in your line of work which enable you to respond accurately and quickly to a clients enquiry. Your presentation (written or verbal) should consider the following:

1. The range of estimates, noting the accuracy, the time to produce and the cost to produce.
2. Separating direct costs from indirect costs which you need to calculate overtime and crashing.
3. The material procurement costs presented as a percentage.
4. The project office costs.
5. The estimating proforma.

"Fill her up please"

7

Planning and Control Cycle

Learning Outcomes

After reading this chapter, you should be able to;

Use a number of planning techniques to produce a baseline plan

Apply a number of project control techniques

Adjust the reporting frequency to reflect the needs of the project

This chapter will overview the project planning and control cycle, which is at the heart of project integration. This is where the project manager is responsible for co-ordinating the contributions of all the project participants to meet the stakeholders needs and expectations. The PMBOK defines project integration management as; '... *the process required to ensure that the various elements of the project are properly co-ordinated.*'

This chapter will outline how the various project management planning and control tools and techniques discussed in this book relate to each other and how the core of project management integration involves making trade-offs between competing objectives and alternatives, in order to meet the stakeholders requirements. It is important to appreciate that a change in one parameter may change other parameters, for example, the late delivery of a drawing, or component could delay the start of an activity which could have resource and cashflow implications.

Planning is an important component of the planning and control cycle, because the planning process not only establishes what is to be done, but also smooths the way to *'make-it-happen'*. The challenge is to select and apply the available planning tools and techniques effectively. Planning asks questions, encourages participation, creates awareness, prompts action, solves problems, and formalises decisions based on consensus.

The planning process communicates planning information to the project team and stakeholders and obliges them to *'sign-on'* and pledge their support. When plans are drawn up by those who are going to implement them, they feel obliged (if not totally committed) to complete as planned. Conversely non-involvement in the planning process may lead to plans being ignored, dragging heels, misinterpretation, and *'not designed here'* attitude - which in turn leads to a time consuming analysis of the behaviour side of project management.

Planning is all about thinking forward in time. What varies is how far ahead the plans stretch and how precise they are. Churchill is reported to have said, *"It's wise to look ahead, but foolish to look further than you can see."*

1. Project Planning Steps

Although the planning steps are outlined here as a sequence of discrete operations, in practice other factors may influence the sequence and there will almost certainly be a number of iterations, compromises and trade-offs before achieving an optimum plan (see figures 7.1 and 7.2).

Project Charter: The project charter officially acknowledges the start of the project, and should outline the purpose of the project, the beneficial changes and key objectives, together with the means of achieving them. (See *Scope Management* chapter).

Feasibility Study: The feasibility study develops the project charter and project brief into a project proposal. It offers a structured approach for identifying the stakeholders and assessing their needs. It reviews closeout reports, together with investigating other options and alternatives to support the project's business viability (see *Feasibility Study* chapter).

Scope Management: The scope of work defines what the project includes and just as importantly, what is not included in order to meet the stated objectives. On an engineering project, for example, the scope of work would be developed into a list of drawings, bill of materials (BOM) and specifications (see *Scope Management* chapter). Scope management also includes a closeout report to document achievements and an opportunity to learn from mistakes.

Build-Method: The build-method outlines how the product will be assembled or implemented, for example, it considers the position of the crane and storage on a high-rise building, or the methods of communication and data storage on an IT project.

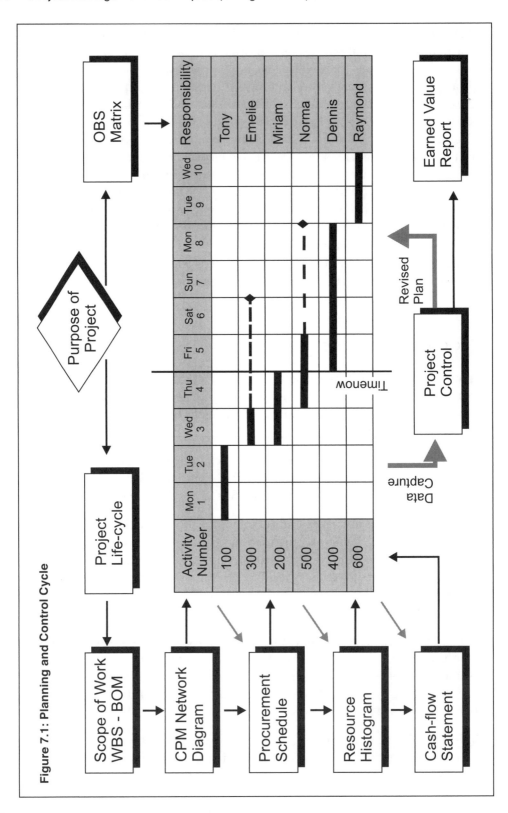

Figure 7.1: Planning and Control Cycle

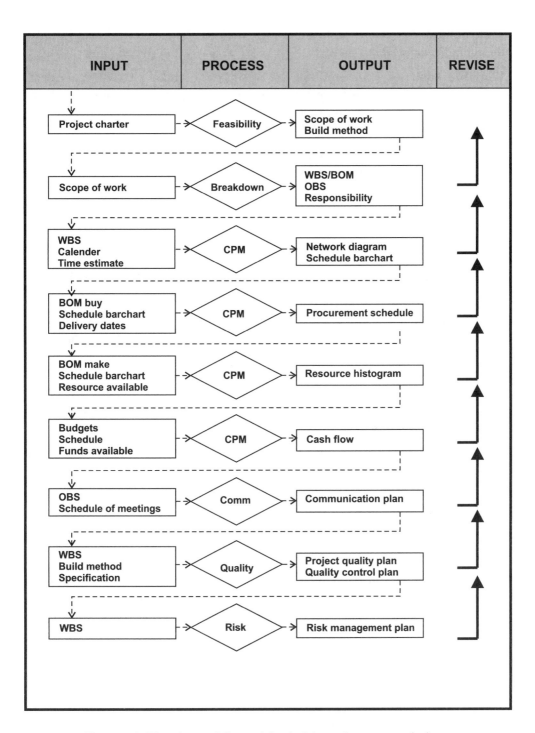

INPUT	PROCESS	OUTPUT	REVISE
Project charter	Feasibility	Scope of work Build method	
Scope of work	Breakdown	WBS/BOM OBS Responsibility	
WBS Calender Time estimate	CPM	Network diagram Schedule barchart	
BOM buy Schedule barchart Delivery dates	CPM	Procurement schedule	
BOM make Schedule barchart Resource available	CPM	Resource histogram	
Budgets Schedule Funds available	CPM	Cash flow	
OBS Schedule of meetings	Comm	Communication plan	
WBS Build method Specification	Quality	Project quality plan Quality control plan	
WBS	Risk	Risk management plan	

Figure 7.2: Planning and Control Cycle (alternative presentation)

Execution Strategy: The execution strategy considers the *'buy-or-make'* decision. If the product is to be purchased this is a procurement issue, but if the product is to be made in-house this is a resource issue where the execution strategy should identify the equipment and labour pool.

Work Breakdown Structure (WBS): The WBS is one of the key scope management tools used to subdivide the scope of work (as outlined by the build-method and the execution strategy), into manageable work packages that can be estimated, planned, assigned and controlled (see *WBS* chapter).

Organisation Breakdown Structure (OBS): The OBS or responsibility matrix is setup to manage the project as outlined in the execution strategy. The OBS links the WBS work packages to the company, department or person who is responsible for performing the work (see *WBS* chapter for diagram). Projects are often managed by a project manager and project team that is specially setup for the project and disbanded on completion. The integration of the project team and company departments is often through a matrix structure where the project team overlays the company's hierarchical structure - achieving *'buy-in'* by all stakeholders is critical for the project to be successful.

Critical Path Method (CPM): The CPM uses a network diagram to present the work packages and activities in a logical sequence of work that is developed from the build-method and other constraints (internal and external). Activity duration and work calendars are estimated, while the availability of procurement and resources are assumed not to constrain the time analysis. The CPM time analysis (forward pass and backward pass) calculates the activities early start, early finish, late start, late finish, float and the critical path (see *CPM* chapter). This information is often presented in an activity table and schedule Gantt chart.

Schedule Gantt Chart: The Gantt chart is one of the most effective and commonly used means of communicating schedule information. It enables the project participants to easily walk through the sequencing of the project's work. The planning structure can be further simplified by focusing on hammocks, key dates and milestones (see *Gantt Charts* chapter).

Procurement Schedule: The execution strategy *'buy-or-make'* decision will determine if the bill of materials is a procurement issue or a resource issue. The procurement function is to supply all the bought-in items at the best price, to meet the project schedule. However, long lead items need to be identified early on so that they can be ordered and/or the Gantt chart revised (see *Procurement Schedule* chapter).

Resource Histogram: The resources required to complete the work outlined in the Gantt chart are forecast and compared with their availability. Resource overloads or resource underloads need to accommodate both project and company requirements. The resource smoothing needs to consider other company projects and outside contractors before revising the scheduled Gantt chart (see *Resource Planning* chapter). The resources can be integrated with time to produce a manpower 'S' curve that forms the baseline plan for earned value calculations.

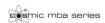

Budgets and Project Cashflow: The project accounting process not only establishes and assigns budgets to all the work packages, but also determines the project's cashflow. There may be cashflow constraints restricting the supply of funds that will require the scheduled Gantt chart to be revised (see *Project Accounts* chapter). The costs can be integrated with time to produce the budgeted cost for work scheduled (BCWS) that forms the baseline plan for the earned value calculation.

Communication Plan: The communication plan includes the process required to ensure proper collection and dissemination of project information. It consists of communication planning, information distribution (lines of communication), a schedule of project meetings, progress reporting and administrative closeout (see *Project Communication* chapter).

Project Quality Plan: The project quality plan outlines a quality management system (quality assurance and quality control), designed to guide and enable the project to meet the required condition. This may include pre-qualifying project personnel and suppliers, developing procedures, quality inspections and quality documentation (see *Quality Management* chapter).

Risk Management Plan: The risk management plan includes the process of identifying risk, quantifying risk impact, response development and risk control. It should also include a disaster recovery plan to accommodate the worst possible scenario. (See the *Risk Management* chapter).

Baseline Plan: The baseline plan may be considered as a portfolio of documents which outline how to achieve the project's objectives. The level of detail and accuracy will depend on the project phase and complexity. The baseline plan should be a coherent document to guide the project through the execution and project control cycle.

2. Project Control Cycle

The project control cycle is presented as a sequence of steps to guide the project to a successful completion. The baseline plan outlines the course to steer, but once the project starts you can be sure things will deviate; be it late deliveries, sickness, absenteeism, or scope creep. The project control cycle monitors project performance and compares it against the baseline plan - it also includes a mechanism for incorporating scope changes. Project control also relates to keeping the project team and personnel interested in the project, together with continuing support and commitment from senior management and all the stakeholders.

Figure 7.3: Project Control Cycle

Work Authorisation: As the *single point of responsibility* the project manager is responsible for delegating and authorising the scope of work. The issuing of instructions to the appointed contractors and other responsible parties signals the start of the execution phase of the project. The methods for authorising work, reporting and applying control should be discussed and agreed at the handover meeting, so that all parties know how the project will be managed. **A record of all decisions and instructions should be kept to provide an audit trail.**

As the project progresses there will be changes to the baseline plan that need to be authorised. These would tend to be authorised by issuing a revised document, typical examples include:

- Issue revised drawing for scope changes
- Issue revised schedule for schedule changes
- Issue revised budget for cost changes.

Expedite: Once instructions, orders and contracts have been issued, project expediting takes a proactive approach to make the instructions happen. It involves the follow up function to confirm that; orders have been received by the subcontractors, internal planning issued, materials have been procured, skilled labour available, work has started as planned and the schedule completion dates will be achieved. Any variance should be reported through the data capture system.

Tracking and Monitoring Progress: The data capture system records the progress and current status of all the work packages and activities. The accuracy of the data capture has a direct bearing on the accuracy of all the subsequent reports (project status, trends and forecast).

The data capture compares actual costs against the budget elements and records are updated and maintained correctly so that performance can be communicated to the relevant stakeholders. Deviations of actual costs against budgeted costs are identified and communicated to higher authority. Opportunities for corrective action or improvement are identified and communicated to relevant individuals (project teams members and client). Financial records are maintained according to agreed standards and procedures.

Change Control: The change control function ensures that all changes to the scope of work are captured and approved by the designated people before being incorporated in the baseline plan. Change control is also concerned with influencing the factors that create changes to ensure that changes are beneficial (see *Scope Management* chapter).

Evaluation and Forecasting: The project's performance is analysed by comparing actual progress against planned progress within the CPM model and extrapolating the trends and use '*what-if*' analysis to forecast the project's position in the future (see *Project Control* and *Earned Value* chapters).

Problem-Solving: The problem-solving function is to generate a list of possible solutions, options and alternatives. This may be achieved through interactive brainstorming sessions and quality circles.

Decision-Making: The decision-making function collates information and decides on an appropriate corrective action. **One of the main management functions is to make decisions**. In-fact it may be argued that the sole purpose of generating information is to make decisions. The following steps outline a typical decision-making process:

- Define project objectives
- Define the problem
- Collect information
- Develop options and alternatives
- Evaluate and decide course of action
- Ensure buy-in of the project team
- Implement the decision.

All these decision-making steps are intrinsically part of the control cycle. The decisions can now be made on what control to apply to keep the project on course.

Revise Baseline Plan: If there are any changes within the project the baseline plan must be revised to reflect the current scope of work and incorporate any corrective action. By saving the old baseline plan an audit trail of changes can be archived. The control cycle is now complete and the next cycle will authorise the changes and corrective action. If the project slips by more than 10%, it can be argued that the whole project should be rescheduled to introduce a sense of realism and attainability.

3. Reporting Frequency

The **frequency** of the reporting cycle should reflect the needs of the project. Short reporting periods, when there is a high level of change and uncertainty in the project, long periods when there is little or no change. For example, during project start up and during the commissioning phase the reporting cycle may be reduced to daily or even hourly, while under normal conditions the reporting cycle is usually weekly or monthly as outlined in the schedule of meetings (see *Project Communication* chapter).

As a rule of thumb the reporting cycle should leave sufficient time to implement corrective action to bring any project deviation back on course without delaying any critical activities. If the reporting is reasonably accurate the worst that can happen in a week, is you lose a week.

Key Points:

- The planning and control cycle integrates and co-ordinates the contributions of all the project participants.
- Although the planning cycle may consist of many separate techniques, collectively a change in one parameter may change another parameter.
- The control cycle guides the project to a successful completion by monitoring performance and applying corrective action where necessary.

Case Study and Exercises:

The planning and control cycle integrates all the planning and control techniques into one document. All the contributions can now be co-ordinated, processed and disseminated. By integrating the techniques the relationship between parameters can be determined and managed (in isolation and together).

You have been appointed project manager to design, build and commission a wind farm on the Isle of Lewis (Scotland). The plan it to line the coast with wind generators that can produce the equivalent power of two nuclear power stations!!! Although the islanders may be willing partners in accepting the project, there could be plenty of other obstacles. Your assignment is to prepare a presentation for a handover / start-up meeting to the project team and stakeholders. Some of the items to be discussed should include:

1. How you intend to develop the planning and control cycle.
2. How you intend to compile the baseline plan, manage it, update it and communicate it to the project team.
3. The role of the expeditor - the project managers' ears and eyes.
4. Reporting cycle, and how it may change during the project.
5. Project integration showing how the various parameters are related.

Project Integration - work in progress

8

Scope Management

Learning Outcomes

After reading this chapter, you should be able to;

Quantify the scope of work

Manage scope change control

Produce a closeout report

Effective scope management is one of the key factors determining project success. Failure to accurately interpret the clients' needs or problems will produce a misleading definition (scope of work). If this causes rework and additional effort there may be project cost and time implications. Therefore, project success will be self-limiting if the scope of work is not adequately defined.

Scope management is defined by the PMBOK as; *'... the processes required to ensure that the project includes all the work required, and only the work required, to complete the project successfully. It is primarily concerned with defining and controlling what is or is not included in the project.'*

Scope management defines what the project will accomplish, what it will deliver, what it will produce and where the work packages start and finish. Since most projects seem to be riddled with fuzzy definitions, scope management takes on a greater importance to avoid scope creep, and avoid adding features and functionality to the product that were not part of the original project contract, without an appropriate increase in time and budget.

1. Project Initiation

The PMBOK defines project initiation as; '... *the process of formally recognising that a new project exists, or that an existing project should continue into its next phase* [of the project lifecycle].'

Projects by definition have a start and finish. For a contracting company the start will probably be simple to identify - invitation to tender, or the award of contract. However, for the client organisation, the start of a project may not be so clear-cut. Some projects evolve as the embryo of an idea responding to market changes and new technology. In this environment, formal project recognition should be in the form of a *project charter* (with authority and budgets). It is important to distinguish between whims and ideas (white elephants) and items that could significantly benefit the company.

Project Charter: Also called **terms of reference**, or **project mission**, should be a tightly worded document outlining what is to be done and the boundaries of the project. For example, the project could be to build an Olympic stadium for 100,000 people, to Olympic standards, to be complete six months before the start of the Olympics, for x million dollars.

Unless the aims of the project can be precisely defined in a few short words it could imply that the client is not clear exactly what they want to achieve. The *project charter* should also include:
- Background to the project
- Key assumptions
- Business needs, and other commercial needs
- Scope of work
- Key activities, budgets and dates
- How the project is to be managed
- Role of the project manager (responsibility and authority) and reporting structure.

The project charter essentially formalises the project and should be documented and signed off. If this is not done by senior management, then the onus falls on the project manager, because the project charter provides the project manager with the authority to apply company resources to the project.

The project charter will help the project manager gain support and commitment from senior management. It may sometimes seem that senior management think that project risks are non-existent; that the project manager does not need any authority and that changes to the scope of work will never occur. Unfortunately, this is not the case, in fact it is just the opposite. Therefore, you need to develop a project charter that addresses these issues early on and get it approved. It will make the project managers job much easier later on, if you get sign-off on these issues at the outset.

2. Scope Planning

The PMBOK defines scope planning as; '... *the process of developing a written scope statement as the basis for future project decisions including, in particular, the criteria used to determine if the project or phase has been completed successfully.*'

The scope planning outlines the project philosophy that:
- Defines the boundary of the project and confirms common understanding of the project scope amongst the stakeholders.
- Forms the basis of agreement between client and contractor by identifying both the project objectives and major deliverables.
- Is a guide and constraint for the configuration management process influencing change control. During the commissioning phase scope planning will help to confirm that the project has been implemented to the required condition.

Scope planning develops a written statement that acts as the basis for future decisions and establishes a criteria for the completion of an activity, completion of a project phase, or the completion of the project itself. As the project progresses, the scope statement may need to be revised to reflect changes to the scope of the project.

3. Scope Definition

The PMBOK defines scope definition as; '... *subdividing the major project deliverables into smaller, more manageable components ...*' This will help to improve the accuracy of the estimate and assign single responsibility to the work packages (see the *Work Breakdown Structure* chapter).

The scope definition outlines the content of the project, how the project will be approached and explains how it will solve the client's needs or problems. Scope definition establishes a method to identify all the items of work that are required to complete the project.

The **build-method** outlines how the product will be built (or implemented) and the WBS can be used to provide a subdivision of the scope of work into manageable work packages. Responsibility can then be assigned to the work packages for accomplishment.

The WBS forms the backbone of the project. The WBS helps you generate a list of work packages against which you can add; costs, time (manhours), procurement (long lead items), resources etc. The importance of this document needs to be stressed, because without it you will be trying to manage an unstructured project.

4. Scope Verification

The PMBOK defines scope verification as; ' ... *the process of formalising acceptance of the project scope by the stakeholders.*' Scope verification can be related to the phases of the project lifecycle. The scope of work should be formally approved at the end of each phase:

Phase 1	Concept and Initiation	Approve the feasibility study
Phase 2	Design and development	Approve the detailed design and the baseline plan
Phase 3	Construction and Implementation	Approve all changes and additional work. Approve the construction is ready for commissioning
Phase 4	Commissioning and Handover	Commission and test the product, and confirm it is ready for handover to client

These controls are essential to establish the required condition before implementation and after implementation to confirm the required condition has been achieved.

5. Scope Change Control

All projects are subjected to scope changes at some time during their lifecycle. The scope change control system, or configuration management, is a system designed to effectively manage the change of scope process. Configuration management is the process of identifying and managing change to the deliverables and other work products as they evolve through the project lifecycle. It helps ensure that the proposed changes are necessary, appropriate and that the integrity of the system is maintained.

The PMBOK defines scope change control as:
> (a) *Influencing the factors which create scope changes to ensure that changes are beneficial* [to the project].
> (b) *Determining that a scope change has occurred.*
> (c) *Managing the actual changes when and if they occur.*

The project manager is responsible for setting up a system to monitor, evaluate and approve the changes (by the designated people) before the change is incorporated into the revised baseline plan. This will ensure that the revised baseline plan always reflects the current status of the project. Change control is also concerned with influencing the factors that create changes to ensure that changes are beneficial. The scope change approval system should be agreed by all stakeholders at the outset and confirmed at the handover meeting. The configuration management system offers:

- A change control system that formally documents a procedure defining the steps by which official project documents may be changed.
- Lists the only people who have the authority to make changes to the scope of work, in both the client and contractor organisations.
- A current and up-to-date description of the product.
- Traceability of previous baseline configurations.

- A record and an audit trail of approved changes.
- A framework to monitor, evaluate and update the scope baseline to accommodate any scope changes. This will ensure that the revised baseline always reflects the current status of the project.
- Automatic approval for emergency situations.

The project lifecycle clearly outlines two aspects of the configuration management system that have a similar scope change approval system, but different budgetary structures:
- Scope design and development
- Scope changes

Scope Design and Development: During the design and development phase, the project brief and project proposal are developed into detailed design drawings and specifications. The configuration management process here guides the design process and develops the scope baseline. The configuration management system formalises the design management process by capturing all the proposed scope developments. Before the scope baseline is revised these developments must be quantified, assessed, verified, integrated and approved by the authorised people. Only then will the scope baseline be updated and work authorised for execution. The financial implications of these scope approvals should be included in the project's budget.

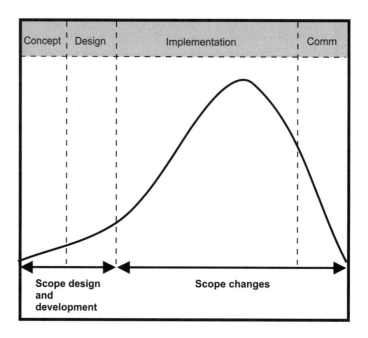

Figure 8.1: Scope Changes - shows scope changes during the design and development phases and the implementation and commissioning phases

Scope Change Control System: These scope changes would need to go through a similar system of approval against the design philosophy, but now the changes may impact on contractual time and budget agreements. If a change falls within the project proposal, this should be considered as a design development. However, if the change falls outside the proposal framework then the change should be considered as additional to contract and may attract a time extension and additional costs. This is why it is most important to establish a comprehensive proposal (scope planning) as a basis to allocate the cost of these changes.

It is important, particularly on large complex projects, that any scope changes are only approved by the nominated technical experts. This will not only prevent scope changes by non-experts, but also ensure that all implications of the proposed changes have been considered. Consider the following (figure 8.2):

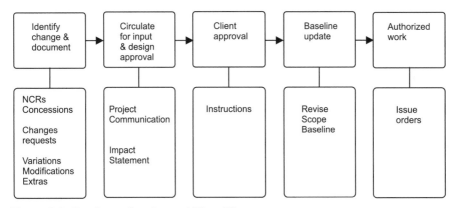

Figure 8.2: Configuration Control Flow Chart

Scope Changes: The control system should allow for scope changes to be motivated by anyone working on the project. Consider the following:

- **Non conformance report** (NCR) is usually initiated by quality control when someone has worked outside a procedure, or the product is outside the required condition. The non-conformance would either be corrected and fall away or motivate a concession.
- A **concession** requests the client to accept an item that has been built and is functional, but out of specification. If approved this would be shown as a scope change for this project only, it would be shown on the as-built drawings, but not on the master drawings.
- **Change requests** modifications and variations request the client to approve a change to the scope baseline.
- Any **verbal** comments or instructions which change the scope of work should be backed up in writing with a **project communication** document, as verbal agreements are open to dispute.

As the project management office (PMO) is the centre of the control system this is the logical place to keep a register of all the approved changes (signed) and their status. These documents may be required later to support invoices for additional work.

Change Request: Using a numbered change request form is the preferred method of motivating a scope change. The form should describe the scope change, list associated drawings and documents, together with the reason for the change (see figure 8.3).

Figure 8.3: Change Request (proforma)

CHANGE REQUEST			
NUMBER :		DATE RAISED :	
INITIATED BY :			
CHANGE REQUESTED (related drawings / work packages):			
REASON FOR CHANGE :			
APPROVAL:			
NAME	POSITION	APPROVAL	DATE

Project Communication: The project communication form enables any stakeholder working on the project, to make a formal statement. This could be a question, identifying a problem or making a suggestion. Once the document has entered the configuration management system this will ensure that it is acknowledged and actioned (see figure 8.4). This essentially puts the ball in the clients court and forces them to give clear written instructions.

Figure 8.4: Project Communication (proforma)

PROJECT COMMUNICATION
NUMBER: DATE RAISED: INITIATED BY: DESCRIPTION (related drawings / work packages):
COMMENTS / INSTRUCTIONS:
WE ACKNOWLEDGE YOUR ENQUIRY / INSTRUCTION: VERBAL FROM: TO: WRITTEN FROM: TO: DATE:
PLEASE ADVISE HOW WE ARE TO PROCEED: 1. START IMMEDIATELY AND QUOTE WITHIN 7 DAYS 2. START IMMEDIATELY ON UNIT RATES 3. DO NOT START, QUOTE WITHIN 7 DAYS 4. OTHER
REQUEST FROM: INSTRUCTION FROM: CONTRACTOR   CLIENT PROJECT MANAGER   PROJECT MANAGER

Impact Statement: The impact statement quantifies the implications of making a proposed change. The impact statement generally follows the clients response from the project communication and change request, but in reality it is usually issued at the same time. An information pack is now compiled by the project office to collect input, information, comments and approval from the responsible parties.

- Design team (prepare information pack)
- Technical impact (can we make it? What is the impact on the build-method)
- Procurement impact (can we buy it?)
- Production impact (do we have the resources?)
- Planning impact (will it delay the project?)
- Cost impact (will it increase the budget?)
- Quality impact (can we achieve the quality requirement?)
- Risk impact (are the risks acceptable?)
- Legal impact (will it change the contract?)
- Project manager (approve / reject)
- Client (approve / reject).

All the above documents should be numbered consecutively with a summary sheet showing the present status (see figure 8.5). The client's approval formally authorizes the scope change into the production system. This completes the configuration management control cycle.

IMPACT STATEMENT

NUMBER: DATE RAISED:
INITIATED BY:
DESCRIPTION:(related drawings / work packages)

REFERENCE PROJECT COMMUNICATION:

IMPACT ON PROJECT:		IF YES QUANTIFY
TECHNICAL:	YES/NO	
PROCUREMENT:	YES/NO	
PRODUCTION:	YES/NO	
SCHEDULE:	YES/NO	
COST:	YES/NO	
QUALITY:	YES/NO	
CONTRACT:	YES/NO	
RISK:	YES/NO	

PLEASE ADVISE IF WE ARE TO PROCEED: YES/NO

REQUEST FROM: INSTRUCTION FROM:

CONTRACTOR   CLIENT
PROJECT MANAGER   PROJECT MANAGER

Figure 8.5: Impact Statement (proforma)

Flow Sheet: A flow sheet is used to control the movement of the change requests and impact statements. The flow sheet determines the sequence of circulation. It logs the documents in and out of departments and collects comments, calculations and information but, most importantly, it notes the acceptance or rejection of the proposed change (see figure 8.6).

IMPACT STATEMENT FLOW SHEET			
IMPACT NUMBER:			
DESCRIPTION:			
POSITION	DATE IN	DATE OUT	COMMENTS
PROJECT MANAGER			
DRAWING OFFICE			
PROJECT ENGINEER			
PROCUREMENT MANAGER			
PRODUCTION MANAGER			
PROJECT PLANNER			
PROJECT ACCOUNTANT			
QA MANAGER			
COMPANY LAWYER			

Figure 8.6: Flow Sheet (proforma)

There are two possible methods of controlling the movement of the document:
    a) Hub and spoke (see figure 8.7)
    b) Consecutive (see figure 8.8)

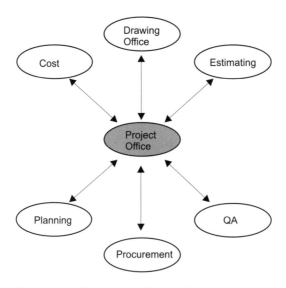

Figure 8.7: Flow Sheet (Hub and Spoke)

Figure 8.8: Flow sheet (Consecutive)

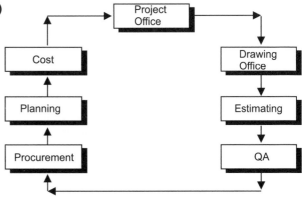

Although the hub and spoke arrangement doubles the movement of the documents, it does enable the project office to know where the documents are at any time. With the consecutive method the lines of communication may be shorter, but if the documents do not reappear timeously, it will require a time consuming witch hunt to find them. Whichever system is used it must be able to update and communicate the status of any change requests.

6. Project Closeout

It is important to not only learn from the mistakes and successes of previous projects, but also learn progressively during the present project. The project closeout report can be subdivided into three sections:

- Compile historical data from previous projects to assist conceptual development, *feasibility study* and estimating on future projects.
- Compile historical data from previous projects and the current project to identify trends and potential problem areas on the current project.
- Recommendations on how to manage future projects.

The lessons learned should be documented and communicated to relevant parties and stakeholders.

Historical Data: The search for historical data from previous projects will clearly show the benefit of effective closeout reports and filing. Learning from previous experiences is the most basic form of development and it is essentially free. There are, however, limitations with historical data, as the correlation between projects may be tenuous. Consider the following:

- The scope of work between projects is unlikely to be exactly the same.
- The cost data will be influenced by inflation.
- The manhours will be influenced by automation.
- The build-methods may be different.
- The project manager and leadership style will probably be different.
- The client and stakeholders will probably be different.

However, having made certain allowances for any limitations there should be a wealth of similarities. Look closely to see what went right and what went wrong together with any recommendations, because the same mistakes have an uncanny habit of happening again particularly if the cause has not been addressed.

Project Closeout Report: A closeout report can be generated at the end of each month, project phase, the end of your contract and the end of the project itself. It is advisable to compile the report before the project participants disperse. For best results a structured report format is recommended - consider the following steps:

- Generate a short questionnaire and circulate it to all the key project participants to capture lessons learnt.
- Analyse responses and debrief the key managers.
- Compile draft closeout report, circulate to relevant parties for comments. This can also be used as an agenda for a formal closeout meeting.
- Hold a formal closeout meeting attended by all the available participants.
- Compile the final closeout report, circulate it and file it.

An evaluation differs from a status report in that it considers the entire project lifecycle; management systems are evaluated, achievement of objectives are noted, budget comparisons are made, outstanding issues are identified, together with the issues that contribute to the success or failure of the project. The emphasis is on feedback with an open forum. However, resistance may be experienced if closeout reports are new to your company and the benefits not fully appreciated.

Questionnaire: The main benefit of the questionnaire approach is to structure the responses. It must be made quite clear that this exercise is not a **search for the guilty** but an attempt to quantify what actually happened on the project. The net should be cast reasonably wide to include a broad range of opinions from:

- Client
- Project team
- Corporate participants
- Suppliers and subcontractors
- Stakeholders

The questionnaire would typically be structured to include the following questions:

- Identify your position in the project organisation structure and comment on the interface with other disciplines.
- Comment on the delegation of responsibility and authority.
- Briefly outline your assigned scope of work.
- Comment on planning schedules, budgets, quality and manpower performance. Where possible quantify performance with statistical data.
- Give a candid assessment of your performance, analysing what went right and what went wrong. Comment on any non conformance reports (NCR) and audits with reasons for deviations and the level of re-work.
- Comment on the lines of communication, the issuing of instructions, the holding of meetings, the availability of information, procedures and reporting.
- Evaluate design, technical changes, as-built drawings and operator manuals.
- Comment on scope changes and concessions; evaluate how smoothly the configuration system worked; were changes approved and timeously.
- Discuss the use of new technology, computerisation and automation.
- Discuss unexpected problems, impact and solutions.
- Comment on the performance of procurement suppliers and subcontractors.
- Comment on manpower performance, their training and any industrial relation problems.

- Evaluate the accuracy of the estimate and list any recommended changes to the company's tariffs.
- Evaluate the contract document and any legal issues.
- Give general recommendations for future projects.

Some participants may be burning to give you their opinion, while others may be reluctant to commit their views on paper. Always be on the lookout for soft data, a simple gesture may speak a thousand words.

Recommendations: Learning from achievements and mistakes and improving productivity are basic economic requirements to fuel sustained commercial competitiveness. These recommendations can provide an invaluable source of direction for future projects. The closeout report should highlight any recommendations simply and clearly, because many years from now this may be the only section that is read.

Besides assisting with the estimating, recommendations from the previous closeout reports should also be tabled at the handover meetings. Validating the project estimate is essential. Over estimating will generate good profits, but in a competitive market will reduce the chance of winning further tenders. While under pricing will simply reduce company profits. Wherever possible the analysis should indicate perceived trends. These may be in technology, build-methods or project management systems. The final statement should comment on the overall success of the project and advise if the company is wise to tender on these types of projects again.

Storage: At the end of the project the files, photographs, all correspondence and particularly the closeout report should not be dumped and lost in the quagmire, but be readily available for inspection. This is the data base for future estimating and is an auditable item.

This concludes the chapter on *Scope Management*, the following chapter will discuss the *Work Breakdown Structure* as a methodology for subdividing the scope of work.

Case Study and Exercises:

Scope management defines the purpose of the project by outlining what the project should achieve; what should be included in the project; and just as importantly - what should be excluded from the project. For your case study you have been appointed to project manage the refit of a 'super yacht'. Outline how you will manage the scope. Your presentation (written or verbal) should consider the following:

1. Outline how the project charter will establish the boundaries of the project, together with the responsibilities and authority of the project manager.
2. Outline how the scope of work will be defined.
3. There will always be changes to the scope of work. Outline how the proposed system will capture and process any changes.
4. Outline how documents associated with scope management will be communicated and controlled.
5. It is important to learn from the mistakes and successes of your projects. Outline how you will progressively closeout your project.

9

Work Breakdown Structure

Learning Outcomes

After reading this chapter, you should be able to;

Subdivide the project into a number of work packages

Use a numbering system to uniquely identify all the work packages

Show the relationship between the top-down and bottom-up estimating

The purpose of the work breakdown structure (WBS) is to subdivide the scope of work into manageable work packages that can be estimated, planned and assigned to a responsible person or department for completion. The breakdown should group similar work together to improve productive efficiency, build-method and executive strategy.

The WBS was originally developed in the 1960's as part of the drive towards improved project definition and it soon became the backbone of the planning and control system. The WBS is an excellent tool for quantifying the scope of work as a list of work packages and is an essential tool for ensuring the estimate or quotation includes the complete scope of work. The WBS can also be considered as a hierarchical form of mind map that helps to break complexity down into simple manageable components.

The main components of the WBS discussed in this chapter are:

- Structure
- Methods of subdivision
- Numbering or coding system
- Level of detail
- Number of WBS levels
- Roll-up
- Integrating the WBS/OBS to assign responsibility.

1. WBS Structure

There are two methods of presenting the WBS:
- Graphically in boxes
- Text indents.

The WBS is a hierarchical structure which is best presented by a **graphical** subdivision of the scope of work in boxes. This logical subdivision of all the work elements is easy to understand and assimilate, thus helping the project participants to quantify their responsibility and gain their commitment and support (see figure 9.1).

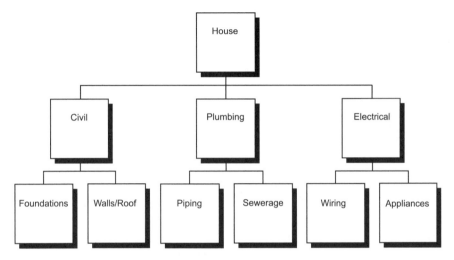

Figure 9.1: House Project WBS Subdivided into Boxes

Although boxes are an excellent means of presentation it is a cumbersome document to develop and edit on the computer. Boxes lend themselves more to graphic software than planning software and the printout for a large project would look best from a commercial printer rather than sticking A4 or A3 sheets together.

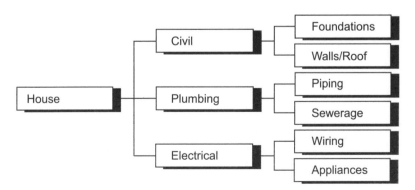

Figure 9.2: WBS Horizontal Presentation - shows a simple rotation of figure 9.1

The other method of presentation shows the scope of work as **text indents**, where each level is tabbed to represent its level in the hierarchy. If you are using planning software you will have to setup this structure anyway as you input the project data.

1.0.0 House Project

    1.1.0 Civil

        1.1.1 Foundations

        1.1.2 Walls and roof

    1.2.0 Plumbing

        1.2.1 Piping

        1.2.2 Sewerage

    1.3.0 Electrical

        1.3.1 Wiring

        1.3.2 Appliances

Here figures 9.1 and 9.2 are now presented as text indents which is how you would input the information into a planning software package.

2. Methods of Subdivision

Designing the WBS requires a delicate balance to address the different needs of the various disciplines and project locations. There is not necessarily a right or wrong structure because what may be an excellent fit for one discipline may be an awkward burden for another.

As you will see there are many methods of subdividing the scope of work, your imagination is the only limiting factor. The best method is the one that works for you, and you may even use more than one method as the project progresses.

Product Breakdown Structure (PBS): This represents a hierarchical view of the physical assemblies, sub-assemblies, components and parts needed to manufacture the product. Consider the subdivision of an aeroplane (see figure 9.3):

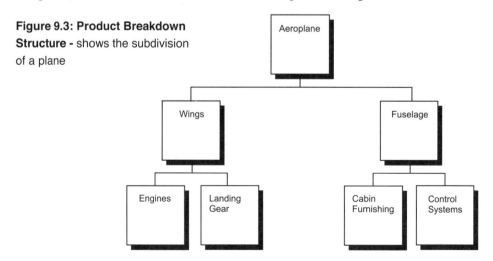

Figure 9.3: Product Breakdown Structure - shows the subdivision of a plane

Organisation Breakdown Structure (OBS): This represents a hierarchy of the company managing the project. By linking the OBS with the WBS or PBS this will identify who is responsible for performing the work packages (see figure 9.17 shown later in this chapter). The OBS could contain any of the following subdivisions (see figure 9.4):

- Department or discipline
- Contractor or supplier
- Project team or person.

**Figure 9.4: Organisation
Breakdown Structure**

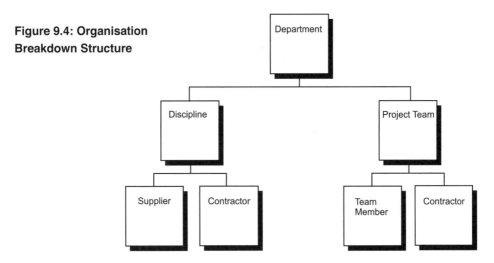

Cost Breakdown Structure (CBS): This represents the financial breakdown of the project into budgets per work package (see figure 9.5). Facilitating top down budgets, and bottom-up estimating.

Figure 9.5: Cost Breakdown Structure
(by cost centre and supplier)

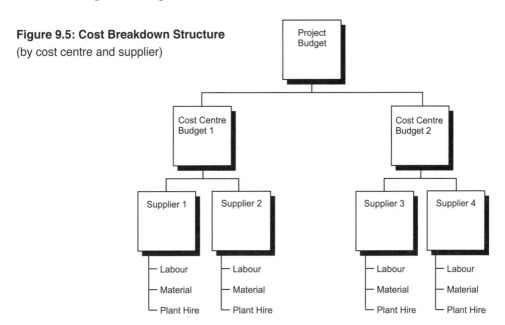

Contract Breakdown Structure: This represents the relationships between the client with the contractor. At the lowest level this could link the purchase orders with the account invoices (see figure 9.6).

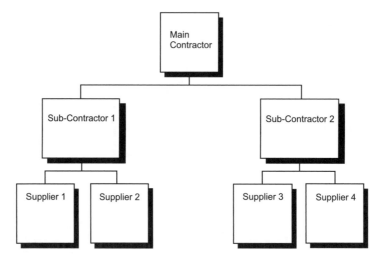

Figure 9.6: Contract Breakdown Structure - shows a breakdown by sub-contractor and supplier

Location Breakdown Structure: This represents the physical location of the work and would be appropriate for a project that has work packages at many sites or locations. Consider a power line project where there may be a number of similar substations along the route (see figure 9.7).

Figure 9.7: Location Breakdown Structure - shows a power line project

Transport Breakdown Structure: Projects that are characterised by large loads may find that transport and cranage limitations determine their breakdown structure (see figure 9.8).

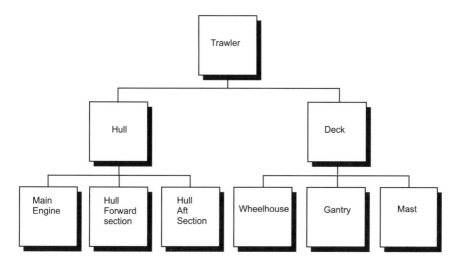

Figure 9.8: Transport Breakdown Structure - shows a breakdown into the largest units that can be transported by road

System Breakdown Structure: This represents a systems breakdown that may cut across other breakdown structures, but would be useful when commissioning the project. Consider the following house building project (see figure 9.9).

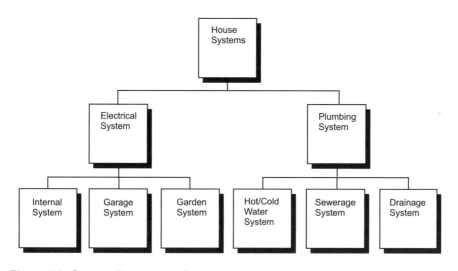

Figure 9.9: System Breakdown Structure - shows a breakdown of household systems

3. WBS Templates

Although location and discipline are popular criteria for subdivision, managers sometimes find difficulty thinking of methods to subdivide their projects. In practice, companies usually set up a standard WBS proforma or template for their projects. Instead of starting each project with a blank sheet of paper, consider using a WBS from a previous project as a template. A standard WBS ensures consistency and completeness as it becomes a planning checklist with all the components that your particular type of project would contain. Having a structured checklist also reduces the risk of omitting the obvious.

Even if the complete WBS template cannot be used, there may be portions of the template which are similar and can be copied across. Using proven structures will greatly speed up the planning process and help to structure your thinking. Figure 9.10 below outlines a WBS where the first level is subdivided by location, the second level by discipline and the third level by expense. This format could be used as a standard WBS for the company. The only changes per project would be to the description rather than the structure.

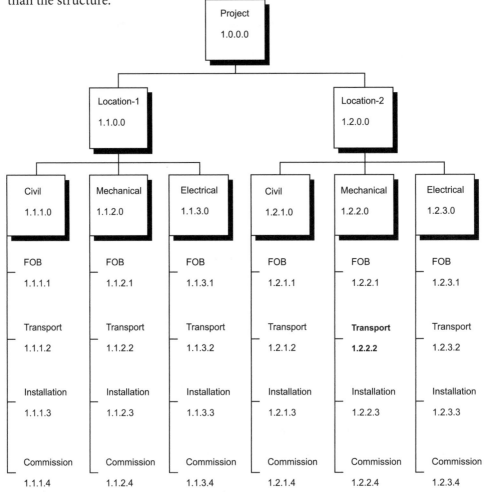

Figure 9.10: WBS Standard Format or Template (this can be used on similar types of projects) Note: FOB = free on board a ship, train or road transport

4. WBS Levels

With each level of the WBS the scope of work is subdivided into more work packages with a corresponding increase in the level of detail. For practical purposes three or four levels should be sufficient to achieve the desired level of planning and control - any more than that and, like a pyramid, the base of the WBS would start to become unwieldy. The number of levels is influenced by:

- Level of detail
- Level of risk
- Level of control
- Estimated accuracy
- Work package value
- Work package manhours.

If more than three or four levels are required this can be addressed by using sub-projects, where the lowest level work package of one project constitutes the highest level of another project. This situation is common on projects where a main contractor uses many subcontractors. In this way, the WBS can effectively increase the number of breakdown levels, with each project manager focusing on their own scope of work and responsibility.

Project Control: The appropriate level of control relates to the complexity and risks embedded in the project. Project control is the ability to steer the project to a successful completion. The earned value technique may suggest an appropriate $ value, duration or workhours for the work packages (see figure 9.11).

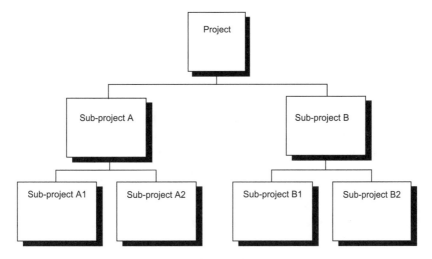

Figure 9.11: WBS Breakdown by Sub-Projects (with each project manager focusing on their own scope of work)

Risk and Uncertainty: The WBS structure should reflect the level of risk and uncertainty in the project. Where the level of risk is high the WBS can be subdivided further to generate more information which should reduce the risk. Consider the figure 9.12, where selected areas of high risk have been subdivided to a lower level.

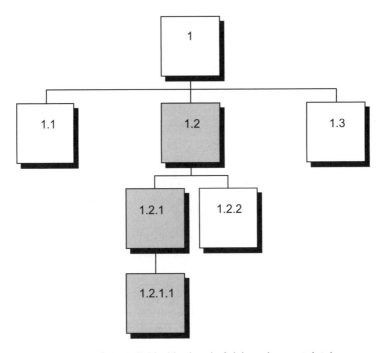

Figure 9.12: WBS (subdivided by level of risk and uncertainty)

5. Estimating

If your company wins contracts by competitive bidding it is important to have a system for generating accurate quotations quickly. The WBS offers a top-down subdivision of the work, while estimating at the work package level, offers a bottom-up roll-up of project costs. The WBS reduces the possibility of overlaps and underlaps. Overlaps of work cause conflict, while underlaps can be expensive - forgetting an item on a fixed price contract would be to your account. The **accuracy** of the estimate will increase progressively as the work package's level of detail increases. As a rough guide the level of accuracy should be at least the same as, or better than, the project's profit margin.

6. Numbering System

One of the beneficial features of the WBS is its ability to uniquely identify by a number or code all the elements of work in a numerical and logical manner. With a unique number or code, all work packages can be linked to the project's schedule, purchase orders, resources, accounts, together with the corporate accounts and the client's accounts. If all your projects use a similar numbering system this will make it easy to retrieve information (actual costs and duration) from past projects' data bases and closeout reports.

The numbering system can be alphabetic, numeric, or alphanumeric (letters and numbers), in most of the examples here the numbering systems will be numeric. Consider the following example:

Level 0: The first number [1.0.0] represents the first work element on the level zero. It is normal practice to have only one item at this level, i.e. the total project. The project may have its own unique number, see figures 9.13 and 9.14.

Level 1: At the first level of subdivision the first work element will be numbered [1.1.0] and the second work element numbered [1.2.0]. Therefore, the other work elements will be numbered sequentially; [1.3.0], [1.4.0], [1.5.0] etc.

Level 2: These numbers are then further subdivided at the second level from the first element at the second level into [1.1.1], [1.1.2], [1.1.3], [1.1.4] etc.

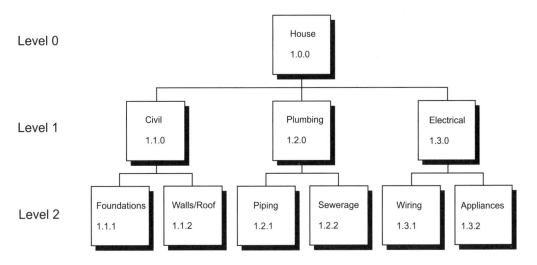

Figure 9.13: WBS Sub-Division by Numbering System

Figure 9.14: WBS Numbering System (this example shows how the numbering system can lead to very long work package numbers)

Project Number: Most projects are given a project number and a description to distinguish them from all the other projects the company may be working on. The project number may come from a number of sources:

- Estimate number
- Quotation number
- Contract number
- Invoice number
- Purchase order number
- Client's order number.

Many projects also have a **name** or humorous nickname to help association. For example, marine projects would use the ship's name, London's city airport was originally known as the STOL port (short take off and landing). With increased computer graphics a project icon is also a consideration.

7. WBS Roll-up

The WBS offers top-down estimating at the project level, and bottom-up estimating and roll-up at the work package level. The accuracy of the estimate will increase progressively as the work packages' level of detail increases. By suitably structuring the WBS, budgets can be established per department, per location or per subcontractor (see figure 9.15).

The WBS roll-up technique lends itself to anything that flows in the project, i.e. manhours, lines of software code, cubic meters of concrete, tonnes of steel erected, bricks laid, drawings completed, square meters of paint, etc. Any of these could be planned, tracked and controlled using the WBS.

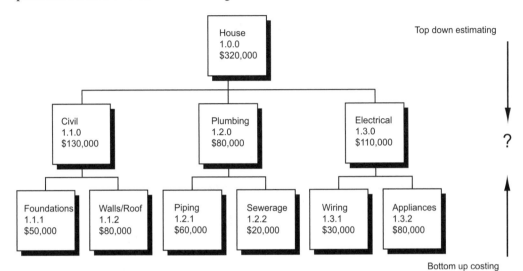

Figure 9.15: Roll-Up House Project

For example, a house building project may be estimated at the project level as 320 m2 at $1000 per square metre. And when the contract is awarded the budget will be developed at the work package level using unit rates and other estimating techniques - will the two figures meet in the middle? (see figure 9.15)

Consider a Drawing Office project where it would be more appropriate to plan and track manhours rather than costs (see figure 9.16).

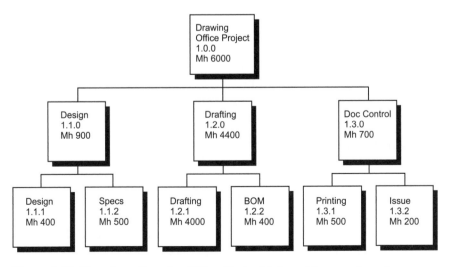

Figure 9.16: Exercise - Drawing Office Project (where Mh = manhours)

8. Responsibility

Assigning responsibility for performing project work is one of the key project management functions. This can be achieved through the interface between the WBS and the organisation breakdown structure (OBS). The WBS / OBS links clearly indicates the work packages and the people responsible for carrying out the work. However, it is a rather cumbersome presentation as the level of detail increases. For this reason it is best suited to high level links (see figure 9.17).

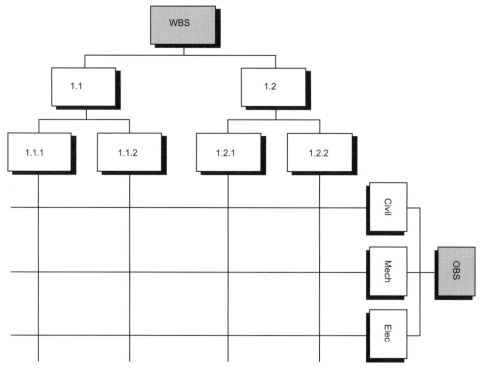

Figure 9.17: WBS / OBS Links

The WBS/OBS links can also be shown more simpler and easier on the Gantt chart, by either using a responsibility field (also called a responsibility matrix) or printing the persons's name after the activity (See *Gantt Charts* chapter).

9. Foreign Currency

Some projects are characterised by international procurement from a number of countries. As these exchange rates are prone to fluctuate, then your risk management analysis will need to determine the extent of your exposure to each foreign currency. This can be achieved by structuring the WBS to roll-up a number of foreign currencies and report the total requirement for each (see figure 9.18).

The WBS does not indicate when the foreign currency is required, for this you will have to develop the cashflow statement through the critical path method (CPM) which is the topic of the following chapter.

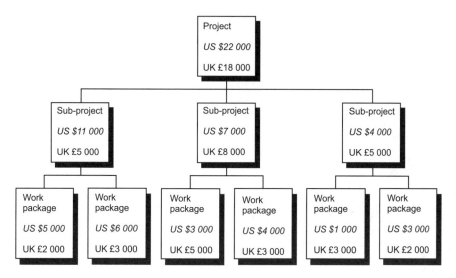

Figure 9.18: WBS by Foreign Currency

Key Points:

- The WBS subdivides the project into manageable work packages.
- On fixed price contracts the WBS helps to ensure the quotation includes the full *scope of work*.
- The WBS numbering system uniquely identifies all the work packages.

Case Study and Exercises:

The WBS subdivides the scope of work into manageable work packages that can be estimated, planned, and assigned to a responsible person or department for completion. You have been appointed project manager (event manager) for a Rolling Stones concert. Outline how you would use the WBS to subdivide the event, considering the following:

1. Methods of subdivision.
2. Develop standard template for future events.
3. Numbering system.
4. Number of levels.
5. What information would you roll-up?

10

Critical Path Method

For project managers to effectively plan and control a project they need to be able to process large amounts of data quickly and accurately to enable them to create order in a complex situation. The critical path method (CPM) offering a structured approach to project planning, has been designed to meet this need.

This chapter will outline the techniques and practical applications of CPM, taking you step-by-step through the planning stages from developing the logical network diagram through to establishing the critical path. Although CPM was originally developed to quantify the **time cost trade-off**, the term is now used interchangeably with PERT. These generic names are understood to mean both time planning on its own, or to incorporate the complete integrated planning and control cycle.

1. Network Diagram (part 1)

The work breakdown structure (WBS) provides a structured breakdown of the scope of work into manageable work packages that can be further developed into a list of activities (see *WBS* chapter). The next process is to establish a logical relationship between the activities using a network diagram.

The network diagram may be defined as a graphical presentation of the project's activities showing the planned sequence of work. In its simplest form only two items of information are required:

- List of activities
- Logic constraints, also called logical links, logical dependency or logical relationships between the activities.

The network diagram, also called precedence diagram method (PDM) is a development of the activity-on-node (AON) (see *History* chapter) concept where each activity is represented as a node or a box.

2. Definition of an Activity (part 1)

An activity may be defined as any task, job or operation that must be performed to complete the work package or project. A WBS work package can be subdivided into one or more activities, with the work packages and activities using different numbering systems. The terms activity, task, work and job are often used interchangeably. In the network diagram an activity is always represented by an identity number, which can be alpha and/or numeric and is presented in a box. The activity should be given a description to ensure the project team members understand the work content - this can be expanded later on a job card.

3. Logical Relationships (part 1)

The network diagram shows the sequence of the activities where these logical relationships can be either mandatory or discretionary. **Mandatory** or hard dependencies are limitations of the build-method, for example, on a construction project the foundations **must** (hard logic) be built before the walls and roof are erected, whereas scheduling the electrical work before the plumbing work is discretionary (soft logic). **Discretionary** logic is the preferred or best practice defined by the body of knowledge. Before we can draw the network diagram we must define the logical relationships between all the activities. There are two basic relationships:

- Activities in series
- Activities in parallel.

Activities in Series: When the activities are in series they are carried out one after the other. When the network is first developed this would probably be the most common type of relationship. An example of activities performed in series on a house project would be the foundation (activity A100), followed by the walls (A200), followed by the roof (A300). Read the network diagram from left to right (see figure 10.1).

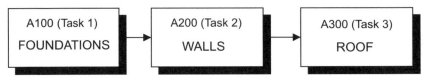

Figure 10.1: Activities in Series

Activities in Parallel: When activities are in parallel they can be performed at the same time, which is a more efficient use of time than activities in series. An example on a house project would be the installation of plumbing (activity A400) and electrical fittings (A500) simultaneously after the roof is fitted (A300), followed by the painting (A600) (see figure 10.2).

Figure 10.2: Activities in Parallel

4. How to Draw the Logical Relationships (part 1)

The terms logical relationship, constraint, dependency and link are all used interchangeably to represent the lines drawn between the activity boxes. The preferred presentation shows the constraint lines drawn from left to right, starting from the right side of one activity box into the left side of the following box. However, many software packages have the lines drawn from the top and bottom of the boxes. Initially an arrow at the end of the constraint may help you to follow the direction of work flow.

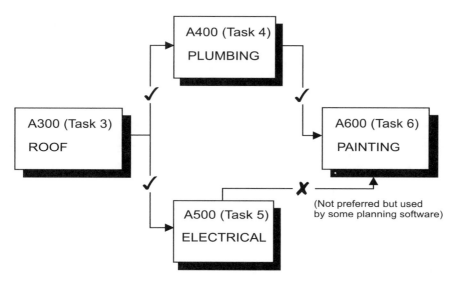

Figure 10.3: How to Draw Activity Constraints

In the past some projects were developed using yellow stickers (as activities) positioned on a large wall. Now with relatively cheap, but powerful planning software it would be rare not to develop a large project on the computer. When viewing the network diagram of large projects on the screen or printing them out, most software offers you the facility to control the amount of information in the boxes, reducing the detail right down to only the activity number for a condensed picture. To print out a detailed network diagram would be a lengthy task - one client showed me their detailed network diagram which would have covered a tennis court!

5. Activity Logic Table (part 1)

For ease of reading, logic information is often compiled in a tabular format, with each record (or line) defining a relationship. Planning software usually names the before and after activities as preceding and succeeding activities as detailed below (see tables 10.1 and 10.2):

Before Activity	Constraint	Following Activity

Table 10.1: Activity Logic Table

Preceding Activity	Constraint	Succeeding Activity

Table 10.2: Activity Logic Table

Using the activity logic in table 10.3, walk through the following worked example (see figure 10.4) where the activities and constraints are labelled.

Preceding Activity	Constraint	Succeeding Activity
Start	C1	A100
A100	C2	A200
A100	C3	A300
A200	C4	A400
A300	C5	A500
A400	C6	A600
A500	C7	A600
A600	C8	Finish

Table 10.3: Activity Logic Table (CPM example)

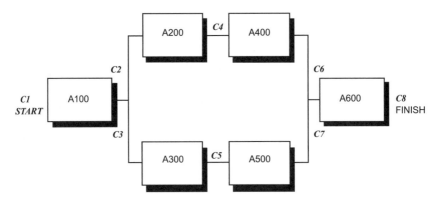

Figure 10.4: Network Diagram (drawn from table 10.3, C = constraint)

Even if the logic table is not manually generated by the planner, the planning software will compile the logic data in this format. It is therefore useful for the planners to be familiar with this presentation to enable them to validate the network data. A common format for both input and presentation is simply to look at an activity and its preceding activity. Consider the above example (table 10.3 and figure 10.4) and transpose the logic into the table 10.4.

Some planners prefer to sketch out a rough draft of the *network diagram* using a pencil and plenty of eraser before loading it on the computer. The intention here is to predict what will happen downstream in the project. A common problem when developing the *network diagram* is to introduce activities on the basis of time rather than logic. At this point in the planning process think only of the sequence of the activities - as the constraints of duration, procurement, resources and costs will be introduced later.

Activity	Preceding Activity	Duration
A100	start	2
A200	A100	2
A300	A100	1
A400	A200	4
A500	A300	2
A600	A400, A500	2

Table 10.4: Solution to Table 10.4

6. Activity Duration (part 1)

We need two more items of information before we can proceed with the CPM time analysis:

- Activity duration
- Activity calendar or work pattern.

Time units can be expressed as hours, days, weeks, months, or shifts depending on the length of the activities and the project. For simplicity, the time units used in this book will be days (unless otherwise stated), and in part 1 of this chapter we will assume continuous working (seven days a week). An activity's duration will run from the start to the finish of the activity. An activity's duration is linked to resources - increasing the resources will obviously shorten the duration. At this point certain assumptions will have to be made and adjusted later.

7. Calendar / Work Pattern (part 1)

Calendar or **work pattern** are common terms used in the planning software to describe an activity's working profile, in other words, on what days of the week the resources or activity will be working. As a first step we will assume the activity is working seven days a week, this is usually termed **continuous** working.

8. Critical Path Method Steps (part 1)

We are now ready to perform the CPM time analysis to establish the start and finish dates for all the activities. Before we do, let us first recap on the CPM steps we have outlined:

- Draw the logic network diagram
- Assign durations to all the activities
- Impose a work calendar.

In addition to the logic table, an activity table would include the following headings (see table 10.5):

Activity Number	Description	Duration	Calendar

Table 10.5: Activity Logic Table (proforma)

Start Date: We need to give the project a start date (this can always be changed later). The CPM analysis needs a start date from which to schedule the work. If no date is given the planning software would use today's date as the default option. By setting the start date the first iteration will give the planner a feel for the end date of the project using the given logic, activity duration and calendar. If a target completion date is given, the above parameters (logic, duration, calendar and start date), can be adjusted accordingly.

Early Start: Is the earliest date by which an activity can start assuming all the preceding activities are completed as planned.

Early Finish: Is the earliest date by which an activity can be completed assuming all the preceding activities are completed as planned.

Late Start: Is the latest date an activity can start to meet the planned completion date.

Late Finish: Is the latest date an activity can finish to meet the planned completion date.

Target Start and **Target Finish:** In addition to the calculated dates there may be a number of imposed dates, influenced by the delivery of materials, access to sub-contractors, or other milestones.

Activity Box: The activity box key indicates where to position the values in the activity box. This layout varies with the software package, but the format in figure 10.5 will be used throughout this book.

EARLY START		EARLY FINISH
FLOAT	ACTIVITY NUMBER DESCRIPTION	DURATION
LATE START		LATE FINISH

Figure 10.5: Activity Box (typical layout)

9. Forward Pass (part 1)

We use the term forward pass to define the process of calculating the early start date (ES) and early finish date (EF) for all the activities. For convenience the early start date of the first activity in all the examples will be either day one or the first day of the month (i.e. 1st May).

Consider a simple project with two activities A and B. The relationship between A and B is *finish-to-start*, this means activity A must be completed before B can start.

Activity Number	Preceding Activity	Duration
A	Start	3
B	A	4

Table 10.6: Activity Logic Table

Figure 10.6: Forward Pass

The early finish date of an activity is calculated by adding the activity duration to the early start date, using the following formula.

EF = ES + Duration - 1

In the equation the minus one is required to keep the mathematics correct. The Gantt chart in figure 10.7, will clarify this requirement. Shown as a Gantt chart it can be clearly seen that a three day activity that starts on day 1 will finish on day 3.

	1	2	3	4	5	6	7
	MON	TUE	WED	THU	FRI	SAT	SUN
ACTIVITY A 3 DAYS DURATION	ES		EF				
ACTIVITY B 4 DAYS DURATION				ES			EF

Figure 10.7: Gantt Chart

Use the above equation to find the early finish date (EF) of activity A (see figure 10.8),

EF(A)   = **ES(A) +Duration (A) - 1**

= 1+3 - 1

= 3

1		3
	A	3

FS

Finish-To-Start

	B	4

Figure 10.8: Forward Pass

To calculate the early start date (ES) of activity B use the following formula (Activity (B) can only start the day after Activity (A) has finished).

ES(B)   = **EF(A) + 1**

= 3 + 1

= 4

1		3
	A	3

FS

Finish-To-Start

4		
	B	4

Figure 10.9: Forward Pass

To calculate the early finish date (EF) of B use the same formula as we used previously on activity A.

EF(B)   = **ES(B) + Duration (B) - 1**

= 4 + 4 - 1

= 7

1		3
	A	3

FS

Finish-To-Start

4		7
	B	4

Figure 10.10: Forward Pass

To recap, the early start date of any activity is a measure of the time required to complete all preceding activities in the logical order outlined in the network diagram.

10. Backward Pass (part 1)

Now that we have completed the forward pass the next step is to perform a backward pass to calculate the late start date (LS) and late finish date (LF) of each activity. The late finish date for the last activity may be assigned, if not, use the early finish date of the last activity (see figure 10.11).

$$\textbf{LF(B)} \qquad = \textbf{EF(B)}$$

$$= 7$$

Figure 10.11: Backward Pass

To calculate the late start date (LS) of activity B use the following formula:

$$\textbf{LS(B)} \qquad = \textbf{LF(B) - Duration (B) + 1}$$

$$= 7 - 4 + 1$$

$$= 4$$

Note the plus one in the formula to keep the mathematics correct.

$$\textbf{LF(A)} \qquad = \textbf{LS(B) - 1}$$

$$= 4 - 1$$

$$= 3$$

$$\textbf{LS(A)} \qquad = \textbf{LF(A) - Duration (A) + 1}$$

$$= 3 - 3 + 1$$

$$= 1$$

Figure 10.12: Backward Pass

To recap, the late start date of any activity is a measure of the time required to complete all succeeding activities, in the logical order outlined in the network diagram.

Note: On large networks, when many activities lead into one activity on the forward pass, take the highest early finish value to calculate the early start date of the succeeding activity. On the backward pass when many activities lead into one activity, take the lowest late start value to calculate the late finish of the preceding activity.

11. Activity Float (part 1)

Activity **float**, also called **slack**, is a measure of flexibility, or inherent surplus time in an activity's scheduling. This indicates how many working days the activity can be delayed or extended before it will extend the completion date of the project or any target finish dates (milestones). Float is calculated by either of the two equations.

Float = Late Start - Early Start

Float = Late Finish - Early Finish

Mathematically they are both the same, therefore select the equation you are most comfortable with. Using the previous example:

Float (A)   = **LS(A) - ES(A)**

= 1 - 1

= 0

The float for activity B is also 0. Where an activity has zero float this indicates it is on the **critical path**.

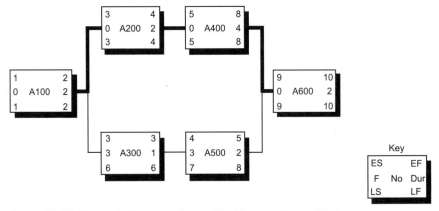

Figure 10.13: Network Diagram - shows the activity float

This now completes the forward pass and backward pass. You are now in a position to complete the CPM time analysis for the logic table 10.3 and figure 10.4, developed earlier in the chapter.

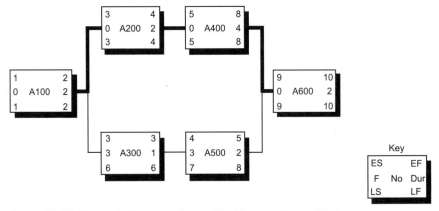

Figure 10.14: Network Diagram (see table 10.3 and figure 10.4)

This completes the first part of the CPM process - the second part will take the planning and control technique a step further.

12. Network Diagrams (part 2)

To develop the network diagram it is advisable that the planner walks through the sequence of work with the managers, supervisors or the people who are going to perform the work, partly to ensure the build-method is correct, but mostly to gain their commitment (*buy-in*) and ensure the project achieves its objectives. Note all the assumptions for hard logic, soft logic, durations, calendars, procurement, resource and budget requirements.

Developing the network diagram can be a juggling act, particularly if you have a long list of work packages. One way to get started is to select a key activity and work outwards:

- What activities must be done before?
- What activities can be done at the same time?
- What activities can be done next?

Feedback from previous projects is also useful particularly if it provides a template that can be applied in whole or part to your project (see the closeout report in the *Scope Management* chapter). Besides the basic *finish-to-start* there are three other types of constraints between activities. The abbreviation is shown in brackets:

- Finish-to-Start (FS)
- Start-to-Start (SS)
- Finish-to-Finish (FF)
- Start-to-Finish (SF)

Finish-to-Start (FS): The *finish-to-start* (FS) constraint is the most common type of relationship. In the example below activity 200 cannot start until activity 100 is finished. So if activity 100 is completed on Monday then 200 can start on Tuesday (see figure 10.15).

Figure 10.15: Finish-to-Start (FS)

This relationship can be further developed by imposing a delay, or lag, between the activities. For example, if the concrete needs 2 days to cure and the foundations (activity 100) are thrown on Monday, then the building of the walls (activity 200) cannot start before Thursday (see figure 10.16).

Figure 10.16: Finish-to-Start (with 2 days lag)

Or in Gantt chart form (see figure 10.17):

	1	2	3	4	5	6	7
	MON	TUE	WED	THU	FRI	SAT	SUN
Foundation 100							
Lag 2 Days							
Walls 200							

Figure 10.17: Finish-to-Start Gantt Chart (with 2 days lag)

Start-to-Start (SS): The *start-to-start* (SS) constraint represents the relationship between the start dates of the two activities. If activity 600 can start 4 days after 500 has started this would represent a *fast tracking* situation, where the project's duration is compressed by overlapping the activities.

An example of a SS constraint would be the laying of a pipe line. When the first km of the trench has been dug, the pipe laying can start. If the digging starts on a Monday and it takes 4 days to dig the first km, then the pipe laying can start on Friday the 5th day (see figure 10.18).

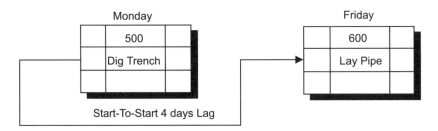

Figure 10.18: Start-to-Start (FS)

Or in Gantt chart form (see figure 10.19):

	1	2	3	4	5	6	7
	MON	TUE	WED	THU	FRI	SAT	SUN
Activity 500 Dig Trench							
Lag 4 Days							
Activity 600 Lay Pipe							

Figure 10.19: Start-to-Start (SS) Gantt Chart

Other SS relationships in this project would be the pipe testing and back-fill of the pipe line. If the start of activity 500 is delayed, then activity 600 will also be delayed. The converse may also be true if resources are available.

Finish-to-Finish (FF): The *finish-to-finish* (FF) constraint represents the relationship between the finish of two activities. For example, activity 2000 can finish 3 days after activity 1000 is complete (see figure 10.20). An example here would be the fabrication and painting of a structure. Although there is no constraint mentioned concerning the start of the painting, the painters cannot start painting the last section until the fabrication is finished and then it will take a further 3 days to complete. If the fabrication is completed on a Monday, then the painting can only be completed by Thursday at the earliest.

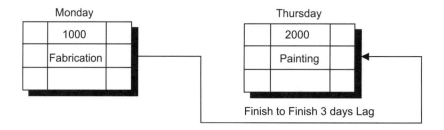

Figure 10.20: Finish-to-Finish (FF)

Or in Gantt chart form (see figure 10.21):

	1	2	3	4	5	6	7
	MON	TUE	WED	THU	FRI	SAT	SUN
Fabrication 1000							
Lag 3 Days							
Painting 2000							

Figure 10.21: Finish-to-Finish (FF) Gantt Chart

Start-to-Finish (SF): The *start-to-finish* (SF) constraint shows the relationship linking the start of an activity with the finish of another activity. This relationship should be avoided like the plague! It is easy to mix-up (SF) and (FS), and then it is virtually impossible to detect. An example of this relationship would be a crane hired for 6 days. The crane has two lifts that must be completed within the 6 days. Therefore 6 days after Activity A100 starts A200 must finish (see figure 10.22).

Figure 10.22: Start-to-Finish (SF)

Or in Gantt chart form (see figure 10.23):

	1	2	3	4	5	6	7
	MON	TUE	WED	THU	FRI	SAT	SUN
Lift 1 A100	→						
Lag 6 Days						→	
Lift 2 A200						→	

Figure 10.23: Start-to-Finish (SF) Gantt Chart

Note: A discontinuous option is available on some software packages where the activity can be constrained both SS and FF. In this case the resource analysis will schedule the activities discontinuously to match the resources available.

Leads and Lags: A delay may be given to the start or finish of an activity by assigning the constraint a duration (the default is zero). These delays are termed **lead time** before an activity and **lag time** after the activity. An example could be *'waiting for plan approval'* or *'the curing time for concrete'*. The planner may want to keep these durations separate from the activities' duration, because if significant, this could distort the cashflow statement and resource histogram.

13. Logical Errors

Before starting the time analysis it is important to validate the network's logic to ensure that there are no logical errors. Some packages perform a **topological sort** to compile the logic relationships into a suitable order, to ensure that no activity is processed before its logical predecessors. There are a number of basic logical errors:

- Logical loop
- Logical dangle
- Redundant precedence relationship.

Logical Loop: Consider the following logical loop that represents an impossible situation. Activity 200 follows 100, activity 300 follows 200, and activity 100 follows 300 (see figure 10.24). The figure indicates that one or more relationships need to be reassigned before processing.

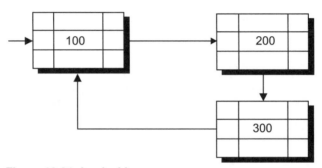

Figure 10.24: Logical Loop

Logical Dangle: As the name suggests a dangling activity is where the activity either comes from nowhere or goes to nowhere. In this example activity 600 follows 500, but what follows 900? Some software packages require the user to define the first and last activities as a start or finish type, as the start does not have a preceding activity and the finish does not have a succeeding activity.

Figure 10.25: Logical Dangle

Redundant Precedence Relationship: When developing the network diagram it is only necessary to indicate an activity's immediate predecessors, for example (figure 10.26), activity 200 is a predecessor of 300 and activity 100 is a predecessor of 200. Therefore implicitly 100 is a predecessor of 300. It is not necessary to explicitly specify this relationship, if you do, this would be an example of a redundant precedence relationship.

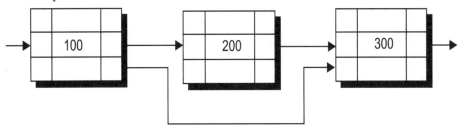

Figure 10.26: Redundant Precedence Relationship

Some project planning software will perform the logical loop, logical dangle and redundant precedence relationship checks as part of the CPM validation. If errors are detected the time analyses (forward and backward pass) will not start and an error message will be sent to the screen. The error messages are usually structured to enable the planner to locate the error quickly. This iterative process may need to be performed a few times before all the bugs are eliminated.

14. Definition of an Activity (part 2)

With the introduction of project planning software, certain terms and norms have been established - these terms will be used wherever possible. The characteristics of an activity include the following:-

- An activity must have a unique activity code or number (A, or 010, or ABC100). The code may be alpha, numeric or alphanumeric. The numbers do not need to be in any sequence because the logical relationships will determine the position of the activity in the network diagram. If the numbers are in sequence, however, this may help readability.
- If multi-project resource scheduling is required the activity numbers from the various projects need to be different, otherwise some data will be over written. This can be achieved by either having a unique project code that forms part of the activity number, or assigning a control digit prior to processing.
- An activity must have a description. The description should be as informative and clear as possible. Some computer packages allow the user to define a short description and a long description to suit the report layouts. The description length is usually restricted to fit into the framework of a report. If longer words are used they may be truncated.
- There will be logical relationships between the activities.
- All activities will have a time duration for completing the task, even if it is zero.

- All activities will have a calendar or work pattern to indicate when the work can be scheduled, even if it is seven days a week (continuous working).
- The activity can have target start and finish dates assigned. Certainly a start date or finish date for the project is required. Target dates would be influenced by delivery of bought-in items, availability of equipment or access to sub-contractors.
- An activity may need items to be procured - by linking the procurement to the activity a procurement schedule can be produced.
- An activity may need resources - by linking the resources to the activity they can be scheduled to produce a resource histogram.
- As time and resources are linked to the activities they can be integrated to generate a manpower S curve against time for planning and control purposes.
- An activity will incur expenses. If these costs are linked to the activities the costs can be scheduled and rolled-up to produce a cashflow statement and planned expenditure curves (BCWS). See *Earned Value* chapter.
- If a WBS is used, the activities can be linked to the work packages. This will enable the costs to be entered at the activity level and rolled-up to be reported at a higher level (see *WBS* chapter).

An example of an activity would be:

Identify	A100
Description	Dig the foundations
Calendar	5 days per week / Mon to Fri
Duration	20 working days
Procurement	Bought in items
Resources	5 men per day
Budget	$20,000
WBS	1.1.1
Logic	List preceding activities
Target date	Assigned start or finish dates

Table 10.7: Activity Details

Activity Duration: A certain amount of inefficiency should be allowed for within the system. As one activity finishes, the next activity may not start immediately, but take a day or so to get organised.

15. Calendar / Work Pattern (part 2)

Up to now all the calculations have assumed the project is working seven days a week. This is usually not the case, so we use a calendar or work pattern to define when work will take place. Before we can calculate an activity's start and finish date we need to know what days of the week the activity will be working. For example, will the activity be working Monday to Friday, or Monday to Saturday or perhaps everyday of the week? We also need to know when the resources will take personal and company holidays together with public holidays.

The planning packages allow the user to define a number of calendars, which can be linked to either the activity or the resource. Listed below are the characteristics associated with a calendar:

- The calendar defines the days on which work can be scheduled.

- A number of calendars can be defined. They can be assigned to any of the trades or even one person if appropriate, each calendar being a unique combination of rest days and holidays.

- Rest days are the days of the week that are always taken off, i.e. weekends, Saturday or Sunday. Planning software packages generally assume continuous work (a default option is a seven day working week) except for the days the activity is not working (i.e. the rest days and holidays).

- Holidays can be defined as public holidays, works holidays, or your own personal holidays. Essentially days on which the resources will not be available in addition to the rest days.

- Activities and resources can be linked to a calendar number.

- If the activity does not have a calendar, the planning software may flag an error or default to a five day week.

Example: The calendar and start date can change the duration of the activity. Consider this example, if the calendar is to work Monday to Friday, an eight working day activity could take either 10 or 12 calendar days depending on where the weekends fall (see figure 10.27).

	Mon	Tue	Wed	Thu	Fri	Sat	Sun	Mon	Tue	Wed	Thu	Fri	Sat	Sun	Mon
	1	2	3	4	5	6	7	8	9	10	11	12	13	14	15
8 Days duration (Takes 10 days)															
8 Days duration (Takes 12 days)															

Figure 10.27: Calendar Gantt Chart

Consider also activity 200 (figure 10.28) which has a Monday to Friday calendar and is dependant on activity 100 which finishes on Friday 5th. Because of the 5 day calendar, activity 200 cannot start before Monday 8th.

ACTIVITY	CALENDAR	FRI	SAT	SUN	MON
DATE		5	6	7	8
100	MON TO FRI				
200	MON TO FRI				

Figure 10.28: Calendar Gantt Chart

16. Activity Float (part 2)

Float is a measure of an activity's flexibility, quantifying how many working days the activity can be delayed before it will extend the completion date of the project, or any target finish dates.

The critical path is defined as the series of activities that have zero float. The critical path always runs through the project from the first activity, to the last activity. As a project approaches completion a number of network arms may become critical, giving more than one critical path.

If a project has a number of 'finish' activities on different arms of the network then each of these arms will become critical if each activity takes its own early finish date as its late finish date. In the example (figure 10.29), activity 300 although indicated as critical could finish up to 7 days earlier. To prevent activity 300 from becoming critical either link it to the latest activity or assign a target finish date nearer the end of the project.

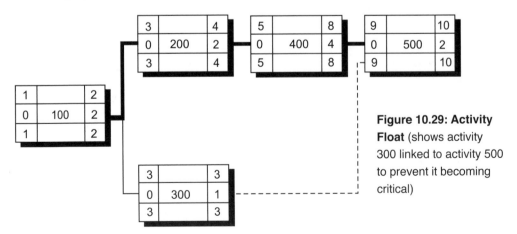

Figure 10.29: Activity Float (shows activity 300 linked to activity 500 to prevent it becoming critical)

The presentation of the critical path is usually highlighted by:

- Heavy print
- Different type of line
- Red line.

There are three main types of float in CPM and it is important to be able to distinguish between them to avoid confusion and errors.

Total Float: Here the float is shared with all the other activities in the arm. If some of the float is used by one activity, this will reduce the amount of float available for the other activities on the arm. **Care must be taken not to assume each activity has all the float to itself** (see appendix 1).

Free Float: This is a measure of the amount of float the activity can use up without effecting the early start of any other activity. This only happens when there is one activity in the network arm linked to a critical activity or milestone.

Negative Float: When calculations show that an activity must start before the preceding activities are finished, this is indicated as negative float. It is an unworkable situation that occurs when an activity falls behind planned progress but the end date remains fixed. The value of the negative float indicates how much the activity's duration or logic must be shortened (or by how much the project is behind schedule).

This concludes the chapter on *Critical Path Method*. The following chapter will show how the output from the CPM analysis can be presented in a Gantt chart.

Key Points:

- The network diagram outlines the logic or sequence of work.
- The calendar outlines when work can be scheduled.
- Activities with zero float are on the critical path.

Case Study and Exercise:

The CPM offers a structured approach to planning and controlling project information. The CPM methodology is best learnt by setting up your own network diagram and calculating all the start and finish dates. For this case study you have been appointed project planner for a drawing office project. Using the techniques in this chapter and appendix 1, 2 and 4, consider the following:

1. Network diagram.
2. Forward and backward pass.
3. Identify the critical path.
4. Adjust the calendar.
5. Change the end date and recalculate.

11

Gantt Charts

Learning Outcomes

After reading this chapter, you should be able to;

Draw a Gantt chart

Understand the benefits of using milestones and Hammock activities

Understand how to use line of balance

Gantt charts are one of the most widely used planning and control documents for communicating schedule information. It was originally designed before the first World War by an American, Henry Gantt, who used it as a visual aid for planning and controlling his shipbuilding projects. In recognition, planning Gantt charts often bear his name and are called Gantt charts.

Gantt charts are widely used on projects because they provide an effective presentation which is not only easy to understand and assimilate by a wide range of people, but also conveys the planning and scheduling information accurately and precisely.

The terms planning and scheduling are often used interchangeably. However, if a distinction is required, planning refers to the process of generating a time framework for the project, which then becomes a schedule when start and finish dates are assigned to the activities. In the past scheduling generally referred to resource scheduling.

The Gantt chart can either be developed on its own for a simple project, or linked to the critical path method to present the schedule of a complex network. Either way the Gantt chart must be developed as a time structure for the procurement schedule, resource histogram and the cashflow statement.

The Gantt chart should be used in conjunction with your daily diary. The daily diary still provides one of the best tools for noting appointments, key dates, reply-by dates and planning your day's activities.

1. How to Draw a Gantt Chart

The Gantt chart lists the activities (scope of work) in the left hand column, against a time scale along the top of the page. The scheduling of each activity is represented by a horizontal line or bar, from the activity's start to finish. The length of the activity line is proportional to its estimated duration. Consider the following list of activity data from a house building project (table 11.1):

Activity Description	Duration	Start Date	Finish Date
Lay foundations	4 days	1 March	4 March
Build Walls	8 days	5 March	12 March
Install roof	3 days	13 March	15 March

Table 11.1: Activity Data (house building project)

The calendar time scale is usually presented in days or weeks, but hours, months and years are also possible. The examples here will use days (see figure 11.1).

Activity Description	Mon 1	Tue 2	Wed 3	Thu 4	Fri 5	Sat 6	Sun 7	Mon 8	Tue 9	Wed 10	Thu 11	Fri 12	Sat 13	Sun 14	Mon 15
Lay Foundations	■	■	■	■											
Build Walls					■	■	■	■	■	■	■	■			
Install Roof													■	■	■

Figure 11.1: Simple Gantt chart (house building project)

2. Tabular Reports

Tabular reports provide the link between the CPM time analysis and the scheduled Gantt chart. On complex projects it is preferable to develop the WBS and network diagram before the schedule Gantt chart, as the network diagram is the best document to establish the logical sequence of work. Table 11.2 is the output from the CPM example (figure 10.14) in the previous chapter, with its corresponding Gantt chart (see figure 11.2). Note how the bars are drawn from each activity's early start to early finish. Tabular reports provide an excellent structure to store and present project information and should be used in conjunction with the other planning documents.

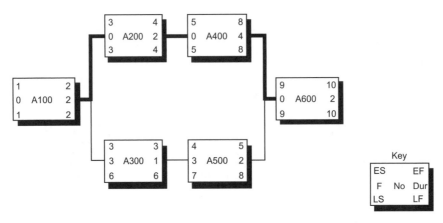

Repeat of Figure 10.14: Network Diagram (Critical Path Method Chapter)

Activity Number	Duration	Early Start	Early Finish	Late Start	Late Finish	Float	Responsibility
A100	2	1	2	1	2	0	Sandra
A200	2	3	4	3	4	0	Linda
A300	1	3	3	6	6	3	Linda
A400	4	5	8	5	8	0	Linda
A500	2	4	5	7	8	3	Sandra
A600	2	9	10	9	10	0	Sandra

Table 11.2: Tabular Format (transferred from figure 10.14 CPM chapter)

Activity Number	Mon 1	Tue 2	Wed 3	Thu 4	Fri 5	Sat 6	Sun 7	Mon 8	Tue 9	Wed 10
100	██	██								
200			██	██						
300			██							
400					██	██	██	██		
500				██	██					
600									██	██

Figure 11.2: Scheduled Gantt chart (note the A has been removed from the activity number to simplify the activity number)

3. Activity Float

The Gantt chart presentation will now be further enhanced with the introduction of activity float (figures 11.3 and 11.4). The accepted presentation is to show the float at the end of the activity from early finish (EF) to late finish (LF), and denote it as a dotted line with a symbol at the end, usually a diamond or upturned triangle. Figure 11.3 shows the float both before and after the activity bar.

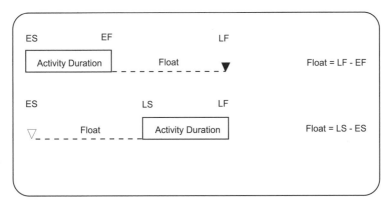

Figure 11.3: Activity Float

Continuing with table 11.2, the Gantt chart can now be drawn with float (see figure 11.4).

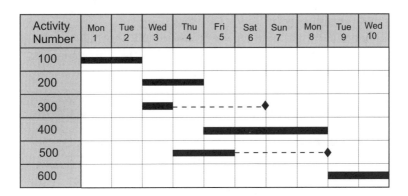

Activity Number	Mon 1	Tue 2	Wed 3	Thu 4	Fri 5	Sat 6	Sun 7	Mon 8	Tue 9	Wed 10
100										
200										
300										
400										
500										
600										

Figure 11.4: Gantt chart (showing activities 300 and 500 with float)

By implication it may be assumed that any activity without float is on the critical path. However, in practice planners are reluctant to show float as it is only human nature for people to work to their late finish, thus making all activities critical.

4. Select and Sort Functions

The 'select' or 'filter' and 'sort' or 'order' functions that are available on software packages, enable the planner to select which activities are included in the Gantt chart and determine the order they are presented. This facility will ensure schedule information is presented to the right person in the appropriate format.

Select: The select function indicates where the schedule information can be found in the project's data base, consider the following:

- 'Select' where activity data is present, this may sound obvious, but if an activity has no schedule information you may not want to show it on the Gantt chart.
- 'Select' where float = 0 (this will select all the activities on the critical path).
- 'Select' where float < (less than) 7 days (this will select all the activities that should be working next week otherwise they will become critical).
- 'Select' where responsibility = 'Sandra' (this will only select Sandra's scope of work).
- 'Select' where early start > (greater than) 1st Jan and < (less than) 1st March (this will select all the activities planned to start in January and February).

These are just a few examples of the select techniques available to extract information from your data base.

Sort: Once the data has been selected the next step is to arrange the data into a suitable order for presentation:

- **Numerical:** Ascending or descending. This could be the WBS or activity numbers, activity duration or float. Also consider ordering by least cost for activity crashing (acceleration) purposes.
- **Alphabetical:** This could separate out schedule information by responsibility - name, department, company or location (this is how company telephone directories are sorted).

Activity Number	Mon 1	Tue 2	Wed 3	Thu 4	Fri 5	Sat 6	Sun 7	Mon 8	Tue 9	Wed 10
100	██	██								
300			██	─ ─	─ ─	─ ◆				
200			██	██						
500				██	██	─ ─	─ ─	─ ◆		
400					██	██	██			
600								██	██	

Figure 11.5: Gantt Chart sorted by Early Start - shows the characteristic cascade effect

- **Date:** Gantt charts are usually sorted by early start (see figure 11.5) to present the activities in the order they are starting. This will arrange the activity bars top left (first) and bottom right (last), giving the characteristic cascade effect.

By skilfully using the above commands the data can be arranged in the format required for calculation or presentation. Sorting is an iterative process, with each sort the data becomes more structured. Using the previous example again (figure 11.2), select information where activity data is present and sort by early start (see figure 11.5). Note the activity numbers are not in sequence any more. Consider now sorting by responsibility and early start (see figure 11.6).

Activity Number	Responsibility	Mon 1	Tue 2	Wed 3	Thu 4	Fri 5	Sat 6	Sun 7	Mon 8	Tue 9	Wed 10
100	Sandra	██									
500	Sandra				███	- - - - - - ◆					
600	Sandra									██	
300	Linda			██	- - - - - - - ◆						
200	Linda			██							
400	Linda				████						

Figure 11.6: Gantt Chart Sorted by Responsibility and Early Start - shows Sandra's and Linda's work grouped separately. This can now be printed out and sent to the responsible person

5. Hammocks

A hammock or **summary activity** is used to gather together a number of sub-activities into one master activity. This is useful for layering or rolling-up the planning presentation and could link in with the WBS structure. Consider the house building project from the beginning of this chapter (see figure 11.1, and table 11.1), with each of the three main activities subdivided into a number of tasks (see table 11.3, and figure 11.7).

Activity Description	Duration	Start Date	Finish Date
Lay foundations	4 days	1 March	4 March
Dig foundations			
Throw concrete			
Build walls	8 days	5 March	12 March
Brickwork			
Fit windows			
Fit roof	3 days	13 March	15 March
Fit roof trusses			
Fit tiles			

Table 11.3: Hammock Activities (with associated tasks)

Activity Description	Mon 1	Tue 2	Wed 3	Thu 4	Fri 5	Sat 6	Sun 7	Mon 8	Tue 9	Wed 10	Thu 11	Fri 12	Sat 13	Sun 14	Mon 15
Lay Foundations	██	██	██	██											
Dig Footings	▭	▭	▭												
Throw concrete				▭											
Build Walls					██	██	██	██	██	██	██				
Brickwork					▭	▭	▭	▭	▭						
Fit Windows											▭	▭			
Fit Roof													██	██	██
Fit Roof Trusses													▭	▭	
Fit Tiles															▭

Figure 11.7: Hammocked Gantt Chart (where the hammock bar is always drawn from the start of the earliest activity to the end of the latest activity)

With hammocks the Gantt chart can now be presented at the appropriate level of detail - less detail for the senior managers - more detail for the people carrying out the activity at the coalface. This ability to vary the level of detail is fundamental to project planning and control.

6. Events, Keydates and Milestones

The principle difference between an **activity** and an **event** is that an event has zero duration - it is a point in time. An event, also called **keydate** or **milestone** represents a happening on a particular day, this could be when the order is placed, the plans are approved, goods are received or, even, the start and finish dates of an activity. Consider the following characteristics:

- An event has no duration, it is a point in time. In Microsoft Project, for example an event is an activity with zero duration and would appear on the screen as a diamond symbol.

- An event may be the start or finish of an activity, WBS work package, project phase or the project itself.

- An event focuses the project on a checkpoint, a major accomplishment, a deliverable result, a stage payment or an approval to proceed.

- An event could be the interface between trades or contractors as one hands over to another.

- Data capture will be more accurate if the scope of work is subdivided into milestones.

An example of an event would be the award of contract (see table 11.4).

Table 11.4: Characteristics of an Event (Award of contract)

Identity	100
Description	Award of contract
Budget	Nil
Duration	0 days
Resources	Nil

Managing events gives a clear focus on when work must be completed and hence a clear measure of progress. Using plenty of milestones pushes the planning down to an appropriate level. Consider figure 11.2 with the start and finish of each activity as an event shown in figure 11.8. This would empower the supervisor to manage their resources to meet these keydates.

Figure 11.8: Event Gantt Chart (house project showing events at the start and finish of all the activities)

Activity Number	Mon 1	Tue 2	Wed 3	Thu 4	Fri 5	Sat 6	Sun 7	Mon 8	Tue 9	Wed 10
100										
200										
300										
400										
500										
600										

◇ = Start   ◆ = Finish

7. Revised Gantt Chart

The Gantt chart was originally designed as a planning and control tool where the actual progress is marked up against the original plan. This progress bar can be drawn above, inside or underneath the original bar. This way the project manager can see at a glance how each activity is progressing and where control may be required to guide the project to completion. There are two ways of drawing the Gantt chart:

- Draw progress bar relative to timenow
- Draw progress bar to timenow and show the knock-on effect.

Consider the following set of two activities at timenow 2 (figures 11.9 and 11.10):

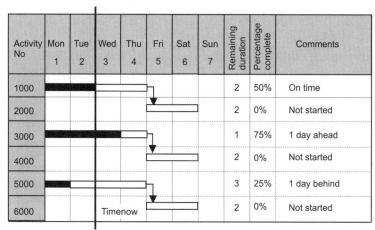

Figure 11. 9: **Revised Gantt Chart** (draw progress bar relative to timenow 2)

Activity No	Mon 1	Tue 2	Wed 3	Thu 4	Fri 5	Sat 6	Sun 7	Remaining duration	Percentage complete	Comments
100								2	50%	On time
200								2	0%	Not started
300								1	75%	1 day ahead
400								2	0%	Not started
500								3	25%	1 day behind
600			Timenow					2	0%	Not started

Figure 11.10: **Revised Gantt Chart** (draw progress bar to timenow 2 and show the knock-on effect)

Drawing the progress relative to timenow (figure 11.9) is easy to mark-up by hand and clearly indicates where control is required. If the progress over successive weeks is marked up on the same document progress trends can also be established (see figure 11.12).

If you are intending to apply control to bring the project back on track the knock-on impact to the end date of the project is of little interest, however, if any keydates are delayed this could disrupt the project. The disruption on the keydates in the short term can be identified by using a three week rolling horizon Gantt chart (see figure 11.11).

The other Gantt chart showing the knock-on effect (figure 11.10) will show the effect on keydates and also identify where activities may have become critical. The computer will produce this revised Gantt chart at the touch of a button, but to revise this document by hand would be a laborious task.

Baseline Plan: For effective control the project's baseline plan must be frozen - accepting only approved changes. Without a baseline plan it would be difficult to calculate progress variances and control would be lost.

Data Capture: To draw the revised Gantt chart the planner needs to capture progress information. This can be achieved by setting-up a progress reporting sheet - consider the following (table 11.5):

WBS	Activity	Start Date	Finish Date	Percentage Complete	Remaining Duration

Table 11.5: Data Capture Format (proforma)

The progress report should start with the reporting date or timenow. The progress should be reported against a WBS number or an activity number. The start and finish dates are important milestones which clearly state if the activity has started and if it has finished.

To draw the revised Gantt chart the planner needs to know the remaining duration as the Gantt chart scale is a time scale not a percentage complete scale. Percentage complete and remaining duration are often directly linked, but this can be misleading or inaccurate - consider the following:

When you state that a 10 day activity will take another 4 days to complete, you have implicitly stated that the material, resources and funds are available to complete the work. However, by stating that the progress is 60% complete, you have said nothing about when you intend to complete the activity.

On a long duration activity, as the work nears completion, the supervisor will have a more accurate feel for the remaining duration as opposed to the percentage complete. Any changes to the activity logic should also be considered when reporting progress.

8. Rolling Horizon Gantt chart

The rolling horizon Gantt chart, or rolling wave Gantt chart is a simplified Gantt chart which focuses on a short period ahead - maybe two weeks ahead for activities being worked on, and four weeks ahead for pre-planning (make sure all the drawings, procedures, job cards, equipment, materials etc. are going to be in place). This type of Gantt chart lends itself to a manual presentation as the scope of work is limited to just the activities that are working.

The rolling horizon Gantt chart can be partly computerised by preparing a planning proforma, as shown below (figure 11.11), which includes the scope of work, but no scheduling. The manager or foreman can then draw up the scheduling data by hand. Drip-feeding the job cards limits the opportunity for the shop-floor to change the logic and conveniently forget some activities.

Figure 11.11: Rolling Horizon Gantt Chart (marked by hand)

The rolling horizon Gantt chart can also be marked-up on the original Gantt chart - this will give a clear indication of progress, but could become cluttered and confusing. The main purpose is to focus on what can be done, rather than what the original Gantt chart says should be done - this is particularly important when the project is significantly behind as unachievable targets can adversely affect morale.

The rolling horizon Gantt charts are generally best produced by the team leader or site manager who is at the work face. The planner should then incorporate the information into a master schedule to check the keydates will still be met - and if they have changed, communicate this to the interested parties.

This type of Gantt chart should be very accurate as it is based on the latest data and drawn up by someone working close to the action. It is quick to draw and only includes relevant information on the activities that are working. Care should be taken, however, not to solely use the rolling horizon Gantt chart on its own, as planned activities which are not being worked on may be conveniently forgotten.

9. Trend Gantt Chart

The progress trend Gantt chart enables the project manager to judge the direction and trend of the project at a glance. This is achieved by marking on the original Gantt chart the successive weekly or monthly progress. The points of interest are:

- Activities which are behind schedule - are they catching up?
- Activities which are ahead - are they maintaining their position?

The progress trend Gantt chart shows a number of possible situations (figure 11.12):

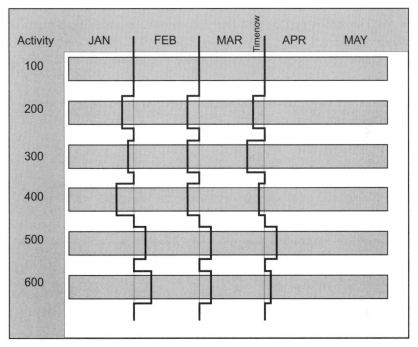

Figure: 11.12. Progress Trend Gantt Chart (progress reported relative to timenow)

Analysis of the trend Gantt chart (figure 11.12):

Activity 100 progress as planned.

Activity 200 progress behind and steady.

Activity 300 progress behind and getting worse (would be an area of concern).

Activity 400 progress behind but catching up.

Activity 500 progress ahead and steady.

Activity 600 ahead but losing ground (keep an eye on this one).

This simple but effective presentation can be drawn by hand on the original Gantt chart and photocopied for circulation. To limit the number of activities, the trend Gantt chart can be drawn at a hammock level. To quantify the overall performance use this progress trend Gantt chart in conjunction with the earned value presentation.

10. Gantt Chart

The positive features of the Gantt chart may be summarised as follows:
- The Gantt chart presentation is easy to assimilate and understand.
- The Gantt chart displays activity progress very clearly and simply.
- Activity float is easier to comprehend when shown on a Gantt chart.
- A scheduled Gantt chart is a prerequisite for forecasting the procurement schedule, the resource histogram and the cashflow statement.
- The revised Gantt chart is an excellent management tool for planning and control.
- A Gantt chart can be used to communicate and disseminate schedule information.
- A Gantt chart is a key document for the management decision-making function.

But the Gantt chart (in its original form) also has two main shortcomings:
- Showing interrelationships.
- Multiple decision-making.

Interrelationships: The Gantt chart does not explicitly indicate the sequences and interrelationships between the activities. If an activity is accelerated or delayed it is not always possible on a complex project to see the effect this will have on the other activities.

Multiple Decision-Making: Before an activity can be placed on the Gantt chart a number of factors have to be considered and decided on simultaneously:
- The logical sequence of the activities.
- The activity's duration which depends on procurement delivery, availability of resources and funds available.

An effective plan must address equally these factors of logic, time, procurement, resources and costs. Unfortunately with larger and more complex projects, the Gantt chart is found to be lacking as a planning and control tool if used on its own. The Gantt chart's problems and shortcomings can, however, be overcome by using it in conjunction with the CPM and its network diagram.

Project Budget   vs   Project Schedule

11. Logic Gantt Chart

The logic Gantt chart or linked Gantt chart shows the activity's logical relationships explicitly on a Gantt chart format. This technique is certainly appropriate for modest sized projects, but as the number of activities increase on large projects so the presentation will become increasingly cluttered. The logic Gantt chart uses the same techniques used to develop the network diagram (see the *CPM* chapter).

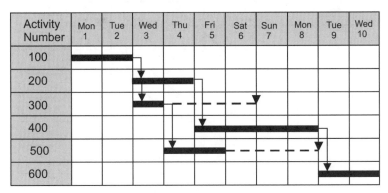

Activity Number	Mon 1	Tue 2	Wed 3	Thu 4	Fri 5	Sat 6	Sun 7	Mon 8	Tue 9	Wed 10
100										
200										
300										
400										
500										
600										

Figure: 11.13. Logical Gantt chart (showing logical links)

12. Line of Balance

The line of balance is a production planning technique developed by Trimble (1968), while he was at the National Building Agency. The purpose of the technique is to calculate the required resources for each stage of production so that the following stages are not delayed and the target output is achieved.

Production systems are usually more efficient than project systems because there is, an economy of scale and a learning curve as the tasks are performed repetitively. It is therefore, in the project's interests to identify areas of manufacture where production planning and control techniques can be applied.

To illustrate the line of balance technique consider a simple pipe laying project which only has two operations per km; dig the trench, and lay the pipe. This has to be repeated 7 times to complete the 7 km pipeline.

The network diagram of the project (see figure 11.14) shows the two activities and a 1 day lag in between.

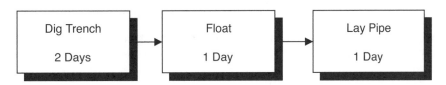

Figure 11.14: Line of Balance Network Diagram - shows the sequence of the activities

When this network diagram is incorporated with the production schedule the start and finish dates for each operation can be established, this is called the line of balance (figure 11.15).

Scope of Work	Mon 1	Tue 2	Wed 3	Thu 4	Fri 5	Sat 6	Sun 7	Mon 8	Tue 9	Wed 10
7										
6										
5										
4										
3										
2										
1		trenches			pipes					
	1	2	3	4	5	6	7	8	9	10

Figure 11.15: Line of Balance - Production Schedule

The next step is to consider the resources required to meet this production schedule. Let us consider the trench diggers on their own and assume that there is only one gang working. The figure 11.16 shows their rate of production drawn on the line of balance.

Scope of Work	Mon 1	Tue 2	Wed 3	Thu 4	Fri 5	Sat 6	Sun 7	Mon 8	Tue 9	Wed 10
7										
6										
5										Gang 1
4						Gang 1				
3					Gang 1					
2			Gang 1							
1	Gang 1									
	1	2	3	4	5	6	7	8	9	10

Figure 11.16: Line of Balance - Rate of Production (one gang)

The line of balance shows that after 10 days only 5 km of trenches have been dug, this will obviously delay the project. Consider the progress when using two gangs (see figure 11.17).

With two gangs the 7m of trenches are dug in 8 days, or 7 days if the two gangs can work together on the last section.

Scope of Work	Mon 1	Tue 2	Wed 3	Thu 4	Fri 5	Sat 6	Sun 7	Mon 8	Tue 9	Wed 10
7								Gang 1		
6						Gang 2				
5						Gang 1				
4			Gang 2							
3			Gang 1							
2	Gang 2									
1	Gang 1									
	1	2	3	4	5	6	7	8	9	10

Figure 11.17: Line of Balance - Rate of Production (two gangs)

The line of balance can be applied to projects such as, low cost housing where each house is the same. The requirements are identifiable production stages, production times are known, deliveries dates are known and the resources can be varied to meet the production schedule.

This concludes the chapter on *Gantt Charts,* which is the key document for issuing planning and control information. General Patton is reported as saying; "*A good plan today is better than a better plan tomorrow*".

Key Points:

- The *Gantt Chart* is the most widely used document to convey planning information.
- The selection and sort functions help to structure the Gantt chart presentation.
- The revised Gantt chart assists project control.

Case Study and Exercises:

The Gantt chart is one of the most widely used planning and control documents for communicating schedule information. You have been appointed project manager or expedition leader of a Royal Geographical Society (RGS) safari in search for the source of the River Nile. You are required to present a Gantt chart which includes the following;

1. Activities sorted and ordered to give the best presentation.
2. Hammocks.
3. Milestones and events.
4. Revised Gantt chart.
5. Rolling horizon Gantt chart.

12

Procurement Schedule

Project procurement management deals with the acquiring of goods and services required to perform the project's scope of work. This could be drawings, materials, equipment or professional services from a number of vendors and suppliers, or company departments outside of the project team.

The PMBOK defines procurement management as; '... *the processes required to acquire goods and services ...*' And the APM bok defines procurement as; '... *the process of acquiring new services or products.*'

The procurement schedule should be considered after the network diagram and schedule Gantt chart have been established, but before the resource histograms and cashflow statements. It is important to identify the items which have a long lead time (particularly those items on the critical path), as the procuring of long lead items may delay the start of its associated activities. These items need to be identified and managed by either:

- Accelerating the procurement cycle, or

- Adjusting the schedule Gantt chart.

The trade-off here is between buying the materials early or *just-in-time* (JIT). Using the JIT approach will reduce the pressure on the cashflow and storage, but will increase the risk of schedule delays.

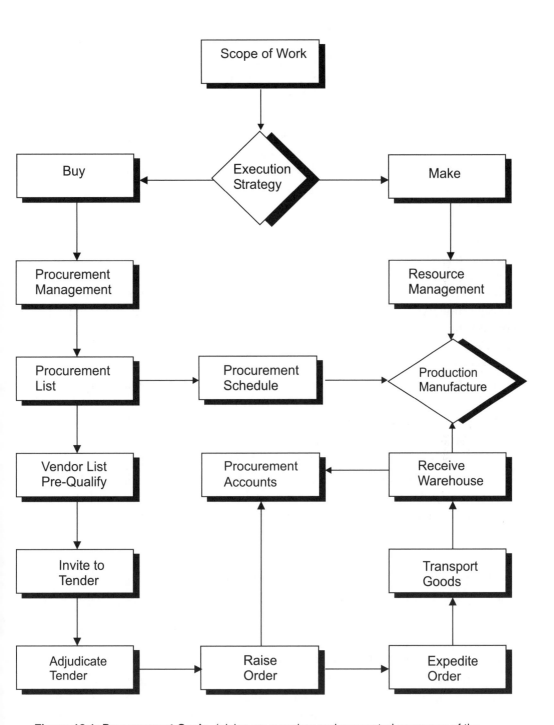

Figure 12.1: Procurement Cycle (giving an overview and suggested sequence of the discrete steps)

1. Procurement Cycle

The procurement process can be effectively presented as a cycle outlining a series of discrete steps. In practice there may be some iteration between certain steps and indeed the steps could even be carried out in a different order. It is the project manager's responsibility to supervise, monitor and control the procurement administration, and ensure the procurement documentation complies with administration procedures and confidentiality is maintained.

Procurement Planning: The procurement planning will be viewed from the buyers perspective, as the process of identifying what products and services are best procured outside the project organisation. This is the **buy-or-make** decision which is a key component of the execution strategy:

- What to procure?
- How much to procure?
- When it is required?
- When to procure?
- How to procure (contract)?

Procurement List: The procurement list is developed from the project's scope of work. On a construction project the drawing office would generate a bill of materials (BOM). This material list should give all the product details; manufacturer, model number, specification, type, colour, rating, level of inspection, etc. From this material list the project manager must decide his execution strategy to **buy-or-make**. This decision may require input from other company departments and outside vendors to assess market conditions and the company's expertise and resource loading.

- **Buy:** When your company resources lack the expertise and machinery, or when your resources are overloaded, or when an outside sub-contractor makes you an offer you cannot refuse.

- **Make:** When your company resources, expertise and machinery are available and under utilised, and the costs are less than using outside contractors.

Procurement Schedule: The procurement schedule is developed after the CPM network diagram and schedule Gantt charts have been produced, but before the resource histograms and cashflow statements have been considered. By working back from the activities early start dates, subtracting the purchase order lead time and the *just-in-time* (JIT) margin, this will give the order by date.

Order Date = ES - Lead Time - JIT (see table 12.1)

Scope	Order Date	Early Start	Lead Time	JIT

Table 12.1: Procurement Order Date

Supplier and Vendor List: All potential suppliers and vendors need to be identified and pre-qualified according to the project quality plan. You need to be satisfied that the supplier has the production and quality management systems to deliver the product to the required specification, quality standards and schedule. The reputation and financial stability of the company should also be considered.

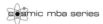

Invite to Tender: Compile a bid package (enquiry document) for the suppliers to quote against. As the initial enquiry document is the basis for the contract, it should be progressively adjusted and marked up as more information becomes available. Monitor the suppliers progress and conformity to the tender requirements. Deviations and exceptions are identified and corrective action initiated, but all the time there is a process of building good supplier relationships. through effective liaison and communication.

Tender Adjudication: Scrutinise the quotations (tenders, proposals), and compile a technical and commercial bid tabulation to ensure you are comparing 'apples with apples'. Record and consider suppliers suggestions and negotiate to achieve the best price and conditions, while striving for a win-win arrangement. This process should take advantage of market conditions, but should also be governed by your company's ethics policy. Recommendations should be documented in the required format and within the agreed time frame, and presented to the adjudication authority.

Raise the Order: The purchase order should be a stand alone document. It should comply with the company's standard terms and conditions of contract and supersede all previous documentation and correspondence, and must be formally accepted by the supplier. Where possible pass on any contractual requirements from your client with a back-to-back agreement with your suppliers. You do not want to be held liable for, a schedule penalty for instance, which you cannot pass on to your supplier who may be the cause of the delay in the first place. For this reason it is risky to finalise your contracts with your sub-contractors before signing a contract with your client.

Expedite: Follow-up the order to ensure and encourage the suppliers to meet their contractual requirements (particularly quality and time). Expediting makes the order happen (see section 3).

Transport: Consider the different methods of transport (see *Project Estimating* chapter). Where possible the product's quality should be checked and confirmed before leaving the factory, this particularly applies to items being exported.

Insurance: Consider placing the order for the transport and insuring yourself so that if there is a problem or claim, you can deal with the transport and insurance companies directly - you will be more motivated to push for a speedy settlement than any middle man.

Receiving: Check the goods against the delivery note, check the delivery note against the order and check the quality of the products against the required condition. A project I was working on received two counter rotating gearboxes for an offshore supply vessel, but on inspection they were found to both rotate the same way! Fortunately this was picked up by the receiving inspection which gave the shipyard time to have the correct type shipped over.

Warehousing: Store the delivered items for safe keeping and retrieval. Check if warehousing requires any special handling equipment and storage facilities. Issue the stock against the required internal requisition order.

Accounts: The accounts should check the budget, purchase order, invoice and delivery note for variances before making payments. Records should be updated and any deviations identified and communicated to higher authority.

2. Procurement Schedule

The procurement schedule integrates the procurement list, the project schedule, the procurement lead time and warehousing *just-in-time* (JIT) stock control. Consider the following house building example (see figure 12.2):

Figure 12.2: Network Diagram (house project)

KEY =

Description	
ID	Dur

ID = Activity Number
Dur = Activity Duration

House Procurement: The shell of the house has been completed and activity 1 (in this case) is the roof inspection. The network diagram (figure 12.2), and Gantt chart (figure 12.3) have been calculated as shown. On **day 1** you decide to procure all the required materials for the next phase of the project. The lead time, which includes **day 1**, is given by the supplier for their scope of supply. The items are required to be on site the day before the activity is scheduled to start (JIT). The required dates have been transferred from the early start Gantt chart to the table of procurement details (table 12.2).

		1	2	3	4	5	6	7	8	9	10	11	12
ID	Task Name	M	T	W	T	F	S	S	M	T	W	T	F
1	Roof Inspection												
2	Electrical wiring												
3	Plumbing piping												
4	Top soil												
5	Electrical fittings												
6	Plumbing fittings												
7	Flowers												
8	Alarm system												
9	Handover												

Figure 12.3: Schedule Gantt Chart (house project)

Activity Number	Description	Lead Time (days)	Deliver Date	Required Date	Variance (days)
1	Roof inspection	-	-	-	-
2	Electrical wiring	1	1	1	0
3	Plumbing pipes	3	3	1	-2
4	Top soil	3	3	1	-2
5	Electrical fittings	3	3	4	1
6	Plumbing fittings	4	4	3	-1
7	Flowers	6	6	3	-3
8	Alarm system	8	8	6	-2
9	Handover	-	-	-	-

Table 12.2: Procurement Details (house project)

= Original plan

= Re-scheduled (for procurement)

Figure 12.4: Revised Schedule Gantt chart (house project)

Procurement Analysis:

Activity 1 - Can start and finish as planned, no procurement required.

Activity 2 - The material should arrive on the **1st day**, therefore it can start and finish as planned.

Activity 3 - The material will not arrive until the **3rd day**, therefore it cannot start until the **4th day** and finish 2 days late.

Activity 4 - The material will not arrive until the **3rd day**, therefore it cannot start until the **4th day**.

Activity 5 - The material arrives on the **3rd day**, but it cannot start until activity 2 has finished.

Activity 6 - Although the material arrives a day late this activity cannot start until activity 3 is complete (logic constraint).

Activity 7 - Although this activity is delayed 2 days by activity 4, it is delayed a further day by the late delivery of materials.

Activity 8 - The material will not arrive until the **8th day**, therefore this activity cannot start before the **9th day**.

Activity 9 - Is delayed by activity 8 and therefore the handover is delayed to the **12th day**.

If any activities are delayed due to late procurement look at the network diagram to see if the knock-on effect delays any other activities. The schedule Gantt chart indicates when the procurement is required, working back, the lead time will indicate when the procurement item must be ordered. If any of the items are going to be late, then the Gantt chart must be re-scheduled.

3. Expediting

The progress expeditor (progress chaser) follows-up on all the purchase orders and instructions encouraging them to happen by continually monitoring the suppliers. On a large project the expeditor becomes the project manager's eyes and ears as he takes on a criminal investigating approach. Consider asking the following questions:

- Have you received the order?
- Is the order understood?
- What is your job number?
- Who is your project manager or foreman?
- Has the job been planned into your production system? (Show me)
- Do you have all the construction drawings, specifications and planning information?
- Have the materials and components been ordered / received / inspected / passed / and are they available? (Show me)
- Have the instructions been received by the foreman?
- Are there suitably qualified resources available? (Name them and show qualifications)
- Is the work progressing as planned?
- Are there any problems?
- Will you meet the contracted delivery date?

By asking all these questions the expeditor becomes an invaluable source of progress information giving early warning of any supply problems so that the project manager has time to respond.

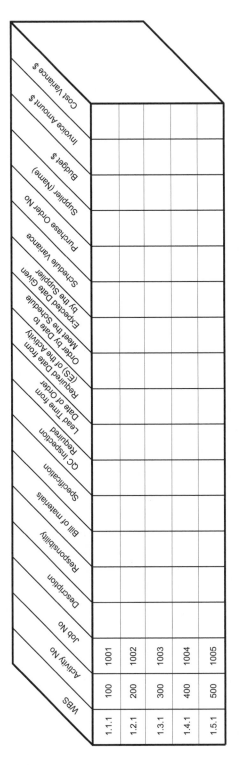

The table columns (read from the cube faces) are:

WBS	Activity No	Job No	Description	Responsibility	Bill of materials	Specification	QC Inspection Required	Lead Time from Date of Order	Required Date from (ES) of the Activity	Order by Date to Meet the Schedule	Expected Date Given by the Supplier	Schedule Variance	Purchase Order No	Supplier (Name)	Budget $	Invoice Amount $	Cost Variance $
1.1.1	100	1001															
1.2.1	200	1002															
1.3.1	300	1003															
1.4.1	400	1004															
1.5.1	500	1005															

Figure 12.5: Procurement Control Cube

4. Procurement Control

Once the *procurement schedule* has been developed, the procurement control function is the project management process to **'make-it-happen'**. This can be effectively achieved by expediting the plan through a procurement control document. The purpose of the procurement control document is to gather all the information together (on one sheet if possible) and summarise all the related functions. These fields may include the following (see figure 12.5):

5. B2B Procurement

B2B (business-to-business) procurement platforms are a type of business facility offered by the Internet. At their simplest, B2B market places are just on-line catalogues. Sellers list their products with prices, specifications and delivery terms. Buyers scan the catalogues, place their orders electronically, and can even make payment on-line.

The potential benefits for buyers include dramatically reducing procurement administration costs and times, lower material prices, faster supply chains, and reduced inventory requirements. The benefit for the sellers include increased sales volume, lower cost of making a sale, and reduced inventory requirements.

Procurement bureaucracy can make orders cost more than the item being bought. Examples in the US military are rife - $600 for hammers, $2400 for a toilet seat, and a staggering $14,000 for a coffee maker for their bombers. On average, e-procurement can reduce the cost of raising an order from $100 to $10 - a significant saving. Procurement cycles can also be reduced - Shell estimates within the oil industry procurement can be reduced from 3 weeks to 30 seconds. Oil supplier's administration costs are also reduced - typically from $5 for processing a telephone order to 20 cents for on-line orders.

The B2B procurement systems are being successfully driven by large companies who are collaborating on a market sector basis, for example, Boeing, Lockheed Martin, BAE Systems, and Raytheon have combined to form <Exostar> a global B2B website for their industry.

B2B procurement, therefore, offers the project manager (project office) the opportunity to;

- Reduce transaction costs
- Generate less paperwork
- Provide an economy of scale through consolidated purchasing
- Reduce the level of unapproved 'rough' purchases.

But the project manager also needs to be aware of the associated risks of accessing this global market. Although web browsing will identify a wider range of products, if these are procured from overseas there will be more links in the supply chain and longer lead times. One of our military clients told us about an administration building they were planning. They recognised that the lift had a long lead time, so they ordered it from a Dutch manufacturer - six months later the project was shelved, six months after that the lift arrived!!! Fortunately they were able to on-sell the lift without a penalty, but it does highlight a problem with procuring long lead items from overseas.

6. Just-In-Time

Just-in-time is a procurement management system that provides the production line with components as they need them. This will reduce stock levels and stock investment, but will also increase the risk of production disruption.

Toyota cars developed the *kanban* system, which is known in the West as *just-in-time* (JIT). This was one of the most spectacular features of the Toyota car production system. To avoid the build-up of huge stocks from suppliers they devised a revolutionary system which would order parts only when they were needed, by simply sending back the empty container for the supplier to fill up. It eliminated huge inventories and waste which cluttered up the car factories. It was a ruthless discipline that squeezed the supplier for even cheaper and faster parts production.

The Toyota system created a greater attention to both the customer who could order their special car without extra cost, and the worker who was much more involved in maintaining quality, much more aware (industry wise) and better educated than their Western contemporaries. However, the downside of JIT is that it makes companies far more sensitive to interruptions - the Kobe earth quake for example, immediately caused supply failures to companies that were not carrying stock!

Another feature of the Toyota production system is continuous improvement. They operate an open system that they are prepared to show foreigners, because they are confident they are five years ahead of the West. *"If we lose confidence we will become closed. If we think there can be no more improvement, the system will perish."*

As the value of the procured goods and services increases, particularity with the trend to outsourcing work, so the procurement function which could be over 50% of the budget, will have a greater influence on project success.

This concludes the chapter on *Procurement Scheduling.* The following chapter will discuss *Resource Planning,* the next technique in the planning and control cycle.

Key Points:

- Subdivide the bill of materials (BOM) into **buy-or-make**.
- Identify long lead items. Order early to meet the schedule, or reschedule to accommodate any delays.
- Expedite all important orders to ensure they happen as planned.

Case Study and Exercises:

The procurement function supplies the goods and services required to perform the project's scope of work. You have been appointed the procurement manager or chief chef for a wedding. Your case study is to outline how you will address the following issues;

1. Outline how you determine the '*buy-or-make*' decision?
2. Outline your procurement cycle.
3. Outline a typical procurement schedule for the wedding, and give examples of how long lead items affect your JIT scheduling.
4. Outline how expediting makes your projects happen.
5. As the power of the Internet grows, so B2B procurement will become more common. Outline how B2B is being used (or could be used) on your project.

13

Resource Planning

Learning Outcomes

After reading this chapter, you should be able to;

Forecast resource requirements

Smooth resource loading to help match requirement with availability

Draw the manpower S curve

Project managers face a challenge with every project, trying to execute the tasks to meet the required quality standards, while expending minimum possible time, cost and resources. The discussions so far have assumed an unlimited supply of resources, however, in reality this is obviously not the case, so here the text will outline methods and techniques for integrating resource planning with time planning.

A resource may be defined as the machine or person who will perform the scope of work. Resource planning is, therefore, a forecast of the resources required to perform the scope of work within the time plan. The resource constraint should be considered after the network diagram, schedule Gantt chart and procurement schedule have been developed, but before the cashflow statement.

1. Resource Estimating

The resource estimate is linked directly to the scope of work and bill of materials (BOM). The scope of work may be expressed as so many tonnes of steel, or so many square metres of wall to be painted. From this description the estimator can convert the scope of work into manhours per unit "X".

The next step is to consider the direct trade-off between the resource requirement and the activity's duration. Consider the following, if the scope of work is to erect 12 tonnes of steel and the estimator knows from past experience that the work can be done in 150 manhours per tonne and the men work 10 hour shifts, then the equation is:

$$\frac{(12 \text{ tonnes x } 150 \text{ man-hrs per tonne})}{10 \text{ hrs per day}} = 180 \text{ man days}$$

The resource / duration trade-off would then be as follows:-

Mandays	Resource Available	Duration (days)
180	10	18
180	11	16.4
180	12	15
180	13	13.8
180	14	12.9

Table 13.1: Resource Duration Trade-Off

By varying the resource availability, the duration of the activity will change. As the time and budget parameters are the first to be planned, the room for resource planning may have already been constrained. In this case the resource analysis function is to forecast the manpower resources required to meet the time and budget (these may already have been agreed in the tender).

In the above example (table 13.1), the duration was expressed as a fraction of a day. In reality you may find that the smallest reasonable time unit is half a day or even a whole day. This will obviously depend on the type of work and the flexibility of your workforce.

In practice the figures are not always so simple - certain industries work in multi-trade gangs, for example, a bricklayer, plasterer, electrician, carpenter and labourer may work together and the estimated total hours may include a contribution from each trade.

2. Resource Forecasting

The next step is to forecast the total resource requirement by discipline or interchangeable resource. An interchangeable resource is when you have a pool of workers and any one of them could perform the work. This is done by compiling all the resource estimates and presenting them in a structured resource table. The following headings for the resource table are typical of those used by the project management software (see table 13.2 and figure 13.1).

Activity Number	Resource Type	Quantity per day	Resource Duration	Lead time
100	Builder	2	2	0
200	Builder	4	4	2
300	Builder	3	2	6

Table 13.2: Resource Table

Activity Number	Mon 1	Tue 2	Wed 3	Thu 4	Fri 5	Sat 6	Sun 7	Mon 8	Tue 9	Wed 10
100	2	2								
200	0	0	4	4	4	4				
300	0	0	0	0	0	0	3	3		

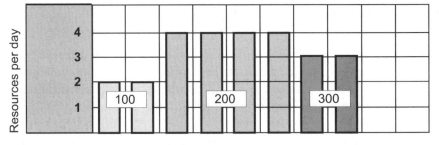

Figure 13.1: Resource Forecast - Gantt chart and Histogram (the Gantt chart shows the number of resources per activity per day, and the histogram shows the total resource required per day)

Activity Number: (from table 13.2) The resource information is addressed through an activity number. Therefore the timing of the resource can be linked directly with the schedule of that activity. This is why it is necessary to perform the CPM analysis, activity scheduling and procurement scheduling before the resource analysis. This way you ensure the logic and sequencing of work is achievable and the materials and equipment are available.

Resource Type: This field is used to distinguish the different types of resources, for example, it could be Mr. Smith, an engineer, a welder or in this case a builder.

Quantity per Day: Use this field to enter the quantity of resource required per day, in this case activity 100 requires 2 builders per day.

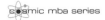

Duration: Use this field to indicate how many days the resource will be working on the activity. This number can be less than the duration of the activity, but obviously not more.

Lead Time: Is the difference between the activity's scheduled start and the resource's start. For activity 200 the builder starts two days after the early start of the activity.

If there is more than one resource working on an activity, use additional lines of information. If the resource quantity per unit time varies, a number of entries are required to define the profile mathematically. The resource table can be developed by taking horizontal or vertical slices through the resource profile.

3. Resource Availability

The next step is to quantify the resources available inside and outside the company. The following points should be considered:

- Other resource commitments - if your company is involved in a number of projects which all draw from a common labour pool, the other projects' requirements must also be considered (multi-project resource scheduling).
- The anticipated sickness and absenteeism rate

Keeping the above points in mind, the resource availability table will be developed. Consider the following example (table 13.3 and figure 13.2):

Resource Type	Quantity Per Day	Available from	Available To
Engineer	3	1 December	15 December
Engineer	3	2 January	31 January

Table 13.3: Resource Availability

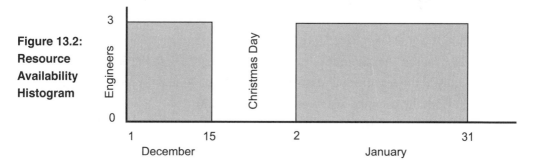

Figure 13.2: Resource Availability Histogram

This resource profile indicates the extent of the Christmas break when no engineers will be available. The resource availability table differs from the resource forecast table in that it is linked to the resource, or resources and not to an activity. It simply identifies the resource and the quantity available between certain dates.

Company holidays, public holidays, religious holidays and maintenance shutdowns can be programmed in. This step ensures that no work can be scheduled when the workforce is not available. A new line will be required in the resource table to define each non-working period.

4. Resource Histogram

The resource histogram is a popular planning tool because it gives a good visual presentation which is easy to assimilate and understand. The prerequisites for drawing the resource histogram are:

- Early start Gantt chart (after considering the procurement requirements which ensures the materials and equipment are available)
- Resource forecast per activity.

By using the early start Gantt chart it is assumed that the planner wishes to start all activities as soon as possible and keep the activity float for flexibility. Once the resource requirements have been added to the early start Gantt chart, the daily requirements are summed by moving forward through the Gantt chart one day at a time to give the total resource required per day.

The total daily resource requirements are then plotted vertically to give the resource histogram. It is important to note that separate resource histograms are required for each resource type. Consider the following example (table 13.4) and steps of how to compile the resource histogram:

Activity No	Start Date	Finish Date	Resource Per Day
100	1	2	2
200	3	4	2
300	3	4	6
400	5	6	3
500	7	10	1
600	11	11	2

Table 13.4: Resource Table

Step 1. Draw the Gantt chart (see figure 13.3).

Step 2. Transfer the resource per day from the table 13.4, to the Gantt chart.

Step 3. Add the resource per day vertically to give a total daily requirement.

Step 4. Plot the resource histogram (see figure 13.3).

Activity Number	Mon 1	Tue 2	Wed 3	Thu 4	Fri 5	Sat 6	Sun 7	Mon 8	Tue 9	Wed 10	Thu 11
100	2	2									
200			2	2							
300			6	6							
400					3	3					
500					1	1	1	1			
600									2		
Total	2	2	8	8	4	4	1	1	2		

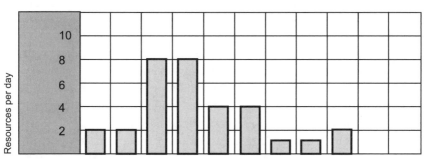

Figure: 13.3. Gantt chart and Resource Histogram

5. Resource Loading

The resource forecast is now compared with the resources available. The ideal situation is when the resource requirement equals the resources available. Unfortunately, in the real world this seldom happens, because it is not always possible to adjust supply with demand, so some form of rescheduling is required.

A resource overload is when the resource forecast requirement exceeds the available resources, while a resource underload is when resource forecast is lower than the available resource. A resource overload will lead to some activities being delayed, which could delay the completion of the project. While a resource underload will under utilise the company's resources, which could have a detrimental effect on the company's profitability.

Consider the example in figure 13.3, when there are only 6 resources available, the resource loading will be as displayed in figure 13.4.

The resource histogram now shows the forecast and available resources both as a histogram and numerically. The overloads and underloads can now be identified and addressed as follows:

- **Resource Smoothing:** Assign resources to critical activities first, then try moving the other activities to ease any overload and under-utilisation.

	Mon 1	Tue 2	Wed 3	Thu 4	Fri 5	Sat 6	Sun 7	Mon 8	Tue 9	Wed 10	Thu 11
Forecast	2	2	8	8	4	4	1	1	2	0	0
Available	6	6	6	6	6	6	6	6	6	6	6
Loading	4	4	-2	-2	2	2	5	5	4	6	6

Figure 13.4: Resource Loading

- **Time-Limited Resource Scheduling:** The end date of the project is fixed, so resources must be increased to address any overloads.
- **Resource-Limited Resource Scheduling:** The maximum number of resources is fixed, so the end date may need to be extended to address any overload.
- **Increase Resources:** To address an overload.
- **Reduce Resources:** To address an underload (under utilised).

6. Resource Smoothing

Resource smoothing is the process of moving activities to improve the resource loading profile. The first step is to select the resource to be smoothed, because it is not possible to smooth for more than one resource at a time. To decide which resource to smooth consider:

- The resource that is most overloaded.
- The resource that is most used on the project.
- The least flexible resource - this could be the resource that comes from overseas, is difficult to get hold of, or is least available.
- The most expensive resource to hire.

After you have smoothed for the chosen resource, the other resources must follow the revised schedule. Unfortunately, you will have to accept this compromise with the other resources, because to smooth for another resource may put the first resource back into overload. Resource smoothing levels the resource overload to meet the resource available. The resource histogram can be levelled by moving activities away from the overloaded area by either:

- Changing the logic of the network.
- Moving non-critical activities within their float so that the end date of the project is not impacted, while making sure the network logic is maintained. This is similar to assigning resources to critical activities first.

Continuing with the example (figures 13.3 and 13.4), the resource overload can be addressed by simply moving activity (task) 200 by two days. However, as the network diagram shows (see figure 13.5), activity 200 has a *finish-to-start* relationship with activity 400, therefore, activity 400 will also have to move forward by two days. The resulting Gantt chart and smoothed resource histogram are shown in figure 13.6.

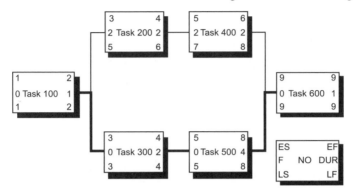

Figure 13.5: Network Diagram

Activity Number	Mon 1	Tue 2	Wed 3	Thu 4	Fri 5	Sat 6	Sun 7	Mon 8	Tue 9	Wed 10	Thu 11
100	2	2									
200					2	2					
300			6	6							
400							3	3			
500					1	1	1	1			
600									2		
Total	2	2	6	6	3	3	4	4	2		
Running Total	2	4	10	16	19	22	26	30	32		

Move >>>> (200)

Move >>>> (400)

Figure 13.6: Gantt chart and Smoothed Histogram

7. Time-Limited Resource Scheduling

Time-limited resource smoothing is used when the end date of the project cannot be exceeded. In which case any resource overloads will have to be addressed by increasing the resources when they are required (see figure 13.7). This situation could occur when:

- The project has heavy time penalties.
- The project is part of another project with critical access dates, for example, an accommodation module for an offshore platform.
- Building a new hotel to meet the summer season.
- Opening an event, i.e. the Olympic Games.

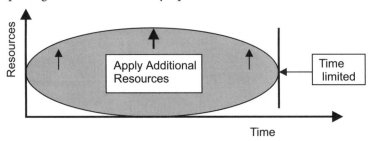

Figure 13.7: Time-Limited Resource Scheduling

Once the end date of the project and milestones have been contractually agreed, time-limited scheduling will become a powerful tool to assist the planner to achieve these commitments.

8. Resource-Limited Resource Scheduling

Resource-limited resource scheduling is when there is a resource limit which cannot be exceeded. If there are any resource overloads then some planned activities will have to be delayed. If this process delays any critical activities, then the end date of the project will be extended (see figure 13.8). This situation could occur in any of the following situations:

- A confined space will limit the number of people able to work there.
- Where there are limited facilities, for example the number of bunks available on an offshore platform.
- Where there are equipment limitations, e.g. the number of computers, machines, drawing boards, lifts or scaffolding.
- Health & safety requirements may limit the number of workers in a certain area.
- Restricted access might limit the movement of materials and equipment, e.g. building a house on a mountain slope or downtown office block.

The frustration of the real world, of course, is that your employer will always expect you to achieve the contractual end date even though the resources are not available (see figure 13.9).

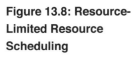

Figure 13.8: Resource-Limited Resource Scheduling

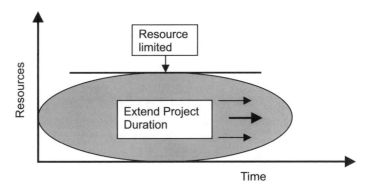

Figure 13.9: Time-limited and Resource-Limited Scheduling (stress - something must give!!)

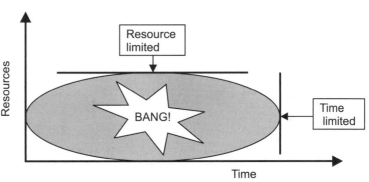

9. How to Increase Resources

When the resources are overloaded there are a number of options to increase the resources available:

- **Working Overtime:** This will increase the number of workhours available without having to employ more staff. This can be achieved by working more hours per day and more days per week, however, working overtime will increase the labour rate and may reduce productivity.

- **Working Shifts:** This will increase the utilisation of machines, equipment and also increase the number of manhours worked in confined spaces.

- **Increase Productivity:** Education and training should improve productivity especially if it incorporates automation. However, this is really a long term strategy, which may not be able to address your short term needs.

- **Job and Knock:** When the workers have finished a job, they can leave the factory, although they will be paid for the full day or shift. Hopefully, this will motivate them to increase their productivity and not drag out the job.

- **Learning Curve:** If the project involves a certain amount of repetitive work, the planner could expect to see the number of manhours reducing on subsequent units. Consider the following example (table 13.5, figure 13.10) from a boatyard manufacturing a series of similar yachts. This example shows a learning curve where the manhours per unit reduce exponentially until it reaches an optimum efficiency.

- **Sub-Contractors:** Using sub-contractors will increase the workforce in the short term. The benefit here is that there are no long term commitments, but the labour costs will be higher. You may need to allow for a learning curve, quality control and supervision issues. Using sub-contractors can also be useful to compare the performance of your in-house workforce.
- **Scope of Work:** If it is not possible to increase resource availability, as a last resort, you may consider reducing the scope of work to meet a fixed end date.

Table 13.5:

Manhours per Hull

Scope	Manhours
Hull 1	15000
Hull 2	13000
Hull 3	10000
Hull 4	9000
Hull 5	9000

Figure 13.10:
Learning Curve
- shows reducing
manhours per hull

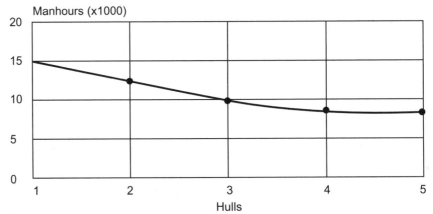

10. Reduce Resources

When the resources are under loaded, or under utilised there are a number of options for reducing the available resources:

- Move unemployed resources to critical activities.
- Move unemployed resources to R&D jobs, or fill-in jobs which either have a resale value or can be used by the company, e.g. building a spec house.
- Hire out resources internally or externally - the hire rate can be competitively reduced to at least make a contribution to their salary.
- Pre-manufacture components before they are needed. However, check the trade-off between resource utilisation and the additional cost of the trial assembly, disassembly and handling.
- Maintenance of equipment during slack periods.
- Train your workforce during slack periods to gain new skills which will make them more productive and flexible in the future, or send them on leave.

The profit of a company in the long term may well depend directly on the efficient utilisation of its resources.

11. Resource Planning and Control

The initial CPM analysis was performed without considering the resource constraint. Now that the resource analysis is complete, certain activities may have been moved during the resource smoothing, the baseline plan will therefore need to be re-scheduled.

The earned value technique often uses resources to gauge a project's performance. In example in figure 13.6, the baseline plan is expressed as the running total to give the characteristic S curve (see figure 13.11). Earned value calls this curve the budgeted cost for work scheduled (BCWS).

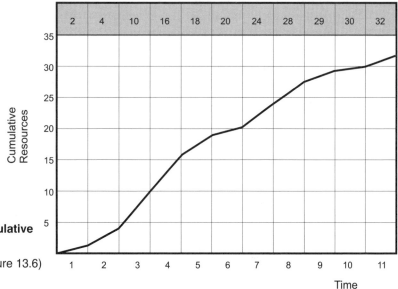

Figure 13.11: Cumulative Resource S Curve
(developed from figure 13.6)

The resource calculations outlined above indicate the optimum resource utilisation to meet project objectives, but they do not address the human element. The project manager must bridge the gap, in terms of communicating explanation and persuasion, between what should be done mathematically and what can be done practically. It is generally accepted that a workforce will tend to be more adaptable and committed when given the opportunity to participate in the planning process. Some planning and control considerations are:

- When a project is running late, bringing in more resources may well delay the project even further.
- It may be possible to split activities which have float. In this situation workers would be moving between unfinished jobs. Concern here would be for the lost production time while moving, setting up and reorganising. However, in reality this is quite common.
- Clients often require a manpower plan to check that the contractors have sufficient resources to meet project objectives.

12. Multi-Project Resource Scheduling

Up to now the manpower resources have only been considered for a single project. Consider what happens when the company is running many projects at the same time, each calling on the same pool of resources.

Multi-project resource scheduling addresses this problem by joining all the projects together to form one large company project. This allows the total requirement of the projects to be compared with the total company pool of resources. Any smoothing will now consider all the projects at the same time.

In the CPM chapter it was recommended that all the activities, even of other projects, should have different numbers. The reason becomes evident when performing multi-project resource smoothing. If two activities have the same number the last activity entered will overwrite the previous one - with disastrous results. It is, however, a problem which can be simply addressed by assigning a prefix or suffix to the activity number or adding the project number.

Multi-project scheduling adds a further dimension to resource management enabling senior management to prioritise the projects, this will assign resources to the high priority projects first.

13. Planning Software

Resource analysis requires a tremendous amount of mathematical calculation. It is therefore desirable to use computer software for this type of analysis. Planning software generally use the following steps:
- Select where the data is located.
- Order the data for the calculation.
- Calculate the resource information using pre-defined algorithms.

Select: Selection of data tells the computer where to look for information in the data base. Typically select where resource information is present.

Order: The ordering of the activities is the first step in building a priority list for the assigning of resources. Although there is no *'right'* or *'optimum'* priority list it is generally accepted that a set of decision rules will produce a better schedule than an *ad-hoc* approach. On a large project it may not be physically possible to manually test all the resource conflicts so some routine must be set up. A typical priority order would be:
    1st priority: Early start
    2nd priority: Total float (critical activities first)
    3rd priority: Duration (least duration first)
    4th priority: Record number

The priority would be established by first looking at the activity's early start. If more than one activity has the same early start, it then looks for the activity with the least amount of float. If there is more than one activity with the same float, it then looks for the activity with the longest duration and if that is not sufficient it then orders the activities by record number. It is not always possible to justify your priority decision rules on logical grounds and the results cannot be assumed to be an optimum solution. The following points should, however, help to establish a framework for your priority.

- On a long project it may not be realistic to schedule in any great detail many months from timenow, because as the project rolls forward the situation and trade-offs may well change. With this line of thinking, early start should have a high priority.
- The size of the float is a measure of the amount of flexibility or movement an activity has before it affects the critical path. Resources should be assigned first to the activity with the least amount of flexibility, i.e. critical activities.
- The duration and cost would be a measure of the size of the activity, therefore, assign resources to the larger and more expensive activities first.
- If no clear priority can be established using the above conditions, simply order by activity number or record number.

During the life of the project it is often found that the priority list might change to accommodate internal and external pressures. This can be easily incorporated during the regular progress revisions. This concludes the chapter on *Resource Planning*, the following chapter will discuss the financial side of project management, particularly the cashflow statement.

Key Points:

- Compile resource histograms to compare resource forecast and resource availability and report loading.
- Allocate resources to the critical activities first.
- The cumulative resource manpower S curve is used for the earned value calculation.

Case Study and Exercises:

The executive strategy *'buy-or-make'* decision will determine if project production is a procurement or resource issue. A *'make'* decision will therefore require resource planning. For this case study you have been appointed project manager for a Water Utility's repair and maintenance project office. Outline how you would address the following:

1. Consider the *'buy-or-make'* decision?
2. Estimate the resource requirements, allowing for a learning curve?
3. Forecast the resource loading and draw the resource histogram?
4. Smooth the resources.
5. Increase or decrease the resources.

14

Project Accounts

The financial success of a project depends not only on the project making a profit, but also financing the project through the project lifecycle. Statistics clearly indicate that more companies go into liquidation because of cashflow problems than for any other reason. The PMBOK defines cost management as; '... *the processes required to ensure that the project is completed within the approved budget.*' And the APM bok as; '... *estimating the proper cost that should reasonably be expected to be incurred against a clear baseline, understanding how and why actual costs occur, and ensuring that the necessary response is taken promptly to ensure actual costs come under budget.*' It is, therefore, essential for the project manager to plan and control the project's cashflow.

Project accounting should not be confused with financial accounting or management accounting which are used within the corporate environment. From the definitions, however, you will see there is some common ground and overlaps.

Financial Accounting: Keeps a record of all the financial transactions, payments in and payments out, together with a list of creditors and debtors. This information gives the financial status of a company using the generally accepted accounting principles. The three main reports are; the balance sheet, the income statement and the cashflow statement.

Management Accounting: Also called **cost accounting**, uses the above financial information particularly from the profit and loss account to analyse company performance. This analysis will assist management decision-making with respect to estimating, planning, budgeting, implementation and control.

Project Accounting: Uses a combination of both financial accounting and management accounting together with some special project management tools (*WBS, CPM* and earned value) to integrate the project accounts with the other project parameters.

1. Cashflow Statement

The cashflow statement is a document which models the flow of money in and out of the project. The time frame is usually monthly, to coincide with the normal business accounting cycle. The cashflow statement is based on the same information used in a typical bank statement, except that here the income (cash inflow) and expenditure (cash outflow) are grouped together and totalled. On a project the sub-contractors' income would come from the monthly progress payments, and the expenses would be wages, materials, overheads, interest and bought-in services. The client's income would come from the operation of the facility (after the project has been completed) and the expenses would be the invoices from the sub-contractors and suppliers. Consider the following example where:

* **Brought forward** amount for January is $5,000
    * **Income:** January $10,000, February $15,000, March $20,000
    * **Expense:** January $8,000, February $12,000, March $16,000

Use the following steps as a guideline to solve the exercise.

Step 1: Set up the cashflow statement headings (see table 14.1). Use monthly headings (fields or columns) to cover the duration of the project.

Step 2: The brought forward (B / F) for January is given at $5,000 (see table 14.2).

	January	February	March
Brought forward			
Income			
Total available			
Expenses:			
Total expenses			
Closing balance			

Table 14.1: Cashflow Statement (proforma)

Step 3: List the inflow of cash items from the income statement for January, February and March, $10,000, $15,000 and $20,000 respectively.

Step 4: Calculate the total funds available for January by adding the total income to the brought forward amount.

Step 5: List the outflow of cash items from the expense statement for January, February and March, $8,000, $12,000 and $16,000 respectively.

Step 6: Calculate the total outflow of funds for January.

Step 7: Calculate the closing statement for January, funds available minus expenditure.

Step 8: The closing statement for January now becomes the B/F, or opening statement for the next month, February.

Repeat this procedure every month for the rest of the project. Follow the calculations through the worked example, note that a mistake in January will have a knock-on impact.

	January	February	March
Brought forward	$5,000	$7,000	$10,000
Income	$10,000	$15,000	$20,000
Total available	**$15,000**	**$22,000**	**$30,000**
Expenses:	$8,000	$12,000	$16,000
Total expenses	**$8,000**	**$12,000**	**$16,000**
Closing balance	$7,000	$10,000	$14,000

Table 14.2: Cashflow Statement (solution)

2. Cashflow Timing

There is a catch unfortunately. The cashflow statement, as the name suggests, is a measure of the cash in and cash out of the project's account. The catch is that this may not be the same as the sales figures or expenses for the month, because of the timing of the payments. Listed below are some typical examples of cashflow timings:

- Part payment with placement of order - this is often used to cover the manufacture's cost of materials and ensure purchaser's commitment particularly on imported goods.
- Stage payments, or progress payments for items which may take many months to complete.
- Payment on purchase - this is normal practice with retailers.
- Monthly payments for labour, rent, telephone and other office expenses.
- 30 or 60 days credit; normal terms for bought-in items.
- 90 days credit - large hypermarkets will pay their suppliers 90 days after delivery, even though they may have an average stock rotation of 20 days or less. This means that even if they sell at cost they can still make a profit on the return from their positive cashflow.

It may help your understanding to look at the data presented the other way round.

- Labour costs are usually paid in the month they are used.
- Material costs can vary from an up-front payment, cash on delivery (COD), to 1 to 3 months credit.
- Bought-in services and plant hire costs can be paid within 1 to 3 months after delivery.
- Income from client could be; up-front payment, stage payments or progress payment one month after invoice.

These figures are usually compiled monthly on a creditors and debtors schedule. It is the project accountant's responsibility to chase up late payments.

Non Cashflow Items: Company assets should not appear on a cashflow statement as they do not represent a movement of cash. Although appreciation and depreciation may represent a flow of value, it does not physically represent an inflow or outflow of cash. This also applies to the revaluation of property, good will and the value of the company's shares.

3. Cost Distribution

The cashflow statement is an integral part of the critical path method (CPM). It combines the WBS, the estimate, project schedule, procurement schedule and resource histogram. At this point we need to make some assumptions about the distribution and profile of the cost and cashflow with respect to the schedule of the activities. For ease of calculation it is usually assumed to be linear unless otherwise stated (see figure 14.1).

Activity No	January	February	March	April	May	June
100	Front end loaded					
200		Linear distribution				
300			End of activity loaded			
400	1 month up front					
500			1 month credit			
600				2 months credit		

Figure 14.1: Cost Distribution

☐ = Cash flow

▬ = Activity schedule

Labour costs are generally uniform over the duration of the activity, whereas, the cost of materials and other bought-in items may need to be qualified. As stated in the previous section, they can vary from up-front payments to 1, 2 or 3 months later depending on the supplier.

Projects with many activities will tend to smooth out any distortions caused by non-linear cashflows. However, if there are activities with disproportionately large material or equipment payments, these can be separated out to form new activities with appropriate duration to match the expense profile.

Worked Example: Before going any further let us consolidate the above information by trying another worked example. Using the following information, produce a cashflow statement for the months January to June.

* Brought forward for January is $5,000.

    * Sales forecast @ $10 each unit. The client takes two months to pay the account.

Nov: 1,000	Mar: 500
Dec: 1,500	Apr: 1,200
Jan: 1,600	May: 1,300
Feb: 900	Jun: 1,400 (units)

* Cost of sales:

    [1] Overheads are $300 per month.

    [2] Material $2 each unit. Supplier gives one month credit.

    [3] Labour $1 each unit. Paid in month used.

    [4] Loan repayment:

February:	$14,000
April:	$16,000
May:	$15,000
June:	$2,000

Before looking at the solution on the following page, try the exercise yourself. Build up the cashflow statement one step at a time.

	January	February	March	April	May	June
Brought forward						
Income						
Total Available						
Expenses: [1]						
[2]						
[3]						
[4]						
Total Expenses						
Closing Balance						

Table 14.3: Cashflow Statement (proforma)

Step 1: Using a cashflow statement proforma (table 14.3) check all column and row headings.

Step 2: The brought forward value for January is given, insert this into the opening balance cell.

Step 3: The income in January will come from sales in November because the client takes 2 months to pay their invoices. The sales for November, being 1,000 units @ $10 each, gives $10,000. Enter this value in the income cell. The sales figures for the remaining months will have the same stagger.

Step 4: The overhead costs are $300 per month running throughout the project. Enter this in the overhead expense row.

Step 5: The material expense for January will come from the purchases made in December since the supplier gives 1 month credit. 1,500 units @ $2 each is $3000. Place $3,000 in the material expense row for January. The other months will once more follow the same stagger.

Step 6: The labour expense occurs in the month of use, so for January 1,600 units @ $1 each gives $1,600. Enter $1,600 in the labour expense row for January and so on for the other months.

Step 7: The loan repayments in this example have been preset by the bank, enter $14,000 in the loan expense row for February and so on for the other repayments.

Step 8: All the data should now be positioned in the cashflow statement. The next step is to run the calculation through the months from January to June. The total funds available for January are the brought forward $5,000 plus the income $10,000 giving $15,000.

Step 9: The total expenses for January are overheads $300, materials $3,000, labour $1,600 and zero for loan payment, giving $4,900.

Step 10: Subtract the total expenses $4,900 from the total funds available $15,000 [step (8) - step (9)], giving $10,100. This is the closing amount for January.

Step 11: The opening amount for February is the same as the closing amount for January, $10,100.

These calculations are repeated for every month of the project (see table 14.4). A negative amount can be printed as -10 or (10). Accountants prefer to use brackets like this (100) to indicate negative cashflow. Any negative cashflow will either need to be avoided or financed by borrowing (overdraft). Unless up-front payments have been organised, the initial stages of a project usually experience negative cashflow due to all the setting up costs and material procurement.

	January	February	March	April	May	June
Brought forward	$5,000	$10,100	$6,700	$20,000	$10,600	$(3,400)
Income	$10,000	$15,000	$16,000	$9,000	$5,000	$12,000
Total Available	**$15,000**	**$25,100**	**$22,700**	**$29,100**	**$15,600**	**$8,600**
Expenses: [1]	$300	$300	$300	$300	$300	$300
[2]	$3,000	$3,200	$1,800	$1,000	$2,400	$2,600
[3]	$1,600	$900	$500	$1,200	$1,300	$1,400
[4]	$0	$14,000	$0	$16,000	$15,000	$2,000
Total Expenses	**$4,900**	**$18,400**	**$2,600**	**18,500**	**$19,000**	**$6,300**
Closing Balance	**$10,100**	**$6,700**	**$20,100**	**$10,600**	**($3,400)**	**$2,300**

Table 14.4: Cashflow Statement (solution)

4. Cashflow (example figure 14.2 and table 14.5)

Consider the following project comprising of only three activities; material, labour and transport. The costs are incurred when the work is performed, however, the cashflow depends on the timing of the income and expenses. The timing of the expenses are shown in the Gantt chart (figure 14.2), where the material supplier gives a one month credit, the labour is paid in the month used and the transport company requires payment one month in advance. The income from the client is a **20%** mark up of the incurred expenses and paid one month after the work is performed (see figure 14.2 and table 14.5).

	May	June	July	Cash flow information
Material (delivered to workshop)	$4000	$5000		1 month credit
Labour		$3000	$6000	Pay in month of use
Transport to site			$2000	Pay 1 month up front
Incurred costs	$4000	$8000	$8000	
Income 20% of expenses	$4800	$9600	$9600	

Figure 14.2: Gantt Chart (example figure 14.2 and table 14.5)

	May	June	July	August
Brought forward	$0	$0	($4,200)	($5,600)
Income	$0	$4,800	$9,600	$9,600
Total Available		$4,800	$5,400	$4,000
Expenses: Material	$0	$4,000	$5,000	
Labour	$0	$3,000	$6,000	
Transport	$0	$2,000	$0	
Total Expenses	$0	$9,000	$11,000	
Closing Balance	$0	($4,200)	($5,600)	

Table 14.5: Cashflow Statement (example figure 14.2 and table 14.5)

5. Cashflow Statement (example figure 14.3, 14.4 and table 14.6)

Consider another example developed from the weekly Gantt chart (figure 14.3). Given the schedule Gantt chart and cashflow, calculate the cashflow statement from April to July. Figure 14.3 outlines the work schedule while figure 14.4 outlines the associated cashflow. The brought forward for April is $10,000 and the forecast rate of invoicing (FRI) for this period of the project has been agreed at $15,000 per month. Calculate the cashflow from figure 14.3 and 14.4 before looking at the solution in table 14.6.

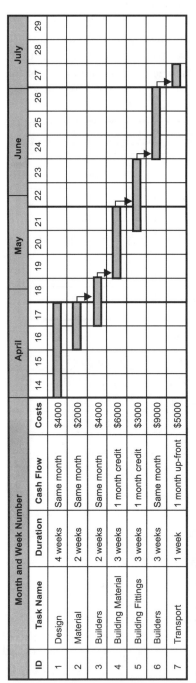

Figure 14.3: Schedule of Work

ID	Task Name	Duration	Cash Flow	Costs
1	Design	4 weeks	Same month	$4000
2	Material	2 weeks	Same month	$2000
3	Builders	2 weeks	Same month	$4000
4	Building Material	3 weeks	1 month credit	$6000
5	Building Fittings	3 weeks	1 month credit	$3000
6	Builders	3 weeks	Same month	$9000
7	Transport	1 week	1 month up-front	$5000

Figure 14.4: Cashflow Imposed on Gantt Chart

ID	Task Name	Duration	Cash Flow	Costs
1	Design	4 weeks	Same month	$4000
2	Material	2 weeks	Same month	$2000
3	Builders	2 weeks	Same month	$4000
4	Building Material	3 weeks	1 month credit	$6000
5	Building Fittings	3 weeks	1 month credit	$3000
6	Builders	3 weeks	Same month	$9000
7	Transport	1 week	1 month up-front	$5000

	April	May	June	July
Brought forward	$10,000	$17,000	$30,000	$24,000
Income	$15,000	$15,000	$15,000	$15,000
Total Available	**$25,000**	**$32,000**	**$45,000**	**$39,000**
Expenses: Material	$8,000	$2,000	$21,000	$2,000
Total Expenses	**$8,000**	**$2,000**	**$21,000**	**$2,000**
Closing Balance	$17,000	$30,000	$24,000	$37,000

Table 14.6: Cashflow Statement
(solution to figures 14.3 and 14.4)

6. Invoicing

Invoices are documents used to request payment. The project office often sits in the middle of the cashflow (between the client and the sub-contractors). An invoice control sheet (figure 14.5) can be setup to summarise all the related documents:

- Scope changes
- Progress report
- Invoice ledger
- Payments ledger

Consider the following invoice control sheet (table 14.7). The scope of work is subdivided by WBS along the top and by expense / income along the left hand side. The sum of agreed

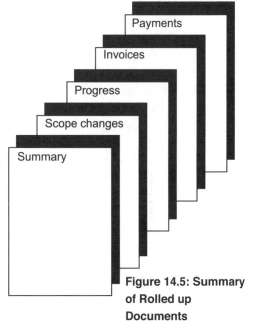

Figure 14.5: Summary of Rolled up Documents

WBS	1.1	1.2	1.3	1.4
Contract value	$100,000	$20,000	$30,000	$25,000
Sum of scope changes	$25,000	$5,000	$20,000	($5,000)
Total contract value	**$125,000**	**$25,000**	**$50,000**	**$20,000**
Progress report				
Percentage complete	15%	20%	80%	60%
Milestone payment				
Total payable	**$18,750**			
Invoice paid to date	$15,000	$4,000	$35,000	$10,000
Retention of performance bond				
Balance () if over paid	$3,750			
Pay latest invoice?	$3,750 (yes)	$1,000	$7,000	$1,500

Table 14.7: Invoice Control Sheet

changes are added to the contract value to give the total contract value. The progress payments can be based on milestones or percentage complete. The percentage complete times the contract value gives the total the client should pay to date. Deduct the total invoices to date plus any retention from the total payable to give the maximum amount the client would be prepared to pay. If the invoice is less than this amount - you can pay the invoice.

Question: From table 14.7 would you pay the invoices for work packages 1.2, 1.3 and 1.4? (Solution at end of chapter)

7. Cost-To-Complete

The *cost-to-complete* should be reported and compared with the expected financial return for the project. If the *cost-to-complete* were to exceed the return, then the future of the project should be reviewed. It may be an option to suspend or abort the project. Consider the following:

- The British Nimrod airborne warning system was scrapped after ten years of development and £800 million sterling. Was this the right decision?
- The Channel Tunnel operations are running at a profit, but the return on the investment is not sufficient to pay the interest on the loans. Should the project have been scrapped half way through?
- When the oil price slumped from $35 a barrel to $15 in 1985, what impact did this have on oil field development?
- Why was the cost of the Sydney Opera House allowed to become 16 times the original budget.
- Should **sunk costs** be considered when considering a project's continuing viability?
- Committed costs are those costs which **will** have to be paid in the near future, either because the work has been performed or the order has been placed.
- The *cost-to-complete* and project return should be rolled-up to give a total picture of the project. At the work package level the project may win some and lose some.

Project Number	Project Budget	Payment To Date	Committed Costs	Cost To Complete	Project Return On Investment
1000	$50,000	$20,000	$0	$20,000	$55,000
1001	$100,000	$30,000	$20,000	$50,000	$80,000
1002	$40,000	$20,000	$10,000	$30,000	$75,000
1003	$120,000	$10,000	$5,000	$90,000	$80,000

Table 14.8: Cost-to-Complete

Question: Consider the progress report (table 14.8) and identify which projects could cause concern (see end of chapter for solutions).

8. How to Draw an Expense S Curve (BCWS)

Another method for modelling the cashflow is to use **S curve** analysis, which provides the link between the CPM and the budget. Experience has shown that a project's accumulated costs tend to follow the **S curve** shape. To draw the **S curve** use the procedure in the Resource Planning chapter and appendix 3.

Step 1: Draw an early start Gantt chart for the project (see figure 14.6).

Activity list	MAY 1	2	3	4	5	6	7	8	9	10	11	12	13	14	15	16
100	50	50														
200			50	50	50	-	-	-	-	- ♦						
300			10	10	10	10	10	10								
400			50	50	-	-	-	-	-	-	-	- ♦				
500					10	10	10	10	10	-	-	-	-	- ♦		
600									30	30	30	30	30	30	30	
700					30	30	30	-	-	-	-	-	-	- ♦		
800																50
Expenses per day	50	50	110	110	90	50	50	20	40	40	30	30	30	30	30	50
Accumulated expenses	50	100	210	320	410	460	510	530	570	610	640	670	700	730	760	810

Figure 14.6: Gantt Chart (showing expenses per day)

Step 2: Assign values linearly per day. Activity 100, for example, is $100 over two days, giving $50 per day.

Step 3: Add the cost values vertically to get daily totals. For the 3rd May add the daily amount for activities 200, 300 and 400, which are $50, $10 and $50 respectively, giving a daily total of $110.

Step 4: Plot the daily total costs on a graph of costs against time, to obtain the daily rate of expenditure curve (see figure 14.7).

Step 5: Accumulate the daily values from left to right to give the total to timenow. Thus the accumulated total for the 3rd May is the sum of the daily totals; $50, $50 and $110, giving $210.

Step 6: Plot accumulated figures on a graph of cost against time (figure 14.7). This will produce the distinctive **S curve**.

Figure 14.7: S Curve (accumulated expenses)

Banana Curve: If the **S curve** for the early start and late start are drawn on the same graph they produce a distinctive banana type curve (see figure 14.8). The banana curve indicates the different timing of the cashflows of activities beginning early start as opposed to activities beginning late start. Project planners normally schedule activities at the early start to ensure all the float time is available. However, the accountant may see things differently and feel that activities should begin at the late start. The advantage with activities beginning late start is that the payments will be delayed and finance charges reduced. This approach, however, could backfire on the accountant in the later stages of the project if there are delays, because now there is no float available to accommodate these delays, so the activities must be crashed if the project is to finish on time. This means the float that was freely given away in the early stages of the project may now be expensive to buy back.

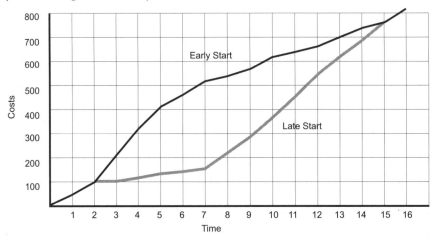

Figure 14.8: Banana Curve (drawn from figure 14.6 in this chapter)

9. Project Cashflow Response

How can the project manager respond to the project cashflow statement, if the closing amount is **negative**, try:
- Delaying expenditure payment or arrange longer credit periods.
- Bring forward the income payments. If your project is financed by stage payments, make sure these are completed as soon as possible.
- If the negative cashflow is being caused by the purchase of materials, ask the client to pay the suppliers directly. (Note: You may lose your mark up and discount).
- Arrange finance well in advance. Bank managers do not like to receive calls on a Friday afternoon to arrange finance for your company salaries. The bank managers also have to plan their cashflow.
- Delay working on activities with float.

If the closing amount is **positive**, try:
- Looking into ways of investing the money at a good rate of return.
- Start activities earlier than planned, thereby finishing the project sooner.
- Make sure the cash flow stays positive.

Having worked through a few examples, you should now appreciate that when there are changes to the income or expenses, all the following values will change.

10. Performance Bonds and Retention

Retention may be defined as holding back payment of a certain amount of a contractor's income for a period of time to ensure they comply with the contract. The normal practice is to withhold 10% per month until 5% of the contract value is reached. This sum will then be held by the client, or arbitrator against agreed defects for a period of up to one year after commissioning. For retention to work effectively, checks must be made to ensure that the contractor is not over claiming. Why use retention ?
- To encourage the contractor to finish the project within the agreed conditions.
- To have something tangible to hold against the contractor in the event of substandard work or default.
- Provide funds to pay another contractor to complete the activity.
- *"Money speaks louder than words"*.

Performance bonds can be used instead of retention. Here a legal document is drawn up by a bank guaranteeing the client the same conditions as a retention. The advantage to the contractor is that they are paid in full (no retention), which should improve their cash-flow.

11. Benefits of Using a Cashflow Statement

Although statistics clearly indicate that more companies go into liquidation because of cashflow problems than for any other reason, the full benefits of cashflow management are not always appreciated. Listed below are some of the many benefits associated with using cashflow modelling techniques.
- The manager can plan ahead knowing what funds are required, when they are required and how much is required.
- It gives timely warning of negative cashflow which needs to be financed and positive cashflow which should be invested.
- It gives a forecast rate of invoicing (FRI) to your client so that they can produce their own cashflow statement. This is often a contractual requirement with some of the larger corporations.
- The cashflow statement is the main item of a business plan, as it will show the bank manager or lender how much you need, when you need it and most importantly when you will pay it back. It will also show that you have done your homework.

- A cashflow loan reduces the amount of paperwork compared with secured lending.
- Cashflow will establish the lending and repayment dates, which usually makes the loan cheaper than an overdraft. With an overdraft the bank has no idea when the company is going to borrow or payback, so the bank has to build up an extra margin to cover its own funding costs.
- 'Secured' lending, even if it is based on the borrower's assets, still depends on the borrower's cashflow to pay for the loan. Assets are only worth as much as an outsider is prepared to pay for them and that valuation is likely to be based on the asset's ability to produce cash.
- The cashflow statement can be developed into expenditure curves, rates of expenditure and accumulated expenditure, all of which are required for earned value project control.
- The cashflow statement can be used to perform a **'what-if'** simulation which will indicate where the project's sensitivity lies. This forms the basis of the sensitivity analysis.
- It can be used as a data source to calculate an investments payback period.
- The discounted cashflow (DCF) introduces a time value to the money.
- The cashflow statement can be the data source for the company's asset register, asset depreciation and company taxes.
- The financial records can be maintained according to agreed standards and procedures.

These benefits clearly indicate why the cashflow statement is axiomatic to effective project cost planning and control. This concludes the chapter on *Project Accounts* and all the planning techniques outlined in the planning and control cycle. The following chapter will discuss *Project Control*.

Solutions: To questions in this chapter.

Invoicing: 6 (1.2) yes

Invoicing: 6 (1.3) no

Invoicing: 6 (1.4) yes

Cost-to-Complete: 7 (1000) okay

Cost-to-Complete: 7 (1001) okay

Cost-to-Complete: 7 (1002) okay

Cost-to-Complete: 7 (1003) investigate

Key Points:

- Statistics clearly indicate that more companies go into liquidation because of cashflow problems than for any other reason.
- Negative cashflows need to financed well in advance.
- The cost S curve forms the basis of the earned value calculation.

Case Study and Exercises:

The financial success of a project depends not only on the project making a profit, but also financing the project through the project lifecycle. As project manager you are responsible for the project accounts. Outline how you would address the following:

1. Develop the cashflow statement. Identify the expenses that could cause negative cashflow.
2. Adjust the timing of the activities to improve the cashflow without unduly increasing the critical path risk.
3. Invoicing work-in-progress.
4. Cost-to-complete.
5. Retention and performance bonds.

"...Projects' cashflow...it never rains but it pours!..."

15

Project Control

The development of a project plan or baseline plan, discussed in the previous chapters, completes the first phase of the planning and control cycle. The next phase is project execution and control using the baseline plan as the means of achieving the project objectives and an outline of the required condition. Needless to say, planning is a pointless exercise unless the execution of the plans are tracked and controlled through accurate reporting on performance.

A structured approach to planning and control is recommended by experienced practitioners, because, through a well disciplined system all parties will know: what is expected of them, their required performance, and the reports they must generate. The baseline plan may be seen as a number of documents which indicate the path the project should follow. Consider the comparison with the course a yacht steers - by taking bearings, the navigator can plot the yacht's position. If the yacht has gone off course they can apply steering control to bring the yacht back on course.

Similarly the project's baseline plan is the course to steer, with the tracking and monitoring functions ascertaining the project's position with respect to time, procurement, resources and costs. **If the project is off course, then control in the form of corrective action must be applied.**

It is essential for effective project control that performance is measured while there is still time to take corrective action. This chapter will show that not only is it cheaper to take effective action early on in the project, but as the project approaches completion, the project manager may in fact be powerless to take any effective corrective action at all.

1. The Need for Project Control

As projects increase in size and complexity, so the progress reporting needs to move from a subjective assessment of progress to a more structured approach. The unsuspecting project manager should beware of the over optimistic reporting trap (the Venus Fly trap!).

Consider this situation - if the progress is consistently over reported during the early stages of the project the managers are only fooling themselves, because the lack of progress will become obvious during the final stages of the project when the over optimistic reporting catches up with itself (see figure 15.1).

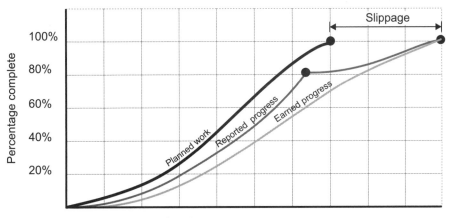

Figure 15.1: Over Optimistic Reporting   Time

This phenomenon is shown in the over optimistic reporting graph (figure 15.1), by the three lines representing planned work, reported progress and earned progress. In this case the reported progress was over stated throughout the project until, at about 80% complete, when it became obvious that the project was only 60% complete, and for the next few weeks the reported progress remained static as the earned progress caught up.

If the reported progress had been accurate at the outset, the under performance trend would have prompted corrective action during the early stages of the project. But now at 80% complete the project manager could be powerless to bring the project in on time, because increasing the workforce will not only increase costs, but could delay the project even more! The US Navy experienced this problem on one of their frigate building projects, which was reported to be 99% complete for over one year!

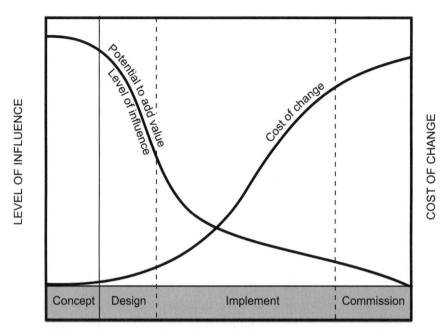

Figure 15.2: Influence / Cost of Change Curve (during the project lifecycle)

If the optimistic reporting curve is overlaid on the influence vs cost of changes curves (see figure 15.2) discussed in the *Project Lifecycle* chapter, then this would further support the argument for accurate reporting at the outset of the project. Not only has the project manager the highest level of influence at the outset, but also the cost of changes are more economical.

2. Scope of Control

It may be argued that as the project manager is the *single point of responsibility*, then he is responsible for everything that happens on the project. Consider the following knowledge areas:

Scope Management: The scope of work (SOW) defines what the project is producing or delivering. The control of the *scope of work* is also called **configuration management.**

Planning documents: Project charter
Work Breakdown Structure (WBS)
Activity list / bill of materials (BOM)
Drawing register
Specification register
Parts list
Contract

Control documents: Project communications
Impact statements
Variations and Modifications

                              Change requests
                              Concessions
                              Closeout report

Technical Support: Technical support from the design office and drawing office extends from interpreting the client's brief to addressing day to day problems within statutory regulations and good building practice.

Planning documents: Client's brief
                           Statutory regulations
                           Specifications
                           Design calculations
                           Build-method
Control documents: Configuration control
                           Impact statements
                           Commissioning
                           As-built drawings

Time Management: Outlines the sequence and timing of the *scope of work*.

Planning documents: Network diagram
                           Scheduled Gantt chart
                           Keydate / milestone schedule
                           Rolling horizon Gantt chart
Control documents: Progress report (actual vs planned)
                           Gantt chart
                           Revised Gantt chart
                           Earned value
                           Trend documents

Procurement Management: The procurement function identifies all the bought-in items. These must be procured to specification, time schedule and budget.

Planning documents: BOM and parts list
                           Procurement schedule
                           Material requirement planning (MRP)
                           Procurement budget
Control documents: Purchase order
                           Expediting status report
                           Revised procurement schedule and budget

Resource Management: Resource management integrates the scope of work, resource estimate with the schedule to produce the resource forecast. This is usually related to manpower requirements.

Planning documents: Resource forecast
                           Resource availability
                           Resource levelled manpower histogram
Control documents: Time sheets
                           Revised manpower histogram

Cost Management: Cost management allocates budgets and cashflows to the work packages.

Planning documents: Cost breakdown structure
Activity budgets
Department budgets
Cashflow statement

Control documents: Expenditure reports (actual vs planned)
Committed costs and cost-to-complete
Revised budgets
Earned value

Change Control: As the project progresses the scope of work is revised and controlled through the following documents:

Project communications
Impact statements
Non Conformance Reports (NCR)
Change Requests and Concessions
Modifications and Variation Orders (VO)
Extras to contract
Drawing revisions
Specification and Configuration revisions.

Quality Management: Outlines how the company will assure the product will achieve the required condition.

Planning documents: Project quality plan (ISO 9000)
Quality control plan
Parts lists and specifications / standards

Control documents: Inspection reports
Non conformance reports (NCR's)
Concessions
Change requests
Commissioning
As-built drawings
Data books and operation manuals

Communication Management: The communication function is to disseminate information and instructions to the responsible parties.

Planning documents: Lines of communication
List of controlled documents
Distribution list
Schedule of meetings and agendas

Control documents: Transmittals
Minutes of meetings

Human Resource Management: This function sets the framework for the human factors.

Planning documents:	Project organisation structure
	Responsibility matrix
	Job descriptions
	Work procedures
Control documents:	Time sheets
	Performance evaluations

Environmental Management: This function considers all the external issues that may impact on the project.

Planning documents:	Laws and regulations
	Environmental issues
	Stakeholders analysis
Control documents:	Environmental report

3. Data Capture

Data capture is part of the progress reporting cycle where information is regularly reported back to the project manager on the project's progress and status. The data capture function may be assumed to be at the start of the information cycle and so the accuracy of the subsequent calculations are based directly on the accuracy of the data capture. It is, therefore, extremely important for the data capture to be at an appropriate level of accuracy. Consider the following points:

- The data capture feedback proforma should be structured in line with the original estimate. This will help to make the data capture less subjective.
- The person responsible for the quality of the data capture needs to be clearly identified by the project manager. One method of improving data capture, is to make the department that uses the information responsible for updating it. This should encourage the users to ensure that the data input is accurate.
- A common integration problem with data capture and the subsequent analysis, occurs when the tracking categories are set up within one

Techniques - Rory Burke

structure, while data is collected through another structure. For example, the planning department being structured by work package or activity, while the procurement department is structured by supplier. In this case, the baseline plan is no longer suitable for tracking the project's progress because there is no basis for comparison.

- The accuracy of the data capture will directly influence the accuracy of any reports generated. Data capture with an accuracy of +/- 20% will give subsequent reports an accuracy of +/- 20%. As a guide the accuracy of the report should be the same or better than the profit margin of the project and in line with the level of risk and level of control required.

- A higher level of accuracy is required on critical activities, because any delays to these activities will extend the project's duration.

- Negotiate the design of your reports with the people who will use them. Try to make the reports simple and easy to use, this will help to ensure accuracy and commitment.

- The use of written communication should be encouraged because it addresses the human failing of misinterpretation and forgetfulness.

- Managers should have a propensity for one page reporting, giving quality not quantity. People are more likely to read a one page document than a 50 page report.

- The data capture should be pertinent and relevant. Managers are busy people, so only ask questions where the feedback will be used.

- If information is received after the decision has been made, the value of the information is reduced to being historical.

- A project manager at NASA advised me to "... *use plenty of milestones to report against - people do not tend to lie, however, they may be economical with the truth, but they won't lie.*"

- The accuracy of data capture can be improved by reporting percentage complete against mini milestones, (see table 15.1).

If these points are used as a guideline for data capture the quality and accuracy of the information should match the appropriate level of control.

Data Capture Example: Consider a drawing office which may need to produce 500 drawings for a project within a short time frame (table 15.1). By setting-up a suitable data capture proforma the project manager will be able to quantify their performance to date and get a feel for *'how they are doing'*.

Data Capture Proforma: The drawing numbers are listed in the left hand column. The scope of work is subdivided into five headings (design, draw, check, correct, re-check) and weighted. As each drawing may require different hours, this is accommodated in the planned hours column. The progress is reported as a percentage of each section, so if on drawing 500 the design is 100% complete, this means they have earned 100% of 25%, which equals 25%. And if the sketching of the drawing is 50% complete, this means they have earned 50% of a 50% weighting, which equals 25%, so overall drawing 500 is 50% complete.

Drawing Number	Design 25%	Draw 50%	Check 10%	Correct 10%	Check 5%	Percentage Complete	Planned Hours	Earned Hours	Actual Hours
100	100%	100%	100%	100%	100%	(Progress)			
	25%	50%	10%	10%	5%	100% (earned)	50	50	50
200	100%	90%	50%						
	25%	45%	5%			75% (earned)	40	30	40
300	100%								
	25%					25% (earned)	60	15	10
400	40%								
	10%					10% (earned)	50	5	5
500	100%	50%							
	25%	25%				50% (earned)	60	30	25
Total						50%	260 hours	130 hours	130 hours

Table 15.1: Data Capture Proforma (Drawing Office)

Analysis of table 15.1: This type of format lends itself to spreadsheet calculations. This project is 50% complete - compare this with the planned progress to see if the rate of work is sufficient to complete the project on time (for this example the data is not given). To measure productivity compare the earned hours with the actual hours. Overall in this case they are the same or a ratio of one. This means the work is being completed at the same rate as the estimate (see *Earned Value* chapter).

Data Capture Formats: The format for a number of other work situations are included for the readers benefit (see tables 15.2, 15.3 and 15.4). Consider designing one for your work environment.

Drawing Number	Sling	Fit and Tack	Weld	Test	Mark-up Butt List	Handover	Percentage Complete
100	20%	20%	35%	15%	5%	15%	100%
200							
300							
400							

Table 15.2: Data Capture Proforma for Pipe Erection

Drawing Number	Column	Beam	Gratings Ladders Handrails	Final Alignment	Punch List and Fix	Handover	Percentage Complete
1000	20%	20%	40%	5%	10%	5%	100%
2000							
3000							
4000							

Table 15.3: Data Capture Proforma for Steel Structures

Location	Removal	Inspection	Repair	Test	Install	Percentage Complete
Port 1	10%	15%	50%	15%	10%	100%
Port 2						
Port 3						

Table 15.4: Data Capture for Ship Repair Valve Maintenance

With all the managers using the same system the accuracy and consistency of the data capture should improve.

Size of Activity: As the size of the work packages, activity and subsections are reduced so the accuracy of the data capture should increase, but so will the effort to capture the data - you will need to strike a balance. As a guide, relate the subsections to the reporting period so that a subsection is completed within each reporting period. Therefore, for weekly reporting the subsection should not be greater than 30/40 hours per person.

Gantt Chart Data Capture: The Gantt chart itself can be a useful format for data capture. Ask the foreman or supervisor to mark-up their progress on the schedule Gantt chart. The Gantt chart will now contain the plan (last week), progress to date and planned work for the next week. This information should be accurate as the foreman is at the operational end of the project. The report is also quick and easy for them to complete in a format they are familiar with.

4. How to Apply Project Control

There are many ways of applying project control, this section has gathered together a number of pointers as a general guide:

- An effective way to achieve commitment is to make the person aware of the cost of any delay to the project.
- When the project involves the repetitive manufacture of components it may be appropriate to change the management style to production management. Production management applies effective control not through activity based planning but through earned manhours. Progress is then monitored and controlled using the production line earned manhours S curve (see *Earned Value* chapter).
- Any changes to the plan should be discussed with the foreman first:
    - To see if the changes are possible
    - To get their input for the planning
    - To gain their commitment.
- If your resources are being under utilised remember that assigning more men to the job may actually slow down production. This is because those already working effectively will have to spend time explaining the job to the newcomers.
- An excuse often used for not feeding progress back to the planner is, *"We don't have the time"*, or *"We are too busy doing the work"*. It is the project manager's responsibility to ensure that all the project members appreciate that data capture is an important aspect of their management function.
- Short training programmes should be developed to ensure that all the managers appreciate and understand how the information is flowing in the project.
- The process of project tracking and analysis should be seen as a tool for the project manager and not a means of removing responsibility. In fact, by identifying future problems, CPM enforces the project manager's authority to apply timely control to keep the project on course.
- Avoid persecution of the responsible parties if there are overruns, otherwise in future the managers will be reluctant to give you any information for fear that it will be held against them. **Project control should be seen as a tool to assist managers reach their objectives, not as a weapon of attack.**
- Failure to coordinate and communicate information between departments may lead to a dissipation of company resources and duplication of effort. It will also limit the amount of cross checking, which is a useful method for identifying discrepancies and future problems.
- It is the project manager's responsibility to establish priorities and differentiate between what is urgent and what is important. If you allow the workforce to set their own priorities they may leave low paying jobs and jobs they dislike until last. This could adversely affect the scheduling of the project.

- Respond early to any variation, before small problems become disasters.
- Encourage the team members to inform you of deviations.
- As the schedule is only an estimate, you must expect activities not to be exactly as per the schedule - introduce a degree of flexibility.
- Although plans should be revised to reflect the current progress, it is important not to forget the original baseline plan to guide the project to completion.
- Contractors could be tempted to over claim to improve their cashflow (in the short term).
- If the project is in serious jeopardy, the client and stakeholders should be involved.

All these decision-making steps are intrinsically part of the control cycle. The decisions can now be made on what control to apply to keep the project on course. As changes occur they could make achieving the baseline plan either impossible or economically unfeasible. If the project slips by over 10% it should be rescheduled to introduce a sense of realism, but most of all to introduce an attainable recovery plan to get the project back on track.

5. Acceleration

Project acceleration, also called **crashing**, is the process of reducing the duration of an activity or project to meet schedule requirements. Consider the following methods of shortening an activity's duration.

- Once the critical path has been identified, resources can be transferred from non-critical activities to critical activities. This will shorten the duration of the critical activities, while extending the duration of the non-critical activities.
- Change the network logic along the critical path. Change activities which are in series to start-to-start (SS) or parallel.
- Recalculate the estimate for activity durations along the critical path. With more information the contingency part of the estimate can be reduced which in turn should reduce the duration of the activity.
- Change the calendar to increase the working hours. For example, work overtime, shifts or change from a 5 day week to 6 days or 7 days. Note, with the longer working hours there may be a fall off in productivity.
- When in-house resources are overloaded employ sub-contractors. Check there is sufficient room to work and consider any impact on industrial relations.
- If an activity's start is being delayed because of access, consider pre-outfit or modularization. In offshore construction the accommodation is often pre-assembled and slotted into place later.

- If an activity is being delayed because of material consider using a faster form of transport (airfreight instead of shipping).
- Incentive payments can speed up production in the short term.
- Technical changes should be considered to make the work simpler and quicker, for example, consider different material or a different build-method.
- If the jobs involve a certain amount of repetition it is reasonable to assume a learning curve.
- Education and training should improve productivity in the long term.
- If time and cost are the main objectives, consider reducing the scope of work.
- Activity duration could be reduced by automation.

By skilfully using a number of these methods the project manager should be able to effectively shorten the duration of the project.

6. Crashing Steps

This section will outline a sequence of steps to crash an activity.

Step 1. Identify the activities that need to be crashed (where an activity has negative float for instance). This can happen at any time from the initial project planning phase to project completion.

Step 2. Identify the critical path. To crash non critical activities is a waste of financial resources because it will simply increase the float on that activity without improving the end date of the project (see figure 15.6).

Step 3. Prioritise the activities to be crashed. When there are many activities which can be crashed which one should you crash first ?

a) Select the activity with the least cost per day to crash.

b) Select the activity which is easiest to crash.

c) Select the activity which can be crashed soonest to bring the project back on course. As project manager you do not want to approach the end of the project with a number of activities running behind schedule and the prospects of further problems during commissioning.

Step 4. Crash activities one day at a time, then re-analyze the network to see if any other activities have gone critical.

Continue this iterative process until there are no activities with negative float. These crashing steps may vary with the different types of projects. It should be evident that cost has been identified as a main consideration, the next section will show how to estimate the crashing expense.

7. Time Cost Trade-Off Theory (relate to triangle of objectives)

This section will explain the theory behind the time cost trade-off concept. The first step is to define some terminology:

Normal Time	The activity duration when working normal office hours, e.g. 8 hours a day, 5 days a week.
Normal Cost	The cost of the activity working normal hours.
Direct Cost	Costs attributed directly to the project, e.g. labour and material. These costs usually go up when crashed due to overtime, shift allowance etc.
Indirect Cost	Overhead costs which cannot be directly attributed to the project e.g. office rent and management salaries. These costs are usually linear with time, therefore if the time reduces the indirect costs reduce.
Crash Time	The duration the activity can be reduced to by working overtime or shift working etc.
Crash Cost	The new cost of the activity after crashing.

We will first discuss the way direct costs and indirect costs react when a critical activity is crashed.

Crashing (direct costs): Crashing direct costs will reduce the duration but increase the costs. These additional costs are caused by overtime, shift work and a reduction in productivity (see figure 15.3).

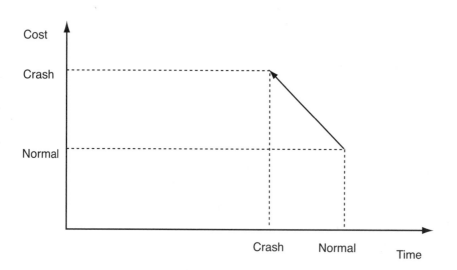

Figure 15.3: Crashing Direct Costs

Crashing (indirect costs): Crashing indirect costs will reduce the duration and also reduce the costs. The benefit has come from reduced office rental, equipment hire etc. Unfortunately project costs are usually split 80% direct, 20% indirect so the benefit of crashing indirect costs is usually overwhelmed by the far greater direct costs.

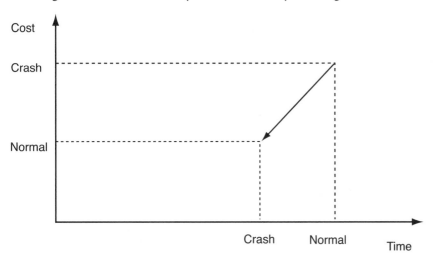

Figure: 15.4. Crashing indirect costs

When the direct costs and indirect costs are combined on the same graph an optimum position is derived.

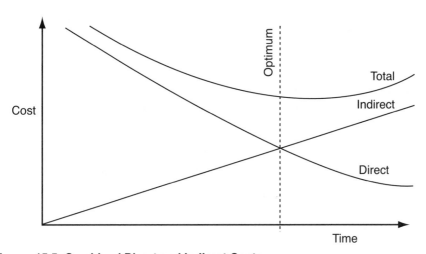

Figure: 15.5: Combined Direct and Indirect Costs

Time cost trade-off: The time cost trade-off figure outlines graphically four different time costs positions. Starting at point A figure 15.6, this point represents normal time and normal cost. Consider first the impact of crashing all the non-critical activities, the project will move to point D. Notice there has been no shortening of the project's duration, but the costs have increased dramatically. This is not a recommended course of action as it only increases the float of non-critical activities.

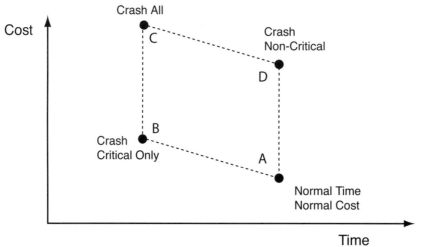

Figure: 15.6: Time Cost Trade-Off

The correct action would be to crash all the critical activities. The project moves to point B. Crashing the critical activities has reduced the duration of the project with a small increase in costs.

The fourth point on the graph, C, indicates the position when all the activities are crashed. Again this is not recommended because there has been no time improvement on point B, yet the costs have increased tremendously.

The moral of the story is only crash critical activities.

Worked Example: The following calculations will show how direct costs increase with crashing, while indirect costs reduce. Consider the following activity to manufacture a garden shed.

When working normal time the activity will take;

5 men working 8 hours per day, 5 days per week for 5 weeks	= 1,000 man hrs
The activity's normal costs will be: Labour @ $20 per hour x 1,000 man hours	= $20,000
Material	= $5,000
Preliminary and General @ $1000 per week $1,000 x 5 weeks	= $5,000
Total	= $30,000

If the client now wants to manufacture the shed in less time, the crash cost can be quantified in steps of one day. To reduce the duration the men will have to work overtime, say 10 hours per day (2 hours overtime @ time and a half). Assume the additional hours do not change the productivity.

The total manhours will still be the same at 1000 man hours / (5 men x 10 hours per day) = 20 days or 4 weeks. The extra hours worked per day will reduce the duration from 25 working days to 20 working days.

The crashing costs will be:

Labour: $20 x 20 days x 5 men x 8 hrs	= $16,000 (normal time)
$20 x 20 days x 5 men x 2 hrs x 1.5 (overtime)	= $6,000 (over time)
Material:	= $5,000 (no change)
P & G: $1,000 x 4 weeks	= $4,000 (reduction)
Total	= $31,000

With this information calculate the additional cost to crash the activity by one day.

Additional crash cost per day $= \dfrac{\text{(Difference in cost)}}{\text{(Difference in time)}}$

$$= (31000 - 30000) / (25 - 20)$$
$$= \$200 \text{ per day}$$

This example clearly shows that to reduce the project by 1 week or 5 days the direct costs will increase while the indirect costs reduce. The overall effect is to increase the costs by $200 per day.

PROJECT MANAGER   SUB-CONTRACTOR

8. Acceleration (Crash) Cost Priority Table

Having decided to crash a project the next step is to set up a priority table to indicate the most cost effective order of crashing, i.e. crash the cheapest activity first.

A crash priority table is developed (figure 15.7). Set-up columns A and B as normal time and normal cost, this information will be available from the original estimate. Assign the crash time and crash costs to columns C and D, this data will have to be calculated as outlined in the above example.

The additional cost to crash per day is calculated from columns A to D. If the table was set up on a spreadsheet this could be calculated automatically. Notice only activities on the critical path are considered and the priority of crashing is to crash the cheapest first.

Although crashing the cheapest first is recommended the timing of that activity should also be taken into count. If the project manager wants to crash the project now then obviously activities that do not start for a few weeks cannot be considered.

	A	B	C	D	(D-B)/(A-C)	
Activity Number	Normal Time	Normal Cost	Crash Time	Crash Cost	Additional cost to crash per day	Crashing Priority
100	25	$30,000	20	$31,000	$200	2
200	10	$5,000	6	$5,400	$100	1
300	12	$9,000	8	$9,200	$50	Not Critical
400	15	$21,000	9	$22,500	$250	3

Figure: 15.7 Crash Cost Estimating Table

Wordsworth is reported to have said; *"It takes less time to do a job right than to explain why you did the job wrong in the first place"*. This concludes the chapter on *Project Control* techniques. The following chapter will take project control a step further outlining the *Earned Value* technique.

Key Points:

- Project control guides the project plan to completion.
- Over optimistic reporting may lull you into a false sense of achievement.
- Develop data capture proformas to accurately capture your earned progress.

Case Study and Exercises:

Project planning is a pointless exercise unless the execution of the plans are tracked and controlled through accurate reporting on performance. As project manager of a marketing project to launch a new Hollywood film discuss how you would address the following;

1. Limit over optimistic reporting.
2. List key planning and control documents.
3. Discuss methods of data capture.
4. Set up a data capture proforma which subdivides the work by percentage.
5. Discuss how you would apply control for schedule delays.

"...I said crash the project....not the car!!..."

16

Earned Value

This chapter continues the project control theme by introducing earned value as an integrated planning and control tool. The earned value approach is a development of the **w** and the **Cost Schedule Control System** criteria (CSCS) introduced in 1967 circa by the US DoD (Dept of Defence), to fully integrate cost and time.

When this approach is combined with forecasting, the project manager has the best of both worlds. For the project manager to answer the basic question, "*How are we doing*?", the performance measuring mechanism should periodically (usually weekly) assess progress and costs in comparable units (compare apples with apples) against a baseline plan. **It is essential for effective project control that performance is measured while there is still time to take corrective action.**

Although the earned value technique was initially set up to track the progress of cost and time, in practice it is often more appropriate to track progress measured as **earned manhours** and time. In fact any parameter that flows through the project can be used; software lines of code, tonnes of steel, cubic meters of concrete, metres of pipe, or pages of a document.

1. The Need for Earned Value

The *Project Control* chapter mentioned a situation where a US Navy shipbuilding project was 99% complete for a year - how could this happen? The likely answer is that they were unable to distinguish between planned manhours, actual manhours and earned manhours. Where:

- Planned manhours are an estimate of how you intend to perform the work.
- The earned manhours are a measure of work done.
- The actual manhours are recorded on the clock cards.

The problem occurs when the actual manhours are assumed to be the same as the earned manhours. In this case, if the actual manhours are 99% of the planned manhours, then it is assumed that the project is 99% complete, but when they look out the window and see the ship is not finished - obviously something is wrong with their reporting.

Separate Reporting: A similar problem arises when expenses and progress are reported separately - consider the following example (figures 16.1 and 16.2):

Figure 16.1: Project Expenses Against Time

From the expense graph (figure 16.1) the accountant would report that the project is under spent, with planned expenditure 50% and actual expenditure 45%. Here the forecast looks good for the project to be completed under budget.

Figure 16.2: Project Progress Against Time

From the progress graph (figure 16.2) the planner on the other hand would not be so optimistic with planned progress 50% and actual progress only 40% complete - the prognosis would predict a project time overrun. But now consider what happens when the two graphs are integrated, the project is 45% spent but has only achieved 40% of the work. The analysis now indicates that not only is the project behind schedule, but is overspent as well, thus giving a strong signal that the project manager needs to apply control to bring the project back on track.

This example clearly shows the **need to integrate** the project's cost and time information. Based on the expense information alone the project manager would have been mislead, believing that the project would meet its objectives without the need for corrective control. As projects grow in size and complexity, so the need for an earned value measuring system quantifying project performance increases. The project manager needs to know if control is required, where and by how much. Earned value provides visibility to the critical areas and identifies the need for further attention.

2. Earned Value Structure

The earned value calculations can be presented as either an earned value table (see table 16.2) or rolled-up to an earned value graph (see figure 16.3). The graph provides an excellent presentation that is easy to assimilate, while the table provides further detail for the project manager to investigate any variances.

Earned value more than any other planning and control technique covered in this book is shrouded in **esoteric terminology**. The key to mastering earned value is to understand and not be intimidated by these terms. It may be argued that if you wish to enter the field of project management, then you must speak the language of project management.

Figure 16.3: Earned Value Curve

2.1 Earned Value Plan

The earned value graph (figure 16.3) is built-up by first outlining the plan.

Budget at Completion (BAC): This is the original cost estimate, budget or quotation, indicating the funds required to complete the work, in this case $2000 (see figure 16.3). Calling this parameter simply *'the budget'* may have been less confusing. At the project management level the BAC does not include profit. The reason for this will become clear later when the actual costs are compared with the planned costs. The BAC becomes a generic term when manhours or another parameter are used.

Budgeted Cost for Work Scheduled (BCWS): Also called planned value (PV), is the integration of cost and time or more commonly manhours and time to give the characteristic S curve, which forms the baseline plan (see the *Project Accounts* and *Resource Planning* chapters which explain how to draw an S curve).

2.2 Earned Value Status

Once the project starts the progress needs to be captured on a regular basis.

Timenow: Also called **data date**, or **progress date** or **progress at week ending** are the terms used to indicate up to what date the progress has been recorded.

Percentage Complete (PC): The PC is a measure of the activities performance and progress up to timenow and is required for the earned value calculation. For this example the PC is 40% at timenow.

Budgeted Cost for Work Performed (BCWP): Also called earned value (EV), is a measure of achievement or value of the work done to timenow. The BCWP is calculated by the equation:

$$BCWP = PC \text{ (earned progress at timenow)} \times BAC$$
$$= 40\% \times \$2000$$
$$= \$800$$

Actual Cost for Work Performed (ACWP): Also called actual value (AV), is the amount payable for the work done to timenow. It is the **real** cost incurred executing the work to achieve the reported progress. Take care to ensure that both **PC** and **ACWP** are based on the same data. A possible mistake is to report progress as the work is performed, but only report costs on receipt of the invoice. This differential cashflow will make the project accounts look deceptively good in the short term. Another mistake is to compare actual work hours with the planned work hours. As mentioned before in the shipbuilding project, this is a meaningless comparison as it says nothing about what work has been performed. For this example the ACWP is $1200 at timenow (see figure 16.3).

2.3 Earned Value Forecast

When the integration of cost and time are combined with forecasting the project manager has the best of both worlds.

Estimate at Completion (EAC): The EAC is a revised budget for the activity, work package or project, based on current productivity. The EAC is calculated by extrapolating the performance trend from timenow to the end of the project. This value assumes that the productivity to-date will continue at the same rate to the end of the project. The productivity is defined by the ratio of costs (ACWP) to earned value (BCWP). If the costs (ACWP) are less than the earned value (BCWP), then the EAC will be less than the BAC and vice versa.

$$EAC = \frac{ACWP \times BAC}{BCWP}$$

But $\qquad BCWP = PC \times BAC$

Therefore $\quad EAC = \dfrac{ACWP \times \cancel{BAC}}{PC \times \cancel{BAC}}$

$$EAC = \frac{ACWP}{PC}$$

For this example at timenow (see figure 16.3)

$$EAC = \frac{\$1200 \times 100}{40\%}$$

$$= \$3000$$

The **budget variance** is therefore BAC - EAC, \$2000 - \$3000 = - \$1000. The project is forecast to be \$1000 over budget.

Estimate-to-Complete (ETC): is defined as;

$$
\begin{aligned}
ETC &= EAC - ACWP \\
&= \$3000 - \$1200 \\
&= \$1800
\end{aligned}
$$

The *estimate-to-complete* is a useful figure for the project manager to compare the funds available (outstanding invoices must also be included) with the *cost-to-complete*. A significant difference should trigger a review of estimates and build-methods to search for a corrective solution.

2.4 Earned Value Variances

A variance is simply the difference between planned and actual values. In the earned value context there are a number of important flags to attract the project manager's attention, consider the following:

- Schedule variance (SV)
- Cost variance (CV)
- Threshold variance

Schedule Variance (SV): The schedule variance calculation is a measure of the time deviation between the planned progress (BCWS) and the earned progress (BCWP). The interesting feature about this time variance is that it is measured in money units.

$$
\begin{aligned}
SV &= BCWP - BCWS \\
&= \$800 - \$1000 \\
&= - \$200
\end{aligned}
$$

The sign of the variance will indicate if the project is ahead or behind the planned progress:

Negative variance: The project is behind the planned progress.
Positive variance: The project is ahead of planned progress.

Schedule Variance Percentage (SV%): Converting the schedule variance to a percentage will address any distortion caused by the size of the activity. For example an SV of $1,000 is 10% of a $10,000 activity, but only 1% of a $100,000 activity.

$$SV\% = SV / BCWS = -\$200 / \$1000 = -20\%$$

Cost Variance (CV): The cost variance is a measure of the deviation between the earned value (BCWP) and the actual cost of doing the work (ACWP) (see figure 16.3).

$$CV = BCWP - ACWP = \$800 - \$1200 = -\$400$$

The sign of the variance will indicate if the costs are under or over the estimate.

Negative variance: The cost is higher than the original estimate (BAC).

Positive variance: The cost is lower than the original estimate (BAC).

Cost Variance Percentage (CV%): Converting the CV to a CV% will reduce the distortion caused by the size of the activity.

$$CV\% = CV / BCWP = -\$400 / \$800 = -50\%$$

Threshold Variance: The threshold variances can be used to flag problem areas and attract the project manager's attention. The threshold limits may be set as a percentage (for example +/- 5%) to give an early indication of an undesirable trend. Tight variance thresholds allow true *management-by-exception*, as negative variances should trigger an immediate response helping supervisors to assign priorities and additional resources. Positive variances identify praiseworthy employee productivity which could have an input into productivity bonuses.

Terminology: The terms outlined here have gained acceptance in the body of knowledge, management press and business schools. They are commonly used in technical articles and management texts. Unfortunately, many of the planning software packages have invented new terminology for some of the above items. This new software terminology serves only to confuse, particularly for those users who are struggling to get to grips with a new concept in the first place.

Performance Indices: Performance indices are ratios used to determine the status of the project.

Cost Performance Index CPI: This is defined as:

$$CPI = BCWP/ACWP = \$800 / \$1200 = 0.66$$

The CPI compares the work earned with the actual cost, if the CPI < 1 then the project is spending more than it is earning and will make a loss if corrective action is not taken.

Schedule Performance Index SPI: is defined as:

$$\text{SPI} = \text{BCWP/BCWS}$$
$$= \$800 / \$1000$$
$$= 0.8$$

The SPI compares the work earned with the work schedule, if the SPI < 1 then the project is behind schedule and if corrective action is not taken it will finish late. The two indices may give results which seem contradictory, for example, CPI>1 and SPI<1. This indicates that the project is under budget, but behind schedule. The question is, *"Can the project be brought back on schedule by expending more resources?"*

Project Control: During the project the activities are usually at various stages of completion; some on target, some ahead of plan, some behind plan, some on budget, some overspent and some under spent. In this situation it is extremely difficult to quantify the project's overall status visually and it may be argued that a subjective assessment of a complex project is bound to be inaccurate. This problem can be addressed by using the earned value model to roll-up all the activity data and report a bottom line for the project giving an overall position. Consider the following example (see table 16.1):

Activity	BAC	BCWS	PC	BCWP	Status
100	$100	$100	100%	$100	On time
200	$400	$400	75%	$300	Behind
300	$1,200	$800	90%	$1,080	Ahead
Totals		$1,300		$1,480	

Table 16.1: Earned Value Progress Report

The status report indicates that overall the earned value BCWP $1480 is ahead of the planned progress BCWS $1300 and if this continues the project should finish early. If the project manager required further information they would look at the variance at the activity level and in this case would have a closer look at activity 200, which is behind. This technique can be further refined by sorting out the critical activities.

3. Earned Value Table

The earned value data can be presented in both a tabular format and a graph. Consider the following steps:

Step 1: Set up an earned value table using the following abbreviated field headings (table 16.2):

WBS	BAC	BCWS	PC	BCWP	ACWP	SV	CV	EAC
1.1	$2,000	$1,000	40%	$800	$1,200	($200)	($400)	$3,000
1.2								
Total								

Table 16.2: Earned Value Table

Step 2: List the full scope of work in the WBS column.

Step 3: Input BAC values for all work packages.

Step 4: Calculate BCWS to timenow.

Step 5: From the data capture sheet transfer the values for PC and ACWP.

Step 6: Calculate BCWP = BAC x PC

Step 7: Calculate SV, CV and EAC

Step 8: Sum the following columns: BAC, BCWS, BCWP, ACWP and EAC.

Step 9: Calculate the total PC, SV and CV.

4. Earned Value Graph

The earned value graph (see figure 16.3) is produced using the following steps:

Step 1: Draw the BCWS curve (see how to draw an S curve in the *Project Accounts* chapter).

Step 2: Draw the BCWP curve to timenow and extrapolate until the line intersects with BAC (see notes on extrapolating - figure 16.4). This intersection will give a forecast completion date. This completion date, however, should not be looked at in isolation because it does not consider the network logic, critical path and timing of the activities.

Step 3: Draw the ACWP curve to timenow and extrapolate to the new end date of the project and EAC. Where EAC = (ACWP / BCWP) x BAC. This equation assumes progress to timenow will continue at the same rate to the end of the project.

Step 4: Draw the SV and CV variances.

Step 5: Determine how far the project is ahead or behind.

Extrapolating: When trying to forecast the trends in the project by extrapolating the earned value curves (BCWP and ACWP), the following considerations should be made (see figure 16.4):

• Will the same performance be maintained?

• Will the performance improve because of a learning curve effect.

• Will the performance reduce because of unforeseen problems and re-work as the project nears completion.

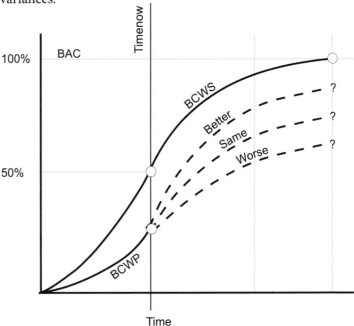

Figure 16.4: BCWP Progress Extrapolations

Earned Value Exercises: There are thirteen different combinations of planned BCWS vs actual ACWP and earned BCWP. These are shown in the table 16.3. First calculate the EAC, then draw the BCWP and ACWP curves. The solutions are given at the end of this section.

Examples	BAC Budget	BCWS Planned Costs	BCWP Earned Value	ACWP Actual Costs	EAC Estimate at Completion
1	$2,000	$1,000	$1,000	$1,000	
2	$2,000	$1,000	$800	$800	
3	$2,000	$1,000	$1,000	$800	
4	$2,000	$1,000	$1,200	$800	
5	$2,000	$1,000	$800	$1,000	
6	$2,000	$1,000	$1,200	$1,000	
7	$2,000	$1,000	$800	$1,200	
8	$2,000	$1,000	$1,000	$1,200	
9	$2,000	$1,000	$1,200	$1,200	
10	$2,000	$1,000	$600	$800	
11	$2,000	$1,000	$800	$600	
12	$2,000	$1,000	$1,400	$1,200	
13	$2,000	$1,000	$1,200	$1,400	

Table 16.3: Earned Value Exercises

Figure 16.5: Exercise Template

Figure 16.6: Solution to Number 4

BAC
$2000
EAC
$1333
$1200
$1000
$800

BCWP
BCWS
ACWP
SV
CV

Timenow

BCWS = $1000
BCWP = $1200
ACWP = $800

Time

Figure 16.7: Solution to Number 7

EAC
$3000
BAC
$2000
$1200
$1000
$800

ACWP
BCWS
BCWP
CV
SV

Timenow

BCWS = $1000
BCWP = $800
ACWP = $1200

Time

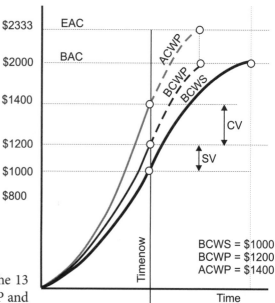

Figure 16.8: Solution to Number 13

BCWS = $1000
BCWP = $1200
ACWP = $1400

Earned Value Solutions: Solutions to the 13 different combinations of BCWS, ACWP and BCWP.

Example 1:   This is the planned situation, where planned and actual are the same.

Example 2:   The project is running late, but the costs are within budget.

Example 3:   The project is on time and the costs are under budget.

Example 4:   The progress is ahead of planned and the costs are under budget. Retire while you are ahead !

Example 5:   The project is running late and the costs are over budget.

Example 6:   The progress is ahead of planned and the costs are under budget.

Example 7:   The project is running late and the costs are well over budget.

Example 8:   The project is on time, but the costs are over budget.

Example 9:   The progress is ahead of planned while the costs are on budget.

Example 10:   The project is seriously behind and the costs are over budget.

Example 11:   The project is behind, but the costs are under budget.

Example 12:   The project is well ahead and the costs are under budget.

Example 13:   The project is ahead, but the costs are over budget.

5. How to Measure Time Deviation

The schedule variance so far has been measured in money units. This section will show a number of methods to translate the variances directly into time units by measuring distances from the earned value graph. Three ways of measuring are (see figure 16.9):

- Horizontally (forwards)
- Horizontally (backwards)
- Vertically

Horizontally (Forwards): The time difference between planned and actual is measured horizontally between the intersection of the planned BCWS at timenow (A) and the horizontal projection to BCWP extrapolated (B).

Horizontally (Backwards): Alternatively the schedule time unit can be measured horizontally from the intersection of BCWP and timenow (C) to the horizontal projection backwards onto the BCWS (D). Note that both of these methods are only an estimate as the actual sequence and timing of the activities are not considered.

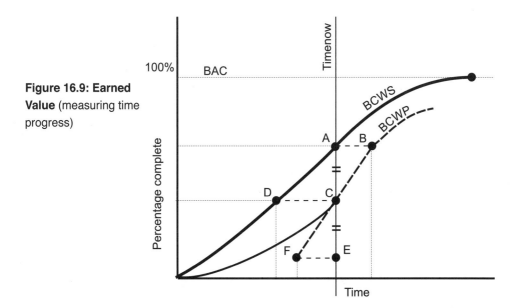

Figure 16.9: Earned Value (measuring time progress)

Vertically: However, even if the sequence and timing of activities were the same as the baseline plan, converting the schedule variance to time units on the BCWP curve would be more accurate if based on the tangential rate (CF), where (CA) = (EC). The reason for this is that future progress is more likely to occur at the current actual rate of progress rather than the planned BCWS slope.

Project Accounts: The project manager will need to ensure that the project accounting system will generate costs to timenow. Corporate accounting departments usually base their reports on invoiced costs which may be 4 to 6 weeks behind timenow. When using earned value the costs will have to be gathered at the order stage, it is essential to compare like with like. Progress to timenow must be compared with the associated costs (ACWP) to achieve that progress.

Extended Site: If costs are being incurred off site, such as stage payments then the progress (PC) must be reported along with the associated cost (ACWP).

Cashflow: The earned value technique is not the same as cashflow. The cashflow only looks at the timing of the inflows and outflows of money, it does not consider committed costs or progress of work.

Project Control: Beware of managers who constantly revise the BCWS to accommodate their lack of performance (see figures 16.10, 16.11 and 16.12). This may make their weekly progress reports look better, but eventually it will extend the end date of the project. If the contractor continually revises the BCWS from the last BCWP then the contractors lack of progress does not look as obvious as comparing it with the original BCWS. The contractors are only fooling themselves because eventually they will have to perform the remaining work on the last day!

Figure 16.10: Timenow 1,
(BCWP falling behind BCWS)

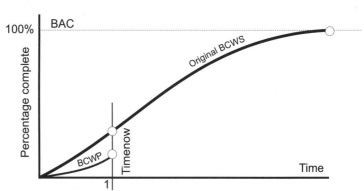

Figure 16.11: Timenow 2,
(BCWP falling further behind, even against revised BCWS)

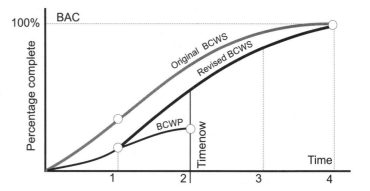

Figure 16.12: Timenow 3,
(BCWP continuing the fall behind second revision of BCWS. Finishing on time looks highly unlikely)

6. Client's View of Earned Value

So far the earned value technique has only been looked at from the sub-contractors' point of view. This section will consider the client's position.
- If the sub-contractors are working to a fixed price contract then BCWP and ACWP will always be the same.
- The client can effectively use earned value to track the progress of their projects in terms of manhours or costs.
- The client must check that sub-contractors do not over claim:
  a) If a sub-contractor has claimed 80% of the contract by value but only completed 50% of the work, there is little financial pressure you can exert. Worse is when it is financially viable for the sub-contractor to walk away without finishing the job. The 10% retention may pale into insignificance.
  b) The sub-contractor's management may not realise their site manager has been over claiming. This could seriously effect the sub-contractor's financial position, which may have a knock-on effect for the project.
- If the sub-contractor under-claims, the client could also be adversely impacted because:
  a) By delaying the claim the sub-contractor could increase income by applying higher escalation rates.
  b) The client could have made arrangements to meet a forecast rate of invoice (FRI) payment and released high interest earning bonds only to find a lower claim is made. The funds must now be invested short term at a lower interest rate.
  c) At year end a late claim could impact the client's fiscal budgeting.

This section clearly shows that earned value can provide the client with a powerful management tool.

7. Earned Value Reporting

The earned value output lends itself to effective reporting for the following reasons.
- The overall status of the project can be seen at a glance on a graph and the tabular reports present more detailed information at the work package and activity levels.
- When reporting to functional management the report should clearly indicate the activities that fall under their responsibility. This information can be separately reported if a responsibility field has been included in the data base.
- The reports can use a management-by-exception (MBE) technique to identify problem areas. The MBE thresholds can be set using any of the following:-
  a) Threshold variance SV% and CV%. Set upper and lower percentages, for example, -5% to +10%.
  b) Activity float = 0 days, identifies the critical path, or set activity float < 5 days, to identify activities which could go critical in the next week.

- The sign of the variance should influence the management response.

  SV (+) The project is ahead of schedule, move labour off the project if they can be used more effectively elsewhere.

  SV (-) The project is behind schedule, move resources on to the project to increase production.

  CV (+) The project costs are less than budget, if significant, amend estimating data base for future projects.

  CV (-) The project costs are greater than budget, try to increase productivity through increased efficiency and effectiveness.

- Plot trends wherever possible to indicate the direction of the project. Extrapolating trends will give an indication of future events and a quick feedback on recent actions. Even if the variances are negative, but reducing, this will show a positive trend indicating that the project is coming back on course.

Determining Percentage Complete: The weakest link in the earned value calculation is determining percentage complete (PC). If the activity has not started it is zero and if it is complete it is 100%, but all points in between are somewhat of a guess even if you use a structure. A quick way to estimate PC is to use the 50/50 rule, if the job has started give it 50% and when it is finished give it 100%. This rule can be distorted to 40/60, 30/70, 20/80 and 10/90. If the work packages or activities are kept small (less than 50 hours), then this method will work well.

- The earned value analysis should not be used in isolation. An activity with a large schedule variance may have plenty of float and not be a problem, while an activity with a small schedule variance may be on the critical path and need prompt action to prevent the project over-running.

- *Estimate-at-completion* (EAC) is based on the ratio of past performance, but if the original estimate is fundamentally flawed, or performance is significantly different to planned, then the rest of the project should be re-estimated.

- EAC includes the actual costs to date plus the forecast *cost-to-complete*.

- Cost reserves are budgeted amounts not assigned to any specific work package.

- NASA manager: "*Earned value is only useful if the difference between planned and actual is 10% to 15%, if greater then use other methods.*" [Rolling horizon Gantt chart]

If the progress indicates that both SV and CV are negative and significant, then ordering a small contractor to increase their resources may actually put the contractor into liquidation quicker! There is obviously a problem which needs to be investigated - is the contractor's estimate over optimistic or is the contractor's workforce under performing? This concludes the chapter on *Earned Value*, the next chapter will discuss *Quality Management*.

Key Points:

- Earned value integrates costs and time or manhours and time.
- The earned value graph and table shows the project's present position and forecasts the completion.
- Threshold variances can be set to flag problem areas.

Case Study and Exercises:

The earned value technique integrates cost and time (or manhours and time) to give the project manager the best of both worlds. For this case study you have been appointed project manager of the drawing office for a military project requiring 1000 drawings. You are required to outline how you will plan, track and control the drawing office project using the earned value technique. Your outline should consider the following:

1. The earned value plan BAC and BCWS.
2. Methods for determining percentage complete.
3. Data capture BCWP and ACWP.
4. Earned value reporting tables and curves.
5. Control of variances.

"Your move"

17

Quality Management

In today's competitive market companies compete on price, quality and customer service. Over the product's lifecycle the project's initial price is only a short term consideration, whereas, the quality of the product and customer service will determine the long term success of the project. Quality products are only expensive once!

The PMBOK defines project quality management as; '... *the processes required to ensure that the project will satisfy the needs for which it was undertaken* [by addressing] *both the management of the project and the product of the project.'* And the APM bok defines quality management as; '... *covering quality planning, quality control and quality assurance.'*

You, therefore, need to consider both the quality management system to assure you are capable of building the product, and also consider the quality control system, which tests and inspects the product, to confirm you have achieved the required condition.

With projects becoming larger, more complex and more technically advanced, the need to assure the product will meet stringent requirements is the focus of quality management. These requirements may be set not only by the client but also by insurance companies, governmental laws and regulations, together with national and international standards.

The development of quality management systems can be traced back to the large military projects of the Second World War where they needed to ensure standardisation. Since then BS 5750 (1979) has established the framework of consistent processes for commercial quality management systems, this has since been adopted internationally as the ISO 9000 standard.

1. Quality Definitions

Quality is a frequently misused term. Be careful not to confuse quality with degree of excellence or grade, where grade is a category of rank given to products which have the same function but different quality requirements. For example, the Rolls Royce and the Mini are often quoted as being at opposite ends of the quality continuum, the Rolls Royce being built to a much higher quality than the Mini. However, if you wish to buy an economical small car that will do 50 miles to the gallon and is easy to park, then the Mini is the car that *conforms to the client's requirements*.

Quality Management Philosophy: Is the involvement of all project participants to ensure the goals and objectives of the project and resulting product, facility or service meet the needs of the client, project team and other stakeholders.

Quality Assurance: Is a systematic process of defining, planning, implementing and reviewing the management processes within a company, in order to provide adequate confidence that the product will be consistently manufactured to the required condition. The body of knowledge defines quality assurance as; '... *the planned and systematic activities implemented within the quality system to provide confidence that the project will satisfy the relevant quality standards.*'

Quality Planning: Is the process of identifying the quality standards the project needs to comply with, to achieve the required condition and satisfy the terms of the contract.

Quality Control: Is the process companies go through to confirm that the product has reached the required condition as determined by the specifications, build-method and the contract. Quality control defines the method of inspection (testing), in-process inspection and final inspection to confirm the product has met the required condition. The body of knowledge defines quality control as; '... *monitoring specific project results to determine if they comply with relevant quality standards and identify ways to eliminate causes of unsatisfactory results.*'

Quality Control Plan (QCP): The quality control plan integrates the project's scope of work with the schedule and with quality control inspection and testing. The QCP achieves this by listing the sequence of work, the performance requirements, the inspection requirements and testing requirements (the quality control plan is developed later in this chapter).

Figure 17.1: Quality Assurance Umbrella - shows quality management systems protecting the company from a range of problems

Quality Circles: Quality circles are a management concept the American government set up for Toyota cars in Japan after the Second World War, to continuously improve their manufacturing process by bringing all the people in a production line together (used in its wider context) to identify and solve problems.

Quality Audit: The body of knowledge defines a quality audit as; '... *a structured review of other quality management activities. The objective is to identify lessons learned that can improve performance.....*' [on this and future projects]. An audit in the project management context should be seen as a search for more information as a basis of the problem-solving and decision-making.

Quality Training: Quality is a company wide issue, from the CEO to the receptionist. Therefore all employees should undertake quality training so that they can contribute to the company's quality of the management system and the quality of the product.

Project Quality Plan: The project quality plan is a detailed document explaining how the company will assure that the product will be made to the client's requirements. The 20 subheadings from the ISO 9000 quality management system can be used to structure the document.

Total Quality Management (TQM): TQM considers the wider aspects of quality by integrating all of the quality management features. Total quality has a people and outcome focus. It first identifies what the client really wants and how it can best be achieved. It keeps an emphasis on continuous improvement, but always endeavours to keep the customer satisfied. For quality to be effective it needs to be introduced to all members and all aspects of the company's operation. TQM advances the rational that just as each organisation has unique products, so each company needs a unique quality management system.

2. Quality Costs

Crosby argues that *quality is free!* Because it costs less to do the job right first time than to have to fix the mistakes. However, it would seem some managers never have the time to get it right first time, yet seem to have the time to re-work the job several times. The cost of this re-work may be two or three times the original cost in terms of manhours, equipment and materials. Consider a weld on a steel fabrication project which has been rejected, the additional costs would include:

- The quality department raises a non-conformance report (NCR).
- The planning department schedules the repair and reschedules the remaining work.
- Removing the rejected weld and surface preparation.
- A quality check of the surface preparation.
- Re-weld
- A quality check of new weld.

And if the second weld fails this may require the whole section to be replaced, the welder retrained together with additional inspection on all his previous welds. This example clearly demonstrates that the cost of failure can be very expensive.

Quality Costs: Quality costs can be subdivided into a number of different types of costs:

- Prevention costs
- Appraisal costs
- Failure costs / internal
- Failure costs / external

Prevention Costs: Prevention costs are those expenses associated with steps taken to make sure the product will be made to the required condition.

- Project Quality Plan.
- Quality planning.
- Quality Control Plan (QCP).
- Quality auditing.
- Assuring vendor and sub-contractors' quality.
- Reviewing and verifying designs.
- In-process control engineering.
- Design and development of quality measurement and test equipment.
- Quality training.
- Acquisition analysis and reporting quality data.
- Quality improvement programs.
- Product recall and liability insurance.
- Planning of product recall.

Appraisal Costs: Appraisal costs relate to expenses incurred while checking and inspecting the work to confirm that it has achieved the required condition.

- Design appraisal.
- Receiving inspection.
- Inspection and non-destructive testing (NDT).
- Procuring inspection and testing equipment.
- Materials consumed during inspection and testing.
- Analysis and reporting of test and inspection results.
- Field performance testing.
- Approval and endorsements.
- Stock evaluations.
- Record storage.

Internal Failure Costs: These costs relate to expenses incurred within the company due to product failure and inefficiencies.

- Replacement, rework or repair.
- Scrap and waste material.
- Re-inspection and retesting.
- Defect diagnosis.
- Downtime.
- Down-grading.

External Failure Costs: These costs relate to expenses incurred outside the company, usually motivated by the client.

- Receiving and actioning complaints.
- Warranty claims.
- Products rejected and returned.
- Concessions.
- Loss of future sales.
- Increased marketing to replace lost clients.
- Recall costs.
- Product liability.

The lists seems frighteningly long, considering all these items may have a cost associated with them. The criteria for success is that the increase in prevention costs should be less than the reduction in failure costs as shown in figure 17.2.

The main problem with the quality management costs diagram (figure 17.2) is that people have a natural propensity to cover up their mistakes, therefore, the figures for the cost of re-work may never be accurately known.

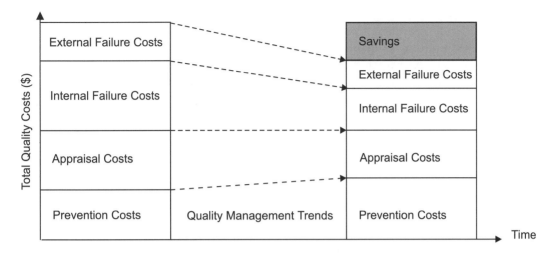

Figure 17.2: **Quality Management Costs** - shows how increased prevention costs can actually reduce the overall quality costs

Quality Costs: When John Eagan joined Jaguar cars in 1980 the company was losing about $5 million a month. Under Eagan's direction, Jaguar set about developing a quality control programme and four years later the dramatic impact could be seen in the company's sales figures, rising morale and a boost to the workers' wage packets. In addition, Jaguar has seen a dramatic reduction in warranty costs, huge gains in productivity and major reductions in finished product defect levels. Once again Jaguar became a profitable company.

"...Two Jags Steyn!..." - Director's meeting at Cranefield College of Project Management

3. Quality Planning

The body of knowledge defines quality planning as; '... *identifying which quality standards are relevant to the project and determining how to satisfy them.*' We need to distinguish between a company's quality policy and the *project quality plan*.

Company Quality Policy: The company's quality policy applies to the whole company and may be formalised through accreditation to ISO 9000 quality management standard, or the national equivalent.

Project Quality Plan: For your project it may be necessary to tailor your company's quality management system to meet the needs of the client and meet the needs of the product - this is achieved through the project quality plan.

For example, the making of your product may include a number of proprietary products. The manufactures and suppliers of these proprietary products will have installation and application requirements that need to be followed. Consider a painting project – the paint supplier will give;

Painting Steps	Comments
Surface preparation	Clean and etched
Preparation of the paint	Stir until well mixed
Temperature and humidity windows	Actual conditions recorded in a log book
Labour qualification	Painting Certificate
Application thickness	Which can be measured
Over coating time (drying time)	Which can be measured

The project quality plan gathers together all the quality standards and manufacturers requirements and presents them in one coherent document. The project quality plan is communicated effectively to all stakeholders to ensure they have been adequately consulted and informed.

4. Quality Control

Quality control is the process projects and companies go through to confirm the product has reached the required condition as determined by the specifications and the contract. For example, this ensures all the components made for a car fit the thousands of cars of that model. Quality control defines the method of inspection (testing), in-process inspection and final inspection to confirm the product has met the required condition. The body of knowledge defines quality control as '... *monitoring specific project results to determine if they comply with relevant quality standards and identify ways to eliminate causes of unsatisfactory results.*'

The required condition should be laid down in the scope of work. The method of testing should be outlined in the project quality plan – this could involve; checklists, inspections, reviews, verification and validation against standards and requirements. Analysis of test results is conducted in accordance with an agreed test plan, which may include statistical analysis, and comparison of results against a baseline or specification.

Quality Testing: Quality testing involves direct testing or measuring of the product or a component, consider the following:

	Test	Comments
Painting	Ambient temperature and humidity, and surface preparation	To comply with paint manufacturers requirements. For example, if the humidity is too high it will adversely impact on the curing process
Welding	Non destructive testing (NDT) this could be die penetrations, ultra sonic tests, or x-rays	To ensure there are no slag inclusions which would weaken the weld
Fitting a door	Dimensional test, +/- 5mm.	To ensure the door and frame are square and the gaps are within the allowable tolerance
Computer screen	Colour check against pantone master	To ensure the end product looks the same as the design on screen
Beer and wine	Measure specific gravity	To ensure you are not drinking coloured water!
Speed	Ships undergo a speed trial over a measured mile. Trawlers undergo a bollard pull	Ways of measuring a ship's performance
Speed trap	30 mph speed trap	Police measure a driver's speed for safety reasons
Dress	Dress size	Dress size standards means you can ask for a dress size in any fashion shop or buy through mail order
Fridge	Thermostat keeps temperature within a narrow range	If the ambient temperature is too warm food will deteriorate - if too cold the food will freeze
Tyre pressure	Check tyre pressure with a pressure gauge	Tyre pressure influences road handling and tyre wear
Traffic noise	Measured in decibels	Noise over a certain limit can cause ear damage

Table 17.1: Quality Testing - shows a range of factors that can be tested to ensure the products are achieving the required condition

The testing instruments themselves need to be calibrated and certified to ensure they are accurate and conform to requirements.

When a non-conformance has been identified, the resulting non-conformance report (NCR) is communicated to the nominated quality stakeholders in accordance with agreed procedures. Records of these deviations, non-conformances and exceptions are maintained in an accurate and complete manner. This may trigger and initiate a quality audit to gather more information before corrective action is authorised to eliminate the causes of unsatisfactory performance of the product, or in some cases the non-conformance is accepted (this time as a concession). In some cases the corrective action may call for quality awareness training.

In the past, quality management focused on the inspection of the product after it was built. There was little involvement with the manufacturers. The emphasis was on *'catching'* defects before they were released – they tended to be inward looking at the product rather than the causes of the non-conformance. But now there is a general acceptance that you cannot inspect quality into a product if the product was not made properly in the first place. The emphasis has shifted to the workers at the 'coalface' assuring they have the support, equipment and training to make the job right the first time.

5. Quality Control Plan

The purpose of the quality management system is to ensure the project delivers the product the client ordered or required. This should be quantified in the contract as the required condition. The project quality plan will then outline how the required condition can be achieved, inspected and documented.

The quality control plan links the quality requirements to the build-method and scheduled Gantt chart. The quality control plan offers you the facility to impose the predetermined work sequence that you want, rather than what the production department may determine as resource efficient. This can be imposed with a quality control plan which lists the sequence of work and the level of inspection and testing. The sequence of work is determined by the build-method and network diagram. The level of inspection is determined by the level of risk and the level of control required – this can be imposed as: surveillance, inspection, witness, testing or hold points. Consider the following project with five key activities to build a warehouse (see figure 17.3):

ID	Description	Duration	Mon 1	Tue 2	Wed 3	Thu 4	Fri 5	Sat 6	Sun 7	Mon 8	Tue 9	Wed 10
1	Foundations	1	▓									
2	Erect steel Columns	3		▓	▓	▓						
3	Install roof trusses	2					▓	▓				
4	Brickwork	3								▓	▓	▓
5	Fit roof tiles	1										▓

Figure 17.3: Gantt Chart (Building a warehouse)

The plan calls for these activities to be carried out in series, but the site foreman decides it is more efficient to start the brickwork before the roof trusses are installed because the scaffolding and men are in position. Shortly after starting the brickwork, the engineer stops this activity when he visits the site because the work is not according to plan. The engineer explains to the foreman that the swaying of the unsupported columns will crack the mortar.

When the roof trusses are installed the foreman decides to fit the roof tiles at the same time because all the men are up on the roof - remember the brickwork has not been completed. That night a storm rips off many of these tiles and besides the cost of damage to property there is a serious risk to life with these giant frisbees flying around.

This example demonstrates a serious lack of understanding between the project management office and the production department. The quality control plan can be used to ensure and enforce compliance to the scheduled Gantt chart. This is achieved by introducing an inspection hold point after each of these key activities. This means no work can commence on a subsequent activity until the previous one has been inspected and approved by the nominated person. A typical QCP is shown below (see table 17.2):

Activity	Description	Spec	Level of Inspection	NC	Sign Off
1	Foundations		Witness pouring / hold		
2	Erect steel columns		Hold		
3	Install roof trusses		Hold		
4	Brickwork		Surveillance / hold		
5	Fit roof tiles		Inspection		

Table 17.2: Quality Control Plan (Building a warehouse)

The quality control plan headings outline the scope of work as a list of activities to be completed. The specification outlines the required condition, standard to be achieved or acceptance criteria. The inspection outlines who is to inspect; client, contractor or third party and the type of inspection; hold point, witness or surveillance. The signature is to confirm compliance. Any non conformance are highlighted in the NC column and communicated to the nominated quality stakeholder for further action.

6. Quality Circles

Quality circles are a management concept the American Government set up for Toyota cars in Japan after the Second World War to continuously improve their manufacturing process, by bringing all the people in a production line together (used in its widest context) to identify and solve problems. Quality circles' methodology ties-in well with the systems breakdown structure (see *WBS* chapter) where there is a need for a number of trades, departments, contractors and suppliers to work together to produce a product, service or solve a problem (see figure 17.4).

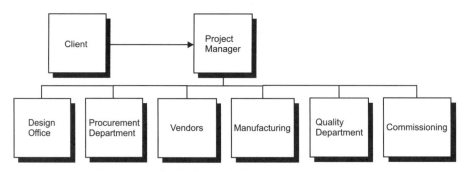

Figure 17.4: System Breakdown Structure (Quality Circles)

Objectives: To improve communication between all parties in the same product line, particularly between planning and production. Also to:

- Identify and solve problems.
- Enhance the product design and manufacturing process and work procedures, leading to increased productivity.
- Improve working conditions and job satisfaction.
- Empower workers to apply their own creative, innovative and entrepreneurial skills, leading to peer recognition which will ultimately improve team morale and commitment.

Organisation: Quality circles generally consist of a team of five or six people who select their own leader. The people should be from the same work area or interfacing work areas, for example planning, procurement, HRM and production. Participation is usually voluntary.

Training: To make the most of quality circles the members may need training in; team building, problem-solving techniques, quality management and customer service.

Scope of Interest: The quality circle should select its own problems. However, initially the quality circle could be encouraged to select problems from its immediate work area. The problems need not be restricted to quality, they can also include productivity, costs, safety, morale, the working environment, new technology and the competition.

Meetings: Usually half an hour per week, held during working hours in a conference room. Use a brainstorming approach to generate ideas and suggestions. Minutes of the meetings should be presented to management for their consideration.

Rewards: Usually no financial benefit. Satisfaction is deemed to be achieved through problem-solving, achieving something worthwhile, observing the implementation of your ideas, having a certain amount of control on your work environment and recognition. Indirectly this may speed up your promotion (see Hertberg's Motivation and Hygiene factors).

The quality circle approach is becoming more pervasive as the benefits are recognised. People at the workface often see problems and solutions their managers cannot see, and the best people to fix a problem are usually those who benefit directly. This working together for the common good of the project creates a dynamic team spirit and camaraderie.

Problem: 15% of components mis - wired

Red

Black

Solution: See end of chapter

Red

Black

Figure 17.5: Quality Circle Question: Consider this production quality problem where 15% of the electrical components were incorrectly wired, even though the wires were colour coded and the terminals staggered.

7. Total Quality Management (TQM)

Total quality management (TQM) considers the wider aspects of quality by integrating all of the quality management components into a quality management system. TQM is a systems approach to quality management that focuses on the system to produce a quality product, and not any particular components of the system.

A system may be defined as a network of interdependent components which operate within a common environment in a manner which will achieve pre-defined objectives. This concept of systems is fundamental to any quality system. All activities of an organisation are interlinked in a systematic manner. Organisational behaviour is constrained by the system, hence, in order to improve performance attention must be focused on the system, not just one particular variable component within the system. A fundamental change to the system will impact on the system as a whole. In order to manage an organisation you must adopt systems thinking.

A quality management system should focus on the organisation, how it functions, and how it is constrained by the environment in which the system operates. A key to this is to recognise that about 85% of all problems are because of the system. You, therefore, need to focus on the system and accept that it is not the people or the machines or the material but the process by which they are specified, selected and maintained that will ultimately ensure specific quality requirements are met.

If a quality system is to be effective, management must learn to apply a systems approach to the way they control the organisation. Improvements and understanding will only commence when top management demonstrate a commitment to the system. You cannot buy a quality system, because a quality culture can only be developed from within the company - guided by the leadership of top management.

Total quality has a people focus and an outcome focus. It first identifies what the client really wants and how it can best be achieved (see *Feasibility Study* chapter). Total quality keeps an emphasis on continuous improvement, but always endeavours to keep the customer satisfied. For quality to be effective it needs to be introduced to all team members and all aspects of the project's operation. TQM advances the rational that just as each organisation has unique products, so each project needs a unique quality management system.

Total quality management was pioneered by Toyota by emphasizing teamwork and catching errors before they were passed down the production line. TQM required the full involvement of suppliers in achieving manufacturing improvements and a product design process that integrates downstream production expertise into production design.

Production equipment is kept sufficiently multi-purpose so that considerable flexibility can be built into the manufacturing line. Customers are offered a greater choice and products match their differing needs more fully and more quickly. Concurrency of design and development enables a fast build to get the product to market before the competition. Die production begins at the same time as the body design by having both sets of designers working as a close knit team.

Consider the following concepts which underpin total quality management:
- Quality is defined by your customers
- There must be a respect for people (the system achieves products through their efforts, therefore the system must be structured so that the people can make a contribution)
- All levels of the project and organisation must want to participate
- There must be an emphasis on continuous improvement
- All those involved must work within the system, therefore, there must be a general understanding of systems thinking
- Management must work on the system, especially to achieve process improvement
- Customers, suppliers and contractor are part of the system, hence there must be a partnership with customers and suppliers in order to achieve a quality outcome
- Prevention is better than detection.

This concludes the section on Total Quality Management (TQM) and the importance of continuous improvement.

8. Quality Audit

An audit may be defined as an investigation, inspection or survey of a system or product, where the actual or measured condition is compared with the planned condition, required condition or declared condition - the difference or variance being reported in the findings and recommendations and communicated to the quality stakeholders. ISO 8402 defines 'quality audit' as; *'... a systematic and independent examination to determine whether quality activities and related results comply with planned arrangements and whether these arrangements are implemented effectively and are suitable to achieve the objective.'*

Audits are not limited to auditing the financial accounts - any aspect of the company or project can be audited. They can be either internal or external to the company, but should definitely be independent to the project. To achieve this the quality manager would normally report to the managing director and not the project manager or general manager (see figure 17.6). This way the quality manager can be held responsible for assuring both the quality management system and the quality of the product.

When a non-conformance is reported or suspected, the quality audit provides the project manager or client with an excellent tool for investigating the root cause of the problem. The right to conduct an audit is usually written into the project's contract. In fact, the procurement department often audit their suppliers to pre-qualify them before tendering. Audits should follow a formal structure, consider the following procedure:

- The auditors organise a pre-audit meeting.
- The pre-audit meeting discusses the scope of the audit - why, what, when, who, how and where?
- The audit is carried out by a series of questionnaires, interviews and inspections.
- The audit data is collected and analysed.
- An audit closeout meeting is held where the audit findings are announced and discussed.
- Corrective actions are carried out and re-audited (if necessary) at a later date.

Auditing the Project Management System: The audit of a project management system can be conducted at three levels:

- Audit the project management system against best practices (body of knowledge) to ensure the management function will be able to achieve the project's objectives.
- Audit the implemented project management system against the declared system.
- Audit against the client's requirements.

Most small contracting companies will probably not have a project management system, so when you audit these companies you are in fact conducting a double audit of:

- What they intend to do against what they should be doing (best practice).
- What they are doing against what they intend to do.

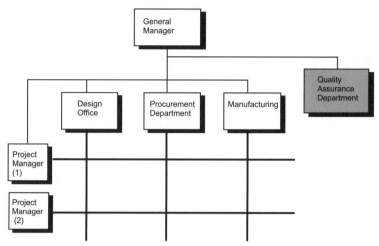

Figure 17.6: Project Matrix Structure - shows the position of the quality department with respect to the other departments working on the project

Audit benefits:

- It provides a wealth of information.
- The data collected is actionable.
- The approach is objective.
- The auditor should be an independent expert with no personal agenda.

Audit problems:

- There may be an unintentional bias on the part of the auditor.
- The auditor's experience may be unique and provide misleading evidence.
- An audit can only be carried out infrequently due to its complexity, time and costs. A small sample could produce misleading results.
- Results may be too detailed - unable to see the wood for the trees.

Audits are not about punishing people who fail, they should be about helping people achieve the required condition and helping them to do their job better. Part of the quality training should consider training people not only how to conduct audits, but also how to be audited.

This concludes the chapter on *Quality Management*, the next chapter will discuss *Risk Management*.

Key Points:

- Quality management includes both the quality of the management of the project and the quality of the product itself.
- It is generally accepted that the cost of prevention will proportionally reduce the cost of failure.
- The *quality control plan* offers a structure to ensure the production will comply with the planned build method.

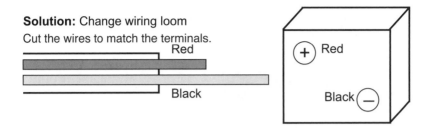

Solution: Change wiring loom
Cut the wires to match the terminals.

Red

Black

Red ⊕

Black ⊖

Case Study and Exercises:

Quality management is the processes required to ensure that the project will satisfy the needs for which it was undertaken, and in today's competitive market companies compete on price, quality and customer service. As project manager of a production line producing DVDs, you are responsible for developing a quality management plan which should consider the following:

1. Quality costs.

2. Quality circles.

3. Quality audit.

4. Quality control plan.

5. TQM.

"...In process control..."

18

Risk
Management

Learning Outcomes

After reading this chapter, you should be able to;

Understand the risk management model

Identify and respond to project risks

Develop a disaster recovery plan

Project management and project risk management both strive to achieve the project's objects – but in different ways. Where project management strives to maximise the chances of success, project risk management strives to minimise the chances of failure.

The purpose of this chapter is to provide an outline of project risk and opportunity, and a methodology for reducing risk to an acceptable level while keeping the entrepreneurial spirit alive to spot marketable opportunities.

Company success is achieved by pursuing entrepreneurial opportunities to gain a competitive advantage. Projects and new ventures have typically been setup to take advantage of these opportunities - to make something new, or change (enhance) an existing facility. Risk management has always been an intrinsic part of managing projects. And, with increasing market competition, increasing new technology and an increasing rate of change, risk management is gaining significance and importance.

A key component of making changes is making decisions - ideally these decisions would be based on complete information with a high degree of certainty of the outcome. However, in the real world most decisions are based on incomplete information with an associated level of uncertainty about the outcome - it is this uncertainty that leads to risk (see figure 18.1).

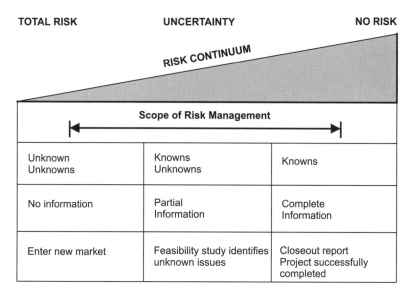

Figure 18.1: Risk Continuum (relating to level of information and uncertainty)

It can be seen that risk, uncertainty and opportunity are closely related. When a risk occurs, with some entrepreneurial ingenuity, this could be turned around to become an opportunity. And, conversely when pursuing an opportunity there will be associated risks that could derail your project (see the risk identification section for further discussion).

Project Risk Management is defined by the PMBOK as; '... *the systematic processes of identifying, analysing and responding to project risk...* [throughout the project lifecycle]'. It includes maximising the results of positive events and minimising the consequences of adverse events. The APM bok defines risk as; '... *factors that may cause a failure to meet the project's objectives...*' or limits the achievement of your objectives as defined at the outset of the project.

1. Risk Management Plan

The generally accepted risk management model subdivides the risk management process into the following headings (see figure 18.2):

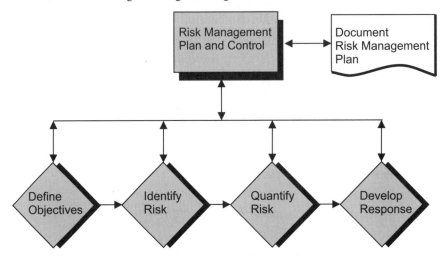

Figure 18.2: Risk Management Model - shows the main components of risk management

The APM bok defines the risk management plan as; '... *a formal approach to the process as opposed to an intuitive approach...*' The risk management plan documents how you propose to tackle risk on your project. Consider using the following headings;

- **Define Objectives:** Defines the goals and objectives the project sets out to achieve. A WBS list of work packages and checklists can be used to define the project objectives at the work package level. This defines what you have to achieve to be successful and establishes a basis for dealing with risk and future decisions.
- **Identify Risk:** Identifies areas of risk, uncertainty and constraints, which may impact on your project, and limit or prevent you achieving your objectives.
- **Quantify Risk:** Evaluates the risks and prioritizes the level of risk and uncertainty and quantifies their frequency of occurrence and impact on the objectives.
- **Develop Response:** Defines how you are going to respond to the identified risks. The response could be a combination of; eliminate, mitigate, deflect or accept.
- **Risk Control:** The risk control function implements the risk management *plan*. This may involve training team members, and communication to all stakeholders. As the project risks and the work environment are continually changing, it is essential to continually monitor and review the level of risk and your ability to effectively respond.

2. Project Lifecycle

The project lifecycle format provides an informative overview of how the level of risk changes as the project progresses through the project phases (concept, design, implement and commission). Figure 18.3a outlines how the risk and the amount at stake change, while figure 18.3b outlines how the level of influence and the cost to make changes varies through the lifecycle.

Level of Risk vs Amount at Stake: Figure 18.3a indicates that the level of risk and opportunity are high at the outset of the project (during the concept and design phases), when there is the greatest degree of uncertainty about the future. As the project progresses these parameters reduce as decisions are made, design freezes are implemented, and the remaining unknowns are translated into knowns. These unknowns are eventually zero when the project is successfully completed. The amount at stake (investment), on the other hand, starts low and steadily rises as capital and resources are invested to complete the project.

Level of Influence vs Cost to Change: Figure 18.3b outlines how the initial phases offer the greatest potential to add value with the least cost, but as the project progresses so the ability to make changes reduces as the cost of changes becomes increasingly expensive.

The period of highest vulnerability to risk, therefore, occurs during the last two phases (implementation and commissioning). During these phases, problems may occur, particularly during commissioning and start-up. This is also when the level of influence is low and the cost to change is high (see *Project Lifecycle* chapter).

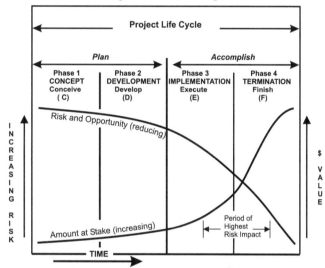

Figure 18.3a: Risk vs Amount at Stake

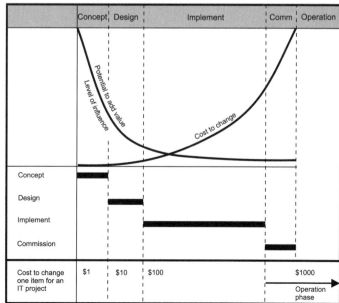

Figure 18.3b: Level of Influence vs Cost to Change

3. Risk Management Responsibility

Who is responsible for managing risk? The managing director is ultimately responsible to the board of directors and the shareholders for managing risk within the company (this includes new ventures and projects). However, this responsibility is usually delegated through the corporate hierarchy with the project managers responsible for project risk and the functional managers responsible for their department's risks (see figure 18.4). This process of pushing risk responsibility down the hierarchy is consistent with risk management being a company wide issue (empowerment).

The respective managers are then responsible for developing a risk management plan to identify, quantify, respond and control risks that impact on their scope of work. As the owners of the risks the managers need to identify the risk triggers, cause and effects in consultation with the appropriate stakeholders and record the situations inline with project procedures.

As with other management techniques, it should be the managers responsibility to ensure that their team members have a working understanding of risk within the context of their scope of work and feel accountable for the consequences of their actions.

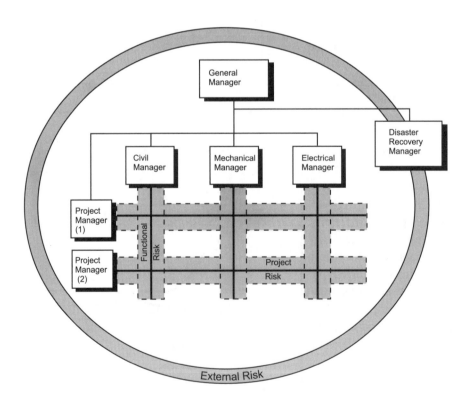

Figure 18.4: Risk Responsibility Organisation Structure

4. Define Objectives

A risk may be defined as any event or constraint that prevents you achieving the project's goals and objectives. It is therefore necessary at the outset to define these goals and objectives in some detail, and indicate who is responsible for achieving them. Consider the project brief, project proposal, project charter and scope of work (SOW) together with the following breakdown structures:

- Subdivide the SOW by stakeholders (see the *Feasibility Study* chapter)
- Subdivide the SOW by project management knowledge areas (see table 18.1)
- Subdivide the SOW by OBS - departments (see table 18.2)
- Subdivide the SOW by WBS - work packages (see table 18.3)
- Subdivide the SOW by constraints (internal and external) (see *Feasibility Study* chapter)

These breakdown structures will provide a logical framework for identifying, quantifying and responding to risk. This systematic approach helps to ensure significant risks and opportunities are not overlooked. The PMBOK knowledge areas can be expanded to include other business operations:

- Sales and marketing
- Design and development
- Education and training
- Computer systems

Project Management Knowledge Areas	Objectives	Responsibility
Scope Management	WBS, Drawing List	
Time Management	CPM, Schedule Gantt chart	
Cost Management	Budget, Cashflow Statement	
Quality Management	Project Quality Plan, Quality Control Plan	
Integration Management	Planning and Control	
Human Resource Management	OBS, Resource Histogram	
Communication Management	Communication Plan	
Risk Management	Risk Management Plan	
Procurement Management	Procurement Schedule	

Table 18.1: Objectives Subdivided by Knowledge Area

Department	Responsibilities and Objectives
Project Office	
Design Office	
Planning Office	
Purchasing Department	
Quality Department	
Accounts Department	

Table 18.2: Objectives by OBS Department

WBS	Objectives
1.1	
1.2	
1.3	
2.1	
2.2	
2.3	

Table 18.3: Establish Objectives by WBS Work Package (proforma)

Develop **Risk Assessment Criteria** against which risks can be assessed and decisions made. These criteria may be based on operational, technical, financial, legal, social and humanitarian requirements. There will be internal and external constraints which set your boundaries (see the *Feasibility Study* chapter):

- Internal project
- Internal corporate
- External.

5. Risk Identification

Having defined your business objectives by one of the above breakdown structures, the next step is to identify what areas of risk, uncertainty and triggers could prevent you achieving these stated objectives - plan to prevent failure. Risk identification is probably the hardest and most important part of the risk management process, because if you cannot identify a risk, it will be excluded from further analysis and, therefore, you will probably not respond to it. The process of risk identification should not be a one time event, but rather a continuous process, its frequency depending on the level of risk on the project and the schedule of meetings.

Using your list of objectives as your starting point, consider adding another two columns to identify cause and impact scenarios. This can be tackled from both directions:

- **Cause of Impact**: If this cause happens what impact will it have on the objectives?
- **Impact caused by:** What could cause this undesirable impact, or failure?

WBS	Objectives	Cause	Impact
1.1			
1.2			

Table 18.4: Cause and Impact (proforma)

Risk identification should be a systematic process to ensure nothing significant is overlooked. By adding another column, combinations of risks can also be considered. Seemingly small risks can combine in complex ways, and under a variety of scenarios to produce significant risks; '*it never rains but it pours*'. Walking through the process should give you an appreciation of these interdependencies. Techniques for identifying risk include:

- Analysing historical records and closeout reports (see *Scope Management* chapter)
- Safety reports (Health and Safety requirements)
- Structured questionnaires
- Structured interviews
- Brainstorming
- Structured checklists (see *WBS* chapter)
- Flow charts (build-method, walk-through)
- Judgement based on knowledge and experience
- System analysis
- Scenario analysis (what-if).

The success of these techniques depends on how the risk management team have been selected and brought together. A balanced team which incorporates; experience, knowledge, judgement, entrepreneurial innovation, creativity, enthusiasm, internal members and external consultants, stands the best chance of identifying the risks.

Experience: The university of life gives us the experience to identify areas of risk, particularly relating to the problems and situations we have experienced or observed in the past. Greater awareness and appreciation is followed by knowledge and judgement.

Historical Data: Learn from the past - access to a comprehensive data base of relevant experience, both internal and external is invaluable. This information should be available internally from previous projects closeout reports.

Questionnaires, interviews and brainstorming are all ways to generate ideas and feedback from your colleagues, stakeholders, clients, engineers, suppliers, legal eagles and governing agencies. Checklists, breakdown structures and flow charts (CPM) are all ways to group and subdivide information for collation and presentation.

Opportunities: The flipside of many risks are entrepreneurial opportunities. We often need a problem, block or challenge as a trigger to force us to investigate and search for solutions and opportunities. Many successful products are the outcome or solution to a problem. Consider setting up a table which lists the objectives, risks and opportunities.

Objective	Risk	Opportunity
Employment	Lose job	Find new career which is better paid
Order Material	Specified material is not available	Find new material which is not only cheaper but a better quality as well
Full workforce	Machine operator leaves	Install automatic machinery

Table 18.5: Table of Opportunities

The risk threat prevention, recovery activities and entrepreneurial opportunity activities are all communicated to relevant parties for inclusion in project's plans and budgets.

6. Why Projects Fail

Projects fail for many reasons, not least due to lack of professional project management. Project managers are often judged on whether their projects achieved; time, cost and quality targets. Another perhaps more telling criteria is whether the project manager was able to steer the project through a minefield of problems and risk triggers, any one of them just waiting to derail the project. Consider these other items:
- **Innovation:** If the level of innovation is too low your product may not be able to compete in the market, but conversely if the level of innovation is too high you may be forever trying to iron out design problems.
- **Concurrency:** Concurrency is developing the product before the client's requirements are fully defined. The USAF now prefers to '*fly-before-buy*' so that prototypes can be tested before making a decision.
- **Stakeholders:** Failing to recognise stakeholders interests, particularly environmentalists. Concorde was an engineering and aviation success, but a commercial disaster because it failed to recognise that the environment lobby would prevent it flying supersonically over land.
- **Communication:** NASA's Mars probe crash landed on the surface of Mars because of a mix up between imperial and metric measurements used by the American and European designers.
- **Scope of work:** Misinterpreting the *scope of work* is a common cause of project failure (states Kerzner). Others include:
  - Mixing and confusing; tasks, specifications, approvals, and special instructions.
  - Using imprecise or vague language, for example; nearly, optimum, about or approximately can lead to confusion, ambiguity or misinterpretation.
  - The project has no pattern, structure, or chronological order - the WBS and CPM techniques have not been used.
  - A wide variation in size of the tasks and work packages, again caused by not using the WBS to subdivide all the work packages to a common level of detail.

- Wide variation in how to describe work details.
- Failing to get a third-party review, or verification from either the client, sub-contractors and suppliers.
- **IT Projects:** (ProjectPro) IT projects have a poor track record for delivering systems within budget:
  - Only 18% of software projects are completed within budget
  - 50% overrun their budget
  - 0% are so expensive that they are abandoned before substantial completion.

Other common reasons for project failure include:
- Not working closely with the client.
- Poor estimating.
- Inadequate planning.
- Insufficient reviews and control.
- A lack of commitment (lack of buy-in from participants and stakeholders) - it is important to gain commitment by involving the responsible people in the planning.
- Incomplete information, for example, during the tendering process the contractor is attempting to assess the correct market price for a project not yet built, for a design which is subject to revision, on a site about which there is little information and a labour force not yet recruited.
- Poor planning - material and equipment not available on time.
- Lack of understanding of project management techniques.
- Lack of support from team members.

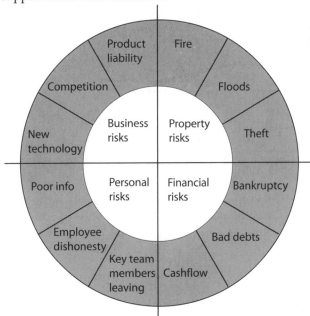

Figure 18.5: Wheel of Misfortune - source adapted from Longenecker.
Besides projects there are a whole range of other risks to consider

7. Risk Quantification

Having identified a range of possible risks, the next step is to quantify the probability (likelihood) of the risk occurring and the impact or consequence to the project, or to the amount at stake; these risks should be assessed in consultation with appropriate stakeholders. Risk quantification is primarily concerned with determining what areas of risk warrant a response and where resources are limited. A risk priority table will determine the areas of risk that should be addressed first. Because with limited resources it is not possible to respond to all risks.

Impact of Risk: Quantifying risk sounds great on paper, but it is very difficult in practice to put an exact number to a risk. Start by ranking the risks (high / medium / low risk) to see if that helps to highlight the high risk work packages. With finite resources it is essential to establish which risks should be addressed first so as to focus your effort.

Frequency of Risk: The frequency of a risk occurring needs to be considered. Low impact risks which occur regularly may well get a higher priority than a high risk which very rarely happens. For example, rain may occur every night during the rainy season, but a tsunami, which could wipe out all the buildings in a coastal region, only occurs very infrequently. The impact of the rain would, therefore, have a high priority for outside jobs, and a tsunami would have a low priority as it probably will not happen during the life of the project.

Probability / Impact Matrix: This matrix plots the probability of the risk occurring against the impact on the project (see figure 18.6). These risks and impacts are quantified as high, medium, or low - this will give a matrix of nine possibilities.

Figure 18.6: Probability / Impact Matrix

For risks that recur on a regular basis there may be statistical information available (e.g. days lost to inclement weather). For non-recurring risks a more subjective analysis will be required to determine probability of occurrence.

Priority: The risk quantification information can be gathered together and presented in a table which can be linked to the WBS (see table 18.6) which identifies, quantifies and prioritizes the risk. With finite resources it is essential to establish which risks should be addressed first so as to focus your effort.

WBS	Objectives	Risk	Probability	Consequence	Priority
1.1					
1.2					
1.3					

Table 18.6: Objective, Risk, Probability, Consequence and Priority (proforma)

In table 18.6 the priority column is a combination of impact (consequence) and frequency (probability). The highest being high impact and high frequency. A high impact, but low frequency would have a lower priority because it might not happen.

8. Risk Response

Having identified, quantified and prioritized the risks, you now need to develop a risk response plan which defines ways to address adverse risk and enhance entrepreneurial opportunities before they occur. The levels of risk should be compared against pre-established criteria, then ranked to establish management priorities. There are a range of responses which should be developed in advance during the planning phase:

- Eliminate risk
- Mitigate risk
- Deflect risk
- Accept risk (with contingency)
- Turn risk into an opportunity.

These are not mutually exclusive - your response may use a combination of them all. A natural sequence would be to first try and eliminate the risk completely - failing that, at least mitigate it. And for the remaining risk the options are to try and deflect them and / or accept them with a contingency. All these responses cost money, so a cost-benefit analysis should be performed as it may be more cost effective to accept a risk rather than taking expensive steps to eliminate it.

Eliminating Risk: Looks into ways of avoiding the risk completely by either removing the cause or taking an alternative course of action. This should initially be considered during the concept and design phases, where the level of influence is high and the cost to change is low (see the *Project Lifecycle* chapter).

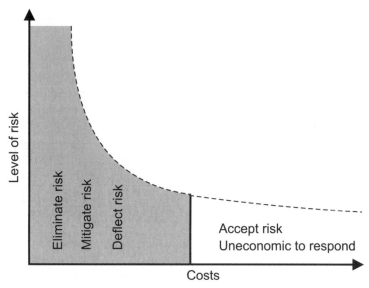

Figure 18.7: Cost Benefit of Reducing Risk

Mitigating Risk: To mitigate a risk means **reducing** the risk's probability and impact. This could be achieved by using proven technology and standards to ensure the product will work. Developing prototypes, simulating and modelling are three methods which share the notion of using a representation to investigate selected aspects of the requirements in order to be more certain of the outcome or suitability. A prototype is a working mock-up of areas under investigation in order to test its acceptance. A model is a miniature representation of physical relationships (often used in ship design).

Deflecting Risk: Transfers the risk (in part or whole) to another party. This can be achieved through contracting, retention, bonding and insurance - these are discussed in the next section.

9. Contracting

Project contracts are a means of deflecting risk, usually away from the client to the contractor. Consider figure 18.8 where the contract determines how the client and the contractor share the risk.

- Fixed price contract
- Cost plus contract
- Unit rates contract
- Turnkey contract
- BOOT contract

Fixed Price Contract: Also called **lump sum price**. This contract requires the contractor to complete the scope of work for a fixed price which is written into the contract. This contract will include all the costs associated with labour, material, plant, inflation and risk. A detailed scope of work is required from the client before the contractor can tender - this effectively prevents fast tracking between design and construction. Once the project has started, any changes in the scope of work will have to be negotiated. This type of contract is becoming more popular with clients because it passes much of the project risk onto the contractor. The inflation risk, however, is often accepted by the client in the form of an escalation clause.

Cost Plus Contract: Also called **reimbursable, plus-fee** contract. The cost plus contract is considered to be the most flexible type of contract, where all the direct costs are paid by the client plus an agreed fee or percentage profit to the contractor. This type of contract is often used at the beginning of a project when there may be many design changes, requiring close client / contractor liaison, thereby allowing work to proceed while the details are still being discussed. Once the scope of work is finalised the type of contract may change, for example, the Channel Tunnel contract changed from cost-plus to a fixed price.

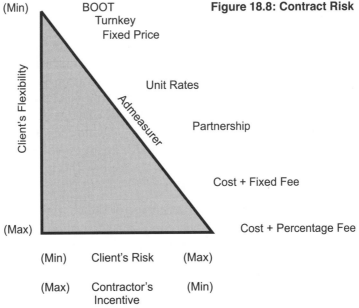

Figure 18.8: Contract Risk

Cost-plus contracts are usually criticised on the grounds that the contractor has little incentive to control costs and increase productivity, since their fee is proportional to the total cost of the project. It is, therefore, up to the client to closely monitor the contractors performance.

Unit Rates: Also called; **billed rates, parameter costs** or **schedule of rates**. This type of contract works on the basis of negotiated rates for specific work. All payments will be based on measurement of the work completed using the unit rates. At the tender stage the quote will be based on a bill of material (BOM). This type of contract is suitable for projects where the client cannot supply sufficient data for the contractor to give a lump sum quote. Thus the client can start their project sooner than a lump sum price and design the project progressively.

Even on a fixed price contract, unit rates can be agreed at the outset as a framework for costing additional work. Unit rates do offer the contractor an incentive to maximise their profits through efficiency. The client will be responsible for the measurement of the work done, which can be integrated with the planning and control function. This type of contract is appropriate for projects where the scope of work cannot be defined at the tender stage - for example, maintenance and ship repair projects.

Turnkey Contract: Also known as the **design and construct** contract. Here the contractor is responsible for the project, from the design phase right through to the commissioning phase. This reduces the client's input to a minimum while contractually ensuring that the contractor is responsible for making the project or facility operational.

The contractor takes the undivided responsibility for the design and construction of the project which invariably leads to a pure lump sum principle, but in practice, this is rarely the case due to variations caused by employer interference as the project proceeds.

Partnership: Or **joint venture** brings client and contractor together to share the risks and benefits on the project.

BOOT Contract (build own operate and transfer): Or BOT contract (build, operate and transfer) or ROT contract (refurbish, operate and transfer), or PPP (public private partnership), transfers the risk completely to the contractor, not only to design and build a facility, but also to finance the building and operation of the facility. The contractor then operates the facility for a period of time and charges the users for the product. For example, a contractor, or consortium would build and operate a power station for 25 years, during which time they will charge their customers for the electricity, and this income will pay for the building of the facility. This process is also used for toll roads, railways, bridges and tunnels.

Retention: The client retains a percentage of the contractors income against the contractor failing to complete their contractual obligations. The retention is usually 10% of the monthly progress payments until the payment reaches 5% of the contract value and then the retention is held until the end of the warranty period.

Bond: The contractor offers the client a bond through a large organisation (bank). The bond could be held against lack of performance or poor quality of work. If the contractor fails to perform, the client is compensated by the bond company, who in turn will take agreed assets from the contractor to cover the bond. Some contractors prefer this arrangement to retention, as they are paid their progress claims in full, thus improving their cashflow.

Insurance: A third party accepts insurable risks for the payment of a premium. The premium is now the quantified impact of this risk on the project. Insurance could cover:

- Direct property damage
- Indirect consequential loss (business interruption - loss of power)
- Legal liability
- Personnel liability.

Acceptance: Some companies may accept the consequence of a risk occurring, also called self-insurance. However, it is more likely the project manager will develop a contingency plan to protect the project from the risk event. A **contingency plan** defines actions to take ahead of time - if **problem A** happens we will do **contingency B.** The contingency plan could be established for:

- Minor internal design changes
- Under estimating the BOM, procurement and resources
- Lack of experience (history, knowledge, judgement)
- Unexpected procurement price changes
- Correcting erroneous assumptions
- Insufficient scope detail resulting in changes
- Implementing and commissioning problems that lead to schedule delays
- Any unforeseen regulations.

A summary table should be developed to gather together all the identified risks and how you intend to respond (see table 18.7).

WBS	Objective	Risk	Response	Mitigate
1.1				
1.2				
1.3				

Table 18.7: Objective, Risk, Response, Mitigating Risk (proforma)

Risk Opportunity: Turning risks into marketable opportunities is one of the corner stones of entrepreneurship. Many innovative products we use everyday are an entrepreneur's direct response to a problem. It is quite possible that problems you are experiencing are impacting on other companies as well. In which case, with some ingenuity your solution may be a marketable product which you can sell to the other companies (see *Entrepreneurs Toolkit*).

Risk Management Plan: The risk management plan, documents the output from the previous sections; identify risk, quantify risk and respond to risk, and assigns responsibility for implementation. The next section - risk control - implements the risk management plan and makes it a working document.

10. Risk Control

The risk control function implements the risk management plan to make it happen - this is the most important part, but surprisingly is often neglected! The risk management plan needs to be communicated to all the project participants and, where necessary, followed up with appropriate training and practice runs. The training should not only ensure that the risk management plan is understood, but also develop a company wide risk management culture and attitude.

The risk management plan should be monitored and updated on a regular basis to ensure everyone learns from reoccurring risks and prevent them from reoccurring again, and further, that the risk management plan is relevant to changing circumstances. The risk management plan should consider;

- Changes in the scope of work
- Changes in the build-method
- Changes in the team members
- Changes in the suppliers.

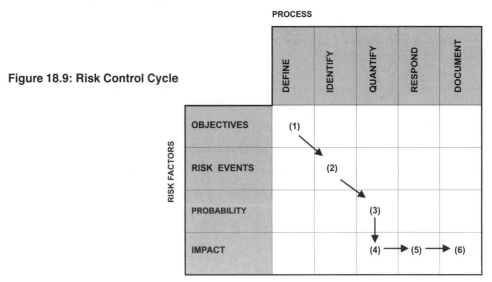

Figure 18.9: Risk Control Cycle

Risk management may become an item on the weekly progress meetings to prompt discussion, identify new areas of risk and develop appropriate responses. It is important to respond to risk quickly (nip it in the bud), so the project can quickly recover from the impact.

11. Disaster Recovery Planning

A disaster is a sudden, unplanned catastrophe that prevents the project (or company) providing its critical business functions for a period of time and could result in significant damage or loss. The time factor will determine whether a problem or service interruption is an inconvenience or a disaster. For example, losing power for a few hours may be an inconvenience, but losing power for a few weeks (on site) could be a financial disaster. It is for this reason that site work is usually self contained. The objective of disaster recovery management is to reduce the consequence of a disaster to an acceptable level. This is the ultimate contingency plan!

Disaster recovery planning is essentially a contingency response from the risk management planning, but due to the unique nature and size of the problems it is probably best managed separately - as a project. The management of the disaster recovery plan should be assigned to a manager with the responsibility to set up a team to:

- Develop the disaster recovery plan
- Control the disaster recovery plan
- (And when the time comes) - Implement the disaster recovery plan quickly and effectively.

"...this project is going to be a disaster - it's going to come crashing down like a pack of cards!..."

Disaster recovery planning essentially follows the same process as the risk management plan, except now the focus is on the major risks, which cannot be eliminated, mitigated or deflected. Controlling the disaster recovery plan may involve training, practice and frequently updating the data base of information (for example, contact details and telephone numbers). The disaster recovery team should meet regularly so that in the event of a disaster they can *hit the ground running*.

A fire, flood, earthquake, or hurricane would be good examples of a disaster where your project, project management office (PMO), factory, or facility could be completely destroyed, or where there is restricted access for a long period of time. How are you going to recover?

Disaster Recovery Implementation: When a disaster happens, this is the time to implement your carefully developed and updated disaster recovery plan. The first step is to mobilise the disaster recovery team, maybe at a prearranged office where all the necessary office equipment, information and communications are ready. Communicate the disaster recovery plan to all the key people and stakeholders using telephone trees (one person rings ten people), this would include:

- Employees
- Clients
- Suppliers
- Media.

If necessary relocate the project office:

- Move to a prearranged office accommodation
- Recover the critical data bases - these should have been regularly backed up and stored off site.

It is essential that you accurately advise your clients how long it will be before you can offer a normal service again. Statistics from America indicate that 43% of American businesses are closed immediately by disasters, 51% for as long as two years, and of these only 6% survive the experience - these are frightening figures. If your company provides an essential business function, then your clients will have to move to another supplier - certainly in the short term.

This concludes the chapter on *Project Risk Management*, the following chapter will discuss *Project Communication*.

Key Points:

- Risks are inherent in all projects
- Project managers need to develop a risk management plan to document how they will respond to risk.
- Project managers need to implement a risk management plan to continually monitor and control the risks until the project is complete.

Case Study and Exercises:

Unplanned catastrophes are always waiting just around the corner to derail your project. For this case study you have been appointed project manager, or risk manager to prepare a risk management plan, and a disaster recovery plan for the project office on an IT project. Your risk management planning should consider how you would address natural disasters (flood, power cut, earth quake, fire). Your presentation should include the following:

1. Identify the risks.
2. Disaster recovery preparation - training.
3. Disaster recovery control.
4. Information back-up and post disaster retrieval.
5. Post disaster communication plan.

"That was a lucky escape!"

19

Project Communication

Learning Outcomes

After reading this chapter, you should be able to;

Understand communication theory

Set-up a document control system

Organize project meetings

Communication is one of those subjects that is hard to separate from what we do naturally everyday, so why does it warrant being a knowledge area? For a project to succeed there is a continuous need for communication to issue instructions, solve problems, make decisions, resolve conflicts, and keep everyone supplied with the information they need.

The PMBOK defines project communication management as; '... *the process required to ensure timely and appropriate generation, collection, dissemination, storage and ultimately disposition* [disposal] *of project information. It provides the critical links among people, ideas and information that are necessary for success.*'

The project manager is in the key position to develop and maintain all the communication links, both inside the company and project team, and outside the company with the client, contractors, suppliers and other stakeholders. The project office is like the *'front door'* to the project. It is estimated that project managers spend about 90% of their working time engaged in some form of communication, be it; meetings, writing memos, emailing, faxes, reading reports, or talking with team members, senior managers, customers, clients, sub-contractors, suppliers and stakeholders.

The ability to communicate well, both verbally and in writing, is the foundation of effective leadership. Through communication team members share information and exchange ideas and influence attitudes, behaviours and understanding. Communication enables the project manager to develop interpersonal relationships; inspire team members, handle conflict, negotiate with stakeholders, chair meetings, and make presentations.

It, therefore, makes sense to rank communication management along with the other knowledge areas, because without effective communication project success will be self-limiting.

It is often stated that *"Information costs money"*, but conversely, *"lack of information could be even more expensive"*. The cost of communication failure may be quantified as; poor problem-solving, poor decision-making based on incomplete information, rework due to the shop-floor using old drawings, downtime due to managers not being advised of late delivery of material, and managers turning up for meetings which have been cancelled. A trade-off needs to be established between the cost of mistakes and the cost of supplying good information.

Projects are particularly prone to communication difficulties because of the unique nature of projects and the matrix organisation through which they are generally managed. There may be overlapping responsibilities, decentralised decision-making and complex interfaces all applying a strain on the communication system. However, if the communication system is well managed it could be the single most important factor determining product quality, efficiency, productivity and customer satisfaction.

The Internet and mobile phones have enhanced the communication mediums - a silent revolution is taking place as we move away from post (snail mail) and faxes. The mobile office and virtual office are now real possibilities for the project team. Consider the facilities:

- Email (one-to-one, or one-to-many)
- Web sites
- B2B procurement
- Real time progress reports
- Video conferences
- Mobile email and internet connections
- Mobile communication nationally and internationally

1. Communication Theory

Communication is essentially the interpersonal process of sending and receiving messages. The key components of the communication process are shown in figure 19.1. They include the sender who encodes and sends (transmits) the message, and the receiver who decodes and interprets the message. The receiver then feeds back a response to the sender and closes the loop. The communication model focuses on each element of the process to identify what should happen and prevent misunderstanding - like the charge of the Light Brigade!!!

Sender: The sender is the originator of the message and the starting point of the communication cycle. The sender will have a purpose to communicate. This may be to; request information, send information, ask a question, issue an instruction, encourage team building, marketing or make a courtesy call.

Encoding: Encoding is the process of converting thoughts, feelings and ideas into '*code or cipher*'. In its broader sense code and cipher are the words and phrases we use to express ourselves, which can, if we are not careful, take on the more devious meaning of a disguised secret way of writing.

Medium: The medium is the vehicle or channel to convey the message. Project communications can be transmitted in many forms; formal or informal, written or verbal, planned or ad-hoc. Consider the following:

- Formal written; letters, faxes, email, memos, minutes, drawings, specifications and reports
- Formal verbal; telephone, voice mail, meetings, video-conferencing
- Informal verbal; casual discussion between friends
- Non-verbal; body language.

The choice of medium will influence the impact of the message, for example, another memo or email will not have the same effect as a discussion face-to-face.

The use of written communication should be encouraged because it addresses misinterpretation and forgetfulness. All important agreements and instructions should be confirmed in writing. You will be thankful for keeping a written trail of agreements if (when) problems develop later in the project. Written communications are acceptable for simple messages that are easy to convey and for those messages that

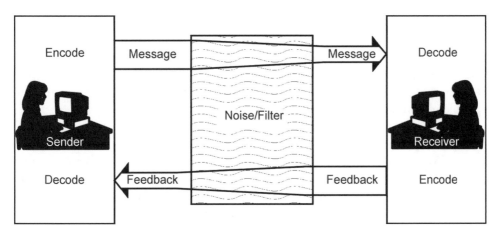

Figure 19.1: Communication Process - shows the communication cycle as a closed loop

require extensive dissemination to all stakeholders. However, verbal channels work best for complex messages that are difficult to convey, may need explanation, and where immediate feedback to the sender is valuable. Verbal communications are also more personal, which helps to create a supportive and inspirational climate.

Non-Verbal Communication: As the phrases suggest; *'a picture is worth a thousand words'*, and *'actions speak louder than words'*, tells us that our non-verbal actions are an important part of our communication process. This could be:

- Body posture
- Hand movements
- Facial expressions
- Eye contact
- Use of interpersonal space.

Eye contact and voice intonation can be used intentionally to accent (enforce) certain words or phases. Body language may express your feelings even though you remain silent. It may also send confusing messages if you are saying one thing, but your body is saying something else. In a meeting a person under attack will unconsciously (instinctively) lean away, or sit back on their chair away from the antagonist. Some researchers claim that gestures can make up more than 50% of communication, a consideration as more and more of our communication moves to emails where non-verbal communications are completely lost.

Receiver: The receiver is the person or persons the message is transmitted to. Their ability to receive will depend on their; hearing and listening skills, selective listening, eyesight and reading skills, visual activity, tactile sensitivity, olfactory sensitivity and extra sensory perception.

Decoding: Decoding is the process of converting the message back into an readable format.

Noise, Filters and Perceptions: These are all factors that interfere with the effectiveness of the communication process. Distortions occur during encoding and decoding; communication channels can be blocked by too many messages; and filters and perceptions may influence our interpretations and impressions.

Physical distractions can interfere with your communication, such as; telephone interruptions, drop-in-visitors, or lack of privacy in an open plan office. It is important to have a place where you can shield yourself from any noise - your cave, a place where you can conceptually think issues through. I personally like to *'sleep on it'*, and I am always pleasantly surprised when I wake up with a more innovative solution to a problem than the one I had the night before.

Our backgrounds and personalities introduce communication filters and perceptions - consider the following; Language (*lost in translation*), semantics, innuendos, intelligence, education, technical experience, knowledge base, cultural background, religion, politics, personal values, ethics, reputation, environment background and organisational position. Consider the OBS block when you tell your boss what he wants to hear, for fear that he will shoot the messenger - this effectively filters the information.

Other factors which will influence your response are: preconceived ideas, frames of reference, needs, interests, attitudes, emotional status, self-interests, assumptions about the sender, existing relationships with the sender, lack of responsive feedback from previous communications with the sender.

Feedback: It is good manners to not only acknowledge receipt of the communication, but also give the sender a time frame for a reply to any questions. It is important to feedback to the sender so that they can gauge how effectively the message was understood, and also for the receiver to confirm they have interpreted the message correctly. No effective communication has occurred until there is a common understanding. But also consider constructive feedback where you critique and add value to the original message.

2. Communication Plan

Communication planning pulls the project together. The project manager and project office are at the heart of the project's information and control system. It is the project manager's responsibility to not only develop the project organisation structure, but also to develop the project's communication plan and lines of communication. The communication plan should outline the following:

- Who (lines of communication- sender and receiver - responsibility and authority)
- What (scope of communication and format)
- How (email, document, telephone, meeting, presentation)
- When (schedule)
- Feedback (confirm message received and understood - document control)
- Filing (retrieval, storing, disaster recovery).

Lines of Communication: A line of communication may be defined as a formal or informal link between two or more; people, departments, companies, suppliers, contractors or stakeholders. The lines of communication tend to follow the organisation chart, which not only outlines the project manager's position, but also implies responsibility, authority and who reports to whom. Further, the stakeholder analysis will identify all the other interested parties, both internal and external to the company (see figure 19.2).

Every effort should be made to include all the key people in the project's lines of communication. To leave out a key person will not only limit their knowledgeable contribution to the project, but may also result in them adopting a hostile and negative attitude to the project. If senior people are included in your circulation list this will add weight to the document's perceived importance.

Scope of Communication: What should be communicated??? This is a tricky issue - if you filter the information, you may be accused of being manipulative. However, if you give everyone all the information, they will be overloaded and are unlikely to read it. The objective should be to communicate sufficient information for the recipient to solve problems, make good decisions and feel involved and part of the project. Certain information should be controlled - contract, specifications, drawings, instructions and scope changes. The art of good communication is to strike a balance with the value of information supplied against the cost and time it takes to collect, process and disseminate it.

Format: The reporting **format and content** should be discussed with the participants, where possible the client should be encouraged to accept the contractors standard forms, which may have been developed over many projects. The information presented should be in an easy to understand format so that the recipient can quickly assimilate the situation and take appropriate action if required.

Timing: The frequency of reports and turnaround time for responses should be discussed and agreed. An information sequence may be established, for example, the progress may be captured on a Friday, processed on a Monday and reported on a Tuesday at the progress meeting.

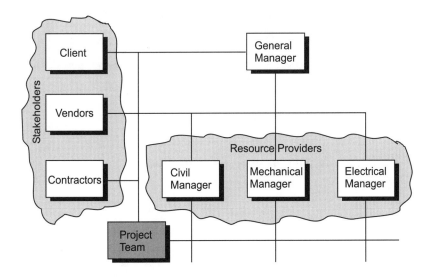

Figure 19.2: Lines of Communication

3. Project Information and Control System

The project's information and control system is the life blood of the communication plan, and the project's planning and control cycle. This information flow applies to each line of communication, which can be considered as separate cycles within the total information and control system.

For the information flow to be effective, all parties must be aware that they are part of a linked system and that the quality of the information (like cogs in a wheel or links in a chain) will directly relate to the weakest link . Further, as the saying goes, 'garbage-in to the system will deliver garbage-out of the system'.

With the advances in computer aided data processing and reporting, the weak link in the information flow is probably located at the human interface with the data capture function where the project's status and progress are quantified (see *Project Control* chapter).

The project manager also needs to encourage communication between other parties - both formal and informal. Informal channels are often essential to ensure the smooth operation, particularly in a matrix situation where there can be considerable ambiguity, and formal channels are required to dot the 'i' and cross the 't'.

Effective communication is more than just people talking to each other and transmission of facts, in the project context much of the communications will be through highly structured documents.

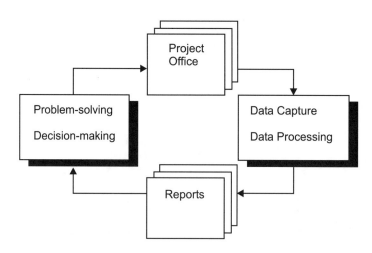

Figure 19.3: Information and Control System

4. Project Reporting

Project data can be collected, processed and reported in many ways; this section will outline a few of the commonly used methods. The format (structure), frequency and circulation of reports needs to be established during the start up phase of the project. The reports should be designed to assist problem-solving and decision-making by the various levels of management so that they can ensure the project will meet its stated goals and objectives.

Status Reports: Status reports simply quantify the position of the project. This data capture function is the first link in the information and control system - all subsequent evaluations are based on this data. Status reports may be specific and focus on the key areas of the project such as, time, cost and quality, or they may be general and include a much wider scope (see table 19.1).

Activity	Description	Status
100	Foundation	Material ordered - work started on Monday

Table 19.1: Status Report

Variance Reports: Variance reports quantify the difference between actual and planned. For example, the revised budget being compared with the original budget. The variance is simply the difference between the two values (see table 19.2).

Activity	Original Budget	Revised Budget	Variance
100	$10,000	$12,000	$2,000
200	$15,000	$13,500	($1,500)

Table 19.2: Budget Variance Report

When a variance is reported as the difference between two values, it does not take the size of the parameter into consideration. This problem can be addressed by converting the variance into a percentage of the planned value. Now the variance is expressed as a percentage of the original base (see table 19.3).

Activity	Original Budget	Revised Budget	Schedule Variance	Schedule Variance %
100	$1,000,000	$1,010,000	$10,000	1%
200	$400,000	$420,000	$20,000	5%

Table 19.3: Schedule Variance Report

Trend Reports: The status report tells the manager where the project is, but not where the project is going. The trend report uses historical data and extrapolates this forward to give the manager a feel for the direction of the project. Figure 19.4 shows the earned value graph where both BCWP and ACWP are extrapolated to show their current trends.

Earned Value: The earned value report integrates the variable parameter of cost with time. This technique can also be used to integrate manhours and time. The integration of data enables the planner to model the various parameters more realistically (see figure 19.4 and the *Earned Value* chapter).

Figure 19.4: Earned Value - shows extrapolated tends

Exception Reports: Exception reports are designed to flag an occurrence or event, which is outside predetermined control limits. This threshold can be set by the project manager as a guideline for the planner to follow and filter out the important information. For example the planner may be requested to report:

- All activities that have a float less than 5 days. This would highlight all the activities that could go critical in the next week.
- All the deliveries that are due in the next week. This would focus on deliveries that could disrupt the work and resource planning.
- All non-conformance reports (NCR) where the product has not attained the required condition as outlined by the specifications or contract. This would focus on the workforce that may need training, or equipment that may need upgrading.

Monthly Reports: On a long project, monthly reports give the project manager an excellent forum to quantify what is happening on the project and report it to senior management and key stakeholders. The monthly report should roll-up the weekly progress meetings and any other special meetings to give an overall picture of the project. The report should highlight any significant trends or variance, particularly those where the CEO's action is required. It should also identify all major events happening in the next month so that the client, CEO and other stakeholders can plan ahead.

Reporting Period: The agreed timing of the reports should link-in with a schedule of meetings and report roll-ups. This would generally be weekly, but should also include key milestones and be adjusted to accommodate risk and the level of control required.

It is important to use structured reports as much as possible, as ad-hoc reports may not include the information the project manager needs - people naturally tend to report the good news while they are economical with the bad news. However, if managers are asked to report against a structured format they will generally answer it honestly.

Reports should be quick, easy to prepare and read. The managers should not spend too much time reporting - about an hour per reporting period would be a reasonable amount. If it takes longer then the managers should rightly complain they are being distracted from productive work.

5. Document Control

The purpose of document control is to ensure that key documents are sent timeously to the key people and there is proof of the delivery. The key documents would include; contract, specifications, drawings, schedules, reports and certain correspondence. The key people would be identified by the project organisation structure and lines of communication. An audit trail of transmittals would demonstrate that the controlled documents (usually marked **controlled copy**) have been sent to the right people and there is a signature confirming date of receipt.

On large projects document control would be handled by the configuration department or a document controller, however on small projects this would be covered by the project manager or project team.

Transmittal Note: A transmittal note or delivery note is sent with every controlled document. The addressee must sign the transmittal note and return a copy to the project office to confirm the document has been received (see figure 19.5).

TRANSMITTAL NOTE	
NUMBER:	DATE ISSUED:
FROM:	TO: RECEIVED BY: DATE:
CONTENT:	

Figure 19.5: Transmittal Note (to confirm receipt)

It is the project office's responsibility to control the flow of these controlled documents. The project office must ensure that these controlled documents reach their destination timeously. A document control sheet is essential (see table 19.4), each week the document controller should confirm receipt by telephone and ensure the signed transmittals are returned. A list of non-returned transmittals can be tabled at the progress meetings to encourage compliance.

Transmittal Number	Date Issued	Document Type	Document Number	To / Destination	Date Transmittal Returned

Table 19.4: Document Control Sheet or Transmittal Summary

6. Project Meetings

'*Meetings Bloody Meetings*' you either love them or hate them, but until the management gurus come up with a better method for communicating project information, we are just going to have to live with them. Our challenge is, therefore, to manage the project meetings efficiently and effectively.

Some managers prefer many small meetings, while others prefer the occasional big meeting with everyone on the project attending; some managers prefer informal ad hoc meetings, while others prefer formal structured meetings. Whichever type of meeting you use there are five basic reasons for holding a meeting:

- Information sharing; exchange of data
- Problem-solving; brainstorming, generating ideas, options and alternatives
- Decision-making; select a course of action, gain commitment from the team
- Planning; what, who, when, how, where and why
- Evaluation; monitoring, measuring, reviewing and forecasting.

Discussing the project at the coffee machine, may be good team building, but it is not effective control. To make the most of a meeting there needs to be structure to make efficient use of your time. There are two different types of meetings I want to focus on; the handover meeting (to initiate a project phase or contractor - it is important to get off to a good start), and the progress meetings (to guide the project to a successful completion).

As the project manager is responsible for establishing the communication plan, he is also responsible for setting up a schedule of meetings. Successful meetings require good planning to ensure genuine participation from the entire team. So advance notice must be given with the purpose, an agenda, venue and time to enable participants to prepare.

7. Handover Meeting

The purpose of the handover meeting is to formally commence the project, phase or subcontract. The attendance would normally include the client, senior management, the project team members and other concerned parties; contractors, suppliers and stakeholders. The purpose of the handover meeting is to set the scene for the project, what it has to achieve and establish how it will be managed. A typical agenda may include:

- **Project Charter:** Outline the purpose of the project, scope of work.
- **Closeout Reports:** Review closeout reports and discuss previous achievements and problems.
- **Project OBS:** Identify all the relevant project participants and stakeholders. Discuss the scope of work and contracts - who does what, responsibilities and authority.
- **Communication:** Discuss the lines of communication and the information and control system.
- **Build-Method:** Discuss how the product will be made, the required quality and hold points.
- **Schedule:** Discuss the project schedule and milestones.

- **Reporting:** Discuss progress reporting - format, content, frequency and circulation.
- **Meetings:** Discuss the schedule of meetings, required attendance, venue, agenda and minutes.
- **Instructions:** Explain the procedure for issuing instructions, the format and who has authorisation. List the documents that will be used for issuing instructions, these could be; drawings, schedules, minutes, memos, letters, faxes and email.
- **Document Control:** Discuss what documents will be controlled and how they will be transmitted.
- **Configuration Management:** Discuss how changes will be incorporated and communicated. Outline procedures for scope changes and identify the people with approved signing power.
- **Payments:** Discuss how progress will be measured and payments will be made.
- **Contract:** Discuss contractual requirements, retention, bonds, penalties and warranties.
- List of client supplied items.
- List of inclusions and exclusions.
- **Commissioning:** Discuss how the product will be run-up, tested, accepted, or rejected.

It is important to get the handover meetings right to set the framework and tone for the project, and then follow-up with progress meetings to keep the momentum going.

8. Project Progress Meetings

Progress meetings are generally held every week to monitor progress and guide the project to a successful completion. Progress meetings provide an effective forum for the project manager to co-ordinate, integrate and manage the project's participants. Meetings provide a dynamic environment where interaction and innovation will enhance the cross flow of ideas and help solve problems. The meetings should also provide the venue for consensus and decision-making. A typical progress meeting would contain the following:

- **Agenda:** The agenda should be circulated before the meeting to list the participants and action points to prepare for the meeting.
- **Minutes:** Approve minutes of previous meeting.
- **Actions:** Report on actions from previous meeting.
- **Progress:** Report progress by work package.
- **Configuration Management:** Discuss scope changes and concessions - their implications and approval.
- **Document Control:** List controlled documents transmitted and police signing of transmittals.
- **Claims:** Discuss any claims since the last meeting.
- **Quality:** Discuss NCRs and quality issues.
- **Payments:** Approve invoices for payment.

The minutes should be produced as soon as possible after the meeting, preferably the next day. The minutes should document discussions and agreements taken during the meeting, together with actions to be done before the next meeting.

This concludes the chapter on *Project Communications*. The next chapter will discuss *Project Organisation Structures*, particularly the matrix structure.

Key Points:

- All lines of communication should pass through the project office - the project's front door.
- Set up a schedule of progress meetings to plan and control your project.
- Set up a fully integrated information and control system to generate progress reports.

Case Study and Exercises:

Projects are run by good communication. For this case study you have been appointed project manager of the construction of an offshore platform. Your presentation should outline how you will approach the following:

1. Communication cycle - data capture, processing, dissemination and storage.
2. Lines of communication.
3. Handover meeting.
4. Progress meetings.
5. Document control.

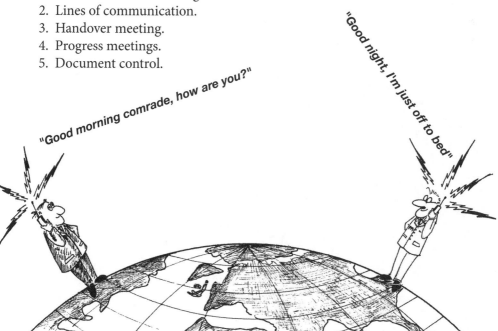

"Good morning comrade, how are you?"

"Good night, I'm just off to bed"

20

Project Organisation Structures (Matrix)

Learning Outcomes

After reading this chapter, you should be able to;

List the range of organisation structures used to manage projects

Understand how to operate within a matrix structure

Understand a range of skills you can use to gain influence

Projects are performed by people and managed through people, so it is essential to develop an organisation structure which reflects the needs of the project (task), the needs of the project team and just as importantly the needs of the individual (see figure 20.1).

Figure 20.1: Intersecting Needs

The PMBOK defines project human resource management as; '... *the process required to make the most of the people involved with the project.*' And the APM bok says; '*Issues typically important in the structuring of a project include the degree of project / functional orientation,* [and] *the extent of the project management (office) authority*'.

Organisation Structures: The project organisation structure identifies the relationship between the project participants, together with defining their duties, responsibilities and authority. Because of the dynamic nature of projects it is possible to have a number of organisation structures running concurrently, and over the duration of the project you may well use all of the organisation structures. These structures outline the relationship between the various participants, lines of authority and the lines of communication, consider:

- Project team
- Project interfaces
- Matrix organisation structure
- Responsibility matrix

Project Team: The project team outlines the relationship between the project manager and the other team members. The membership of this structure may be dynamic, as seconded members move in and out of the project office (see figure 20.2).

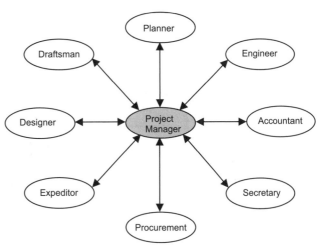

Figure 20.2: Project Team (centred on the project manager)

Project Interfaces: The project interface diagram outlines the contact (communication) between the project manager with the internal and external stakeholders (see figure 20.3).

- Internal contacts - the functional managers and all the other internal departments that may be associated with the project.
- External contacts - the client and all the other outside companies (contractors and suppliers) used on the project.

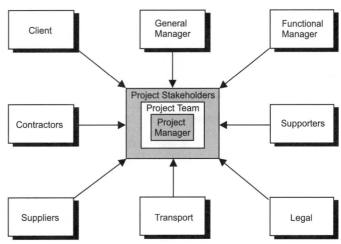

Figure 20.3: Project Interfaces

Matrix Organisation Structure: The matrix structure presents the temporary project lines of responsibility overlaying the functional lines of responsibility, and outlines the relationship between the project manager, functional managers and their subordinates (figure 20. 4).

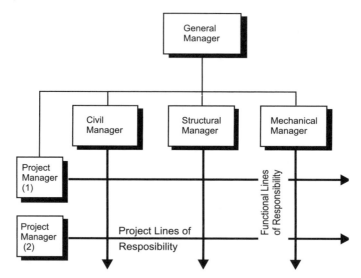

Figure 20.4: Matrix Organisation Structure (showing lines of responsibility)

Responsibility Matrix: The responsibility matrix is a development of the schedule Gantt chart which clearly links the work (WBS and/or activities) to the responsible person (OBS). This is an easier document to use than the matrix WBS/OBS (see figure 20.5).

Activity Number	Mon 1	Tue 2	Wed 3	Thu 4	Fri 5	Sat 6	Sun 7	Mon 8	Project Manager	Functional Man	General Manager	Stakeholders
100	▬								•	•		
300		▬							•		•	•
200			▬						•			
500				▬					•	•		•
400					▬				•			
600						▬			•			•

Responsibility Matrix

Figure 20.5: Responsibility Matrix (adds a responsibility field to the schedule Gantt Chart)

WBS / OBS Matrix: The WBS / OBS matrix is another format outlining the integration of the scope of work (work package) with the responsible person or department. This matrix ensures that the full scope of work is assigned and the responsible person for each work package is identified. The earned value bubble indicates the planning and control function at the work package level (figure 20. 6).

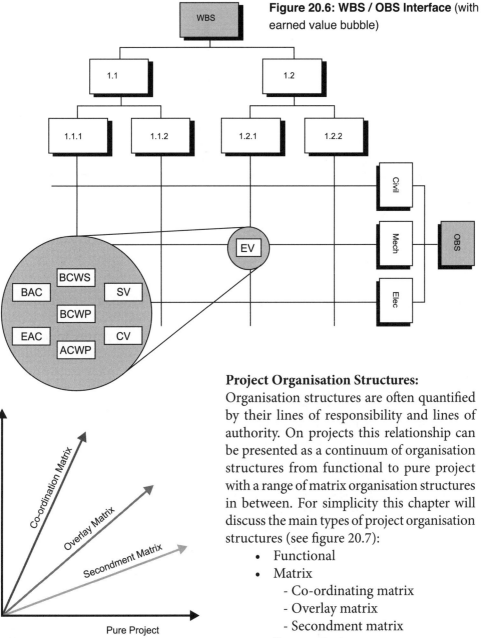

Figure 20.6: WBS / OBS Interface (with earned value bubble)

Project Organisation Structures:

Organisation structures are often quantified by their lines of responsibility and lines of authority. On projects this relationship can be presented as a continuum of organisation structures from functional to pure project with a range of matrix organisation structures in between. For simplicity this chapter will discuss the main types of project organisation structures (see figure 20.7):

- Functional
- Matrix
  - Co-ordinating matrix
  - Overlay matrix
  - Secondment matrix
- Pure project

Figure 20.7: Project Organisation Structure Continuum

1. Functional Organisation Structure

This **traditional** organisation structure is based on the subdivision of product lines or disciplines into separate departments, together with a vertical hierarchy. Figure 20.8 outlines a typical structure with a number of functional departments reporting to the general manager. Also called **wedding-cake** corporate structure.

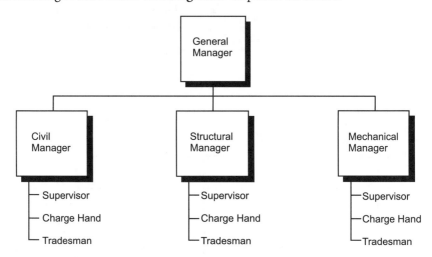

Figure 20.8: Functional Organisation Structure

The **advantages** of the functional organisation structure (particularly for projects within a department) are:

- Functional departments provide a **home** for technical expertise which offers technical support and continuing development.
- Functional departments provide good **support** as the work is usually carried out in the department.
- Functional departments can achieve a high degree of flexibility, because people in the department can be assigned to the project, then immediately reassigned to other work. Switching back and forth between projects is easily achieved.
- Functional departments provide the normal **career path** for advancement and promotion.
- Functional departments' work is **simpler** to estimate and manage as the scope of work is usually restricted to its own field and the functional data base should contain information from previous projects (closeout reports).
- Lines of **communication** within the department are short and well established.
- There is quick **reaction time** to problems within the department.
- Some employees prefer working in a consistent work routine, rather than the challenge of diverse projects.
- Functional departments offer clearly defined responsibility and authority for work within the department.

The **disadvantages** of the functional organisation structure (particularly when being used on multi-disciplined projects) are:

- No *single point of responsibility* as the project scope moves from one department to another, this can lead to co-ordinating chaos. Without a nominated project manager the co-ordinating role will become the responsibility of the general manager, but the general manager should really be more concerned with corporate issues and not project operations. As projects become larger and more complex, it becomes increasingly difficult for senior management to co-ordinate the day-to-day problems of individual projects.

- On multi-disciplined projects there are no formal **lines of communication** between the workers within the different departments - like a stovepipe, information flows straight up and down. Generally, the only formal line of communication is through the functional managers, which will lengthen the lines of communication and slow down the response time. With these long communication cycles problem-solving and decision-making will be self-limiting. In practice, out of necessity, informal links may be established between the people working on the project.

- Competition and conflict between functional departments could limit effective communication of important project information.

- Departmental work could take **priority** over project work. If there is a resource overload the project's schedule might be pushed out, which could delay the handover to the next department and ultimately delay the project's completion.

- For functional managers the project is not always their main focus of concern, particularly when the work has moved to another department. The client might well feel like a football being passed from one department to another.

- The responsibility for external co-ordination with the client, suppliers and other stakeholders may become muddled because of overlap, underlap and inadequately defined **responsibilities**.

- Without a clear project manager the client could end up personally **co-ordinating** the different functional departments.

- The department might myopically focus only on their scope of work in preference to a holistic view of the project and a departmental solution to a problem may not be the best solution for the project as a whole. For example, the production department might want standardisation, while the marketing department might want to offer a range of products.

- Functional structures are not effective in a **multi-project** environment because of the conflicts associated with assessing the relative importance and priorities as each project competes for limited resources.

- No single department is responsible for the overall project's success, this could lead to decisions by committee.

The functional organisation structure offers excellent facilities within its own department, but where a multi-disciplined scope of work calls for interaction with other departments then the system may be found lacking. To address this problem the matrix organisation structure offers an interaction of both functional and project interests.

2. Matrix Organisation Structures

The topology of the matrix structure has the same format as a mathematical matrix, in this case the vertical lines represent the functional department's responsibility and authority, while the horizontal lines represent the project's responsibility and authority, thus giving the matrix structure its unique appearance and name.

The matrix structure is considered by many practitioners to be the natural project organisation structure, as it formalises the informal links (mentioned in the previous section). On multi-disciplined projects employees need to communicate at the operational level to perform their tasks. Where the lines of responsibility intersect, this represents people to people contact, thus providing shorter formal lines of communication.

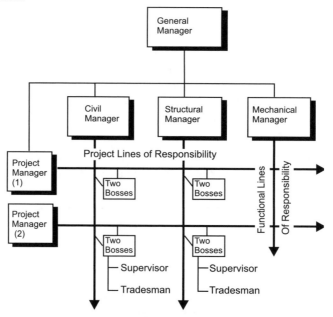

Figure 20.9: Matrix Organisation Structure

A characteristic of project management is that it relies on a number of functional departments and sub-contractors to supply the resources to produce the product, each appearing to act autonomously and yet requiring strong communication links with each other. The project manager needs to cut across organisational lines to co-ordinate and integrate specific resources located in different departments. To achieve this the project manager must have appropriate tools, particularly an information system that not only accommodates interdisciplinary tasks but also the cross-functional capability of retrieving data from the different departments. Within this matrix structure there are a number of variants influenced mainly by the distribution of power (authority) - namely:

- Co-ordination matrix (weak matrix)
- Overlay matrix (balanced matrix)
- Secondment matrix (strong matrix)

Consider some of the **advantages** inherent in the typical matrix organisation structure:

- The project has a clear *single point of responsibility* - the project manager.
- The project can draw on the entire resources of the company. The matrix structure allows a time-share of expertise which should lead to a higher degree of resource utilisation.
- By sharing the use of equipment, the capital costs can be shared between projects and functional departments.
- With seconded resources project termination is not necessarily a traumatic event (worrying about continuing employment) - the resources can return to their original functional department.
- Rapid response to the client's needs - the client communicates directly with the project manager.
- The corporate link will ensure consistency with company policies, strategies and procedures, yet give the flexibility to tailor these to the project's needs.
- The matrix structure can be tailored to the needs of the project with respect to; job descriptions, procedures, work instructions and lines of communication.
- Good flow of information (dissemination) within the project as there is a provision for both horizontal (project information) from function to function and vertical (functional information) through the organisation structure.
- The needs of the project and functional departments can be addressed simultaneously by negotiation and trade-off. The project is mainly concerned with what and when (scope and planning), while the functional department is concerned with who and how (resources and technical).
- Problem-solving can draw on a much wider input for ideas and innovative options - brainstorming.
- Teams of experts within the functional department are kept together as the projects come and go. Therefore technology, know-how, expertise and experience are not lost when the project is completed and the project team disbanded. Specialists like to work with other specialists in the same discipline, thus increasing innovation, problem-solving ability and synergy.
- The multi-disciplinary environment exposes people to a wider range of considerations.
- By retaining their functional home, specialists keep their career path. If they work well in a multi-disciplined environment then a new career in the project office may open up.
- The matrix structure is a good training ground for project managers working in multi-functional and cross-functional environments.
- The matrix structure integrates the WBS with the OBS (see figure 20.6).

The following **disadvantages** are inherent with the matrix structure:

- The matrix structure is complex and more difficult for the participants to understand than the simpler functional or pure project organisations.
- More communication links are required to keep the additional number of managers informed and consulted.
- Dual responsibility and authority leads to confusion, divided loyalties, unclear responsibilities, and conflicts over priorities and allocation of resources.
- The two boss situation is a recipe for conflict over the allocation of employees. The conflict could be between the project manager, functional manager and employee.
- Matrix structures do not encourage strong staff commitment to the project, particularly when staff from functional departments are assigned on an as-needed basis. Also the staff may be working on a number of projects, further limiting their commitment to any one project.
- The reward system of a matrix structure does not encourage staff to put in long hours in a project. Why should they when they have no personal stake and no additional payments. Further, the project manager does not usually write their appraisal reports.
- Reaction times, although faster than the functional structure, may get bogged down in negotiation (there is considerably more negotiation) so decisions could take longer to make as more people must be consulted. This problem is more acute with the weaker matrix structures where the project managers do not have the authority to make decisions on their own.
- A company with a number of projects calling on the same resources faces real problems establishing priorities and resource allocation, as the project manager and functional manager are likely to claim their work should have the highest priority. In this situation the priority will have to be made at a senior management level.
- The cost of running a matrix organisation is higher than a functional or pure project organisation because of the increased number of managers involved in the administration and decision-making process.
- Project integration between departments is more involved and complex than integrating people within one functional department.

- With functional projects and pure projects it is clear who has the power to make decisions, however, with the matrix structure the power may be balanced between departments. If this causes doubt and confusion then the productivity of the project may suffer.
- After a secondment of a few years personnel may find they either do not have a functional department to return to, or their position has been reappointed. *"Someone is sitting at my desk!!"*
- The corporate employees' career path is usually within the functional department. Therefore, while working on projects they may miss-out on functional promotion.
- In the matrix structure the project manager controls the administration decisions, while the functional managers control the technical decisions - this division of power and responsibility could lead to an overly complex situation.
- Where the project and functional lines of influence cross there exists a two boss situation which is a recipe for conflict.
- Where project and functional reporting is required, this double reporting may lead to additional work and, therefore, additional costs.
- The functional departments are unlikely to give up their best personnel to the project, so team selection may be self-limiting.

For the matrix organisation structure to work successfully the functional departments may have to make some major adjustments in the way they work. The matrix structure introduces new management interfaces and these will increase the potential for conflict. New management skills will be required for the functional managers to accommodate conflicting goals, priorities and resource demands.

3. Co-ordinating Matrix

Referring to the matrix organisation structure (figure 20.9), this is the nearest structure to the traditional functional hierarchy where the project manager (more likely called project co-ordinator, progress chaser, or expediter) co-ordinates the resources across functional departments. The project co-ordinator may come from the department that initiates the project, or the department with the largest scope of work. Although the project co-ordinator is generally in a junior position with little formal power, as titular head of the project the project co-ordinator may well be held responsible for the project meeting its objectives.

This arrangement gives little formal authority to the project co-ordinator to manage the project, control resources, or make decisions. Due to this lack of formal authority the project co-ordinator usually ends up performing more project administration work than managing the project. In this situation the best approach may be to offer a co-ordinating service, identify problem areas, and facilitate the project management process through communication skills and interpersonal skills - this way earning appreciation and perhaps some power!

4. Overlay Matrix

Also called the **balanced matrix**. This is the commonest type of matrix structure, where the project manager through a project office would negotiate with the functional departments for resources to implement the project. The project manager would be on the same level of seniority as the functional managers which puts the project manager in an interesting position - because the project manager may now be deemed to have sufficient seniority to be held responsible for the project, but at the same time does not have formal authority over the functional managers who **own** the resources.

The onus is on the project manager to practice an appropriate leadership style towards the functional managers, which would certainly include negotiation to address the trade-off between who controls the what, when, who and how.

5. Secondment Matrix

This is the nearest type of organisation structure to the pure project where the project manager has a wide range of powers over the whole project. Although the project manager would usually be senior to the functional managers, it would still be necessary to negotiate with them for the use of their resources. During the secondment the functional personnel would formally report to the project manager.

The project office would develop an information and control system tailored to the needs of the project, together with procedures and work instructions. This ability to either modify existing systems or develop new systems from scratch is a characteristic of project management.

Although the functional personnel will return to their department after their involvement in the project, to help gain commitment and respect from the seconded staff, it is in the project manager's interest to ensure their continuing employment after the project.

6. Pure Project Organisation Structure

The pure project organisation structure is similar in shape to the functional organisational structure except now all the departments are dedicated to the project. It has autonomy from the rest of the company, as a self-contained unit with its own technical staff and administration. This type of structure is typical of large capital projects - Channel Tunnel, NASA and offshore projects (see figure 20.10). The project manager has a high level of authority to manage and control the project's resources and constraints. The **advantages** with the pure project structure include:
- The project manager has full line authority over the project.
- Team members have increased project commitment and loyalty.
- It promotes more effective communication between the project manager and the team members.
- All members of the workforce report directly to the project manager. There are no functional department heads whose permission must be sought.

Figure 20.10: Pure Project Structure
- shows all the managers reporting to the project manager

- The lines of communication are shorter than the multi-disciplined functional route.
- If there are a series of similar projects, the team of skilled experts can be kept together.
- Because the project team tends to have a strong separate identity, this encourages a high level of communication between members. Inspiration and motivation is high and task orientated.
- With centralised authority, decisions are made quickly.
- With the one boss situation the lines of communication, responsibility and authority are clear and undisputed.
- A pure project presents a simple structure which is easy to understand, implement and operate.
- There is a holistic approach to the project.

The **disadvantages** with the pure project structure include:
- If the parent company has a number of projects running concurrently, with pure project structures this could lead to duplication of effort in many areas and an inefficient use of company resources.
- To ensure access to technical know-how and skills there may be a propensity to stockpile equipment and personnel. This may lead to resources staying on the project longer than required.
- Project team members work themselves out of a job at the end of the project.
- If the project divorces itself from the functional departments and other projects, this could sever the cross flow of ideas and information within the company.
- As the project cannot offer continuity of employment, this may encourage the company to use sub-contractors. If a detailed closeout report is not generated by the sub-contractors the company would lose valuable experience and information.

7. Job Descriptions

The job description develops the organisation structure's positions into a further level of detail. The job description should contain the job title, the supervisor, a job summary, duties, level of responsibilities and authority. A job description should include:

- Who the person reports to, and who reports to that person
- What duties the person is responsible for
- What authority the person has to solve problems, make decisions and issue instructions.

Using this basic framework consider an example of a project manager's job description - reporting to the general manager, the project manager is delegated with responsibility and authority to:

- Achieve all the targets set out in the baseline plan.
- Select and manage the project team.
- Set up the project office management system to plan and control the project.
- Represent the company at the client meetings.
- Process all project related correspondence.
- Authorise all reimbursable procurement and services required by the project.
- Negotiate and award all the sub-contracts.
- Process all non-conformance reports (NCRs).
- Issue the necessary project procedures.
- Issue weekly / monthly progress reports and financial statements.
- Approve all changes on behalf of the company.
- During the development of the scope of work it is the project manager's responsibility to structure and co-ordinate the input and involve all interested parties (internal and external stakeholders). This involvement is required to determine the technical and managerial requirements.
- Some of the qualities the project manager requires include; an ability to communicate, negotiate, deduce, quantify dreams, quantify wish lists and interpret the client's needs correctly.

As the project manager is responsible for selecting the project team it can be assumed that the project manager is also responsible for defining their job descriptions. These would normally include the following positions:

- Project Accountant
- Project Planner
- Project Engineer
- Project QA Manager
- Project Procurement Manager
- Configuration Manager
- Document Controller
- Progress Expeditor
- HRM.

The size of the project would determine the number of people in the team. On a small project one person may cover all these positions, while on a large project there may be a number of people per position. The bottom line is that the project manager is the *single point of responsibility* and as such has a blanket responsibility for the project. The project manager's authority, however, may be limited. The key word here is to strive for authority **commensurate** with your responsibility.

8. Organisation Structure Selection

Selecting the right organisation structure is essentially a balancing act between addressing the project's needs (scope), the project team's needs, and stakeholders needs and, just as importantly, the individuals' needs (see figure 20.1). On some projects, the client may request or instruct the contractor to use a certain type of management structure.

The choice can be further complicated by an organisation structure which is appropriate for one company but could be a burden for another. The project could therefore evolve into many different structures running concurrently. The project manager is often selected from a functional department, but which one?

- The department that initiated the project.
- The department with the largest part of the project.
- The department with the initial phase of the project.
- The department with the least work on at the time.

The selection is often influenced in favour of the department with the appropriate technical background. This organisation structure would be called **lead technical**. When the project requires input from a number of different departments the **matrix** structure offers a real solution to the functional division of responsibility and authority. If the project is a large capital project which will run for a few years, setting up a **pure project** structure may be the most expedient and appropriate decision.

9. Responsibility - Authority Gap

A characteristic of the matrix organisation structure is that it relies on the functional departments for resources. Although the project and functional departments may appear to work autonomously, for project success, they need strong communication links with each other. The project manager needs to cut across organisational lines to co-ordinate and integrate specific resources located in the functional departments. To achieve this the project manager must have both a fully integrated information and control system and the means of addressing the responsibility - authority gap.

Responsibility may be defined as feeling obliged to perform assigned work, while authority is the power to carry out the work. The authority gap is when you are given responsibility but do not have sufficient authority to issue instructions to make the work happen. It is often stated that authority should be commensurate with responsibility, but feedback suggests that CEOs are often reluctant to assign sufficient formal power to project managers. In which case, the project managers need to address the authority gap in other ways. Consider the following ways to gain influence:

Formal Authority: Or position power is automatically conferred on you with your appointment to the project. While position power can be exerted over subordinates, this type of power is very limited in its acceptance and often does little to influence behaviour particularly with the functional managers who own the resources the project manager needs, and do not report to the project manager.

Budget Authority: If the project manager holds the purse strings this will confer some financial power over the functional managers, particularly if the departments are run as cost centres. This is certainly powerful when dealing with outside suppliers and contractors who depend on the payments for their existence. Budget authority can lie with both the carrot and the stick - the promise of future business, an incentive bonus and threats of withholding payment for poor work.

Coercive Power: Coercive power uses the fear and the avoidance of punishment and threats to influence behaviour. This may be seen as; power not to reward, or threaten demotion, withholding overtime, limiting salary increase, or transfer to another job. Use of coercive power is linked to organisation position, and if used excessively tends to inhibit creativity and can have a negative impact on team morale.

Information Power: Expert knowledge and technical ability are effective if perceived as valuable and shared appropriately with functional managers and project participants, however, it will erode trust and create resentment if hoarded. As project manager you should be at the centre of the information and control system and, therefore, in an ideal position to capture, process, file and disseminate useful information.

Reward Power: The ability to provide positive rewards for performance. To be effective, it must properly correspond to participants' values and expectations. Since money is not always available, project managers must consider a variety of potentially satisfying sanctions especially those related to work challenge and recognition (see Herzberg's motivation and hygiene factors in the *Project Leadership* chapter).

Cognitive Persuasion: The logical (cognitive) approach includes the use of reasoned argument, evidence and logical consistency. How can you encourage the functional managers to part with their best people??? Perhaps you can persuade them that their contribution is needed for the success of the project, the success of their department and for the success of the company.

Emotional Persuasion: Beg the functional managers for their assistance; appeal to their sense of compassion; request a favour, say please, appeal to their better nature - *go down on your knees!*

Personal Power: Charismatic project managers can compel people to listen and follow them. They are natural leaders who can persuade and encourage others to follow a certain course of action. They have a sense of mission, a sense of purpose, have a good sense of humour, are empathetic to staff needs, enthusiastic and self-confident.

Ideally project managers should be competent in all areas of authority for continuing success. Charismatic managers for example, may have initial appeal, but as problems arise, if they are not able to assist technically, their power will be undermined. Project managers' leadership ability is usually expressed in terms of influencing the behaviour and attitudes of the project team members, the effectiveness of leaders is, therefore, dependant to some extent on their power.

This concludes the chapter on *Project Organisation Structures*. The following chapters will discuss *Project Teams* and the human factors associated with *Project Leadership*.

Key Points:

- The matrix structure is considered by many practitioners to be the natural project organisation structure.
- Clients prefer to deal with one manager - the project manager as the *single point of responsibility*.
- Acquiring power outside formal authority is the key to successful project management.

Case Study and Exercises:

Projects are performed by people and managed through people, so it is essential to develop an organisation structure which reflects these needs. For this case study you have been appointed project manager for the fabrication and erection of a steel bridge to link a coastal island to the mainland. You are required to design a multi-disciplined OBS which should consider the following:

1. Benefits of a matrix OBS for this type of project.
2. Benefits of secondment OBS for this type of project.
3. Benefits of pure project OBS for this type of project.
4. Job descriptions.
5. Methods of addressing the responsibility - authority power gap.

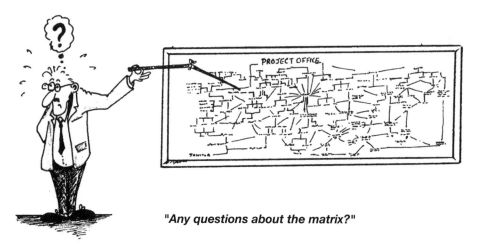

"Any questions about the matrix?"

21

Project Teams

Learning Outcomes

After reading this chapter, you should be able to;

Demonstrate an understanding of the criteria for working as a member of a team

Collaborate with other team members to improve performance

Understand the benefits of working in teams

The PMBOK defines team development [managerial and technical] as; '... *both enhancing the ability of stakeholders to contribute as individuals as well as enhancing the ability of the team to function as a team.*' And the APM bok defines teamwork as; '... *effective teamwork is generally at the heart of effective project management.*'

A project team may be defined as a number of people who work closely together to achieve shared common goals (see figure 21.1). Through interaction they strive to enhance their creativity, innovation, problem-solving, decision-making, morale and job performance. A team implies a number of people working together to achieve results.

Whereas, a group implies a collection of individuals who, although they may be working on the same project, do not necessarily interact with each other. This is often the case when the project manager co-ordinates the project with the people individually. Under such conditions, unity of purpose is a myth.

Figure 21.1: Project Team Structure - shows the interface between the team members and the project manager - this can be further overlaid with interfaces between the team members themselves

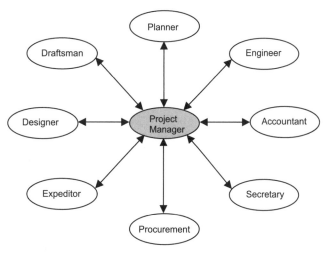

Teams are not always associated with projects, but as companies move to a management-by-projects approach, so the link will become better recognised. The implementation of the project planning and control techniques is through people, therefore, to effectively implement the system one must gain support and commitment from the project team and other stakeholders. Many projects fail to reach their optimum level of performance, not because of any lack of equipment or project systems, but purely because the human factors were not addressed.

The growth of new technology, increased complexity and competition, has generated a need for multi-disciplined teams to work closely together. Teamwork should aim to bring individuals together in such a way that they increase their effectiveness without losing their individuality - an orchestra is a good example of this criteria.

1. Purpose of Project Teams

Project teams are an efficient and effective way of managing projects, where efficiency implies performing the work well, and effectiveness implies performing the right work. Consider the following reasons to form a team:

- To achieve the schedule and project objectives the **volume of work** must be distributed (shared) amongst a number of people.
- The scope of the project may require a broad **range of ideas and skills** which any one person is unlikely to have. Consider an orchestra - this is an excellent example of a set of complementary skills and talents (functional skills) which are required to produce the music.
- To improve communication and information sharing.
- **Brainstorming** and discussions are a good example of interactive team work and collaboration with other team members to improve performance, and particularly to generate creative ideas and **solve problems**. Through cross-fertilisation and synergy a small team can generate many innovative options and alternatives - a suggestion from one person can stimulate spontaneous ideas from the others (particularly if there is no evaluation).

- Collaboration, consultation and joint decision-making help to ensure the whole team is fully committed to the chosen course of action.
- Project teams generally take riskier decisions than an individual would on their own. There is a feeling of mutual support.
- Project teams enhance motivation - the members do not want to let the side down.
- Team members are held collectively accountable and responsible for achieving targets.
- Project teams support other team members when they need help both technically and emotionally.

Management tests show that teams repeatedly make better decisions than the team members would make individually with the same information. This has been attributed to the teams' wider range of skills and experiences than any one individual would have, and the cross-fertilisation of ideas that stimulate creativity and innovation. To make the most of teams we need to understand the complex nature of teams, and their internal dynamics.

2. Individual's Purpose for Team Membership

Why should an individual wish to be part of a project team? Consider the following constructive and non-disruptive behaviours:
- It is a means of satisfying an individual's social or affiliation needs, to belong to something or be part of a team.
- It is a means of sharing risk with other team members - spread the load.
- It is a means of establishing self-esteem. People like to introduce themselves as Joe Bloggs from Eurobuilders Ltd. This way they are defining themselves in terms of their relationship to others, as a member of a team or company.
- It is a means of gaining **support** to carry out their particular goals. It also allows the individual to bounce ideas off other team members who can offer support, constructive criticism and alternative suggestions.
- It encourages the individual to build relationships with other team members and stakeholders.
- It encourages the individual to respect personal, ethical, religious and cultural differences and so enhance interaction between team members.
- It helps the individual develop a variety of strategies to deal with potential or actual conflict between team members.
- The team provides a psychological home for the individual and a warm feeling of moral and camaraderie.

These criteria and behaviours make working as a team member more conducive. It should be mentioned, however, that not everyone wants to work in a team - many people prefer to work on their own. And with the increasing use of email, the Internet and video-conferencing, working from home or away from the project office is becoming more feasible and popular.

3. Benefits of Teams

In the past, corporations have been preoccupied with the qualities of individual people. Any attempt to list the qualities of a good manager would demonstrate abilities that are almost certainly mutually exclusive to any individual:

- They must be **highly intelligent** but not **too clever**.
- They must be **forceful** but also **sensitive** to people's feelings.
- They must be **dynamic** but also **patient**.
- They must be a **fluent communicator** but also a **good listener.**
- They must be **decisive** but also **reflective**.
- They must be an **expert** on a wide range of different fields.

And if a manager is found with all the above attributes, a paragon of mutually compatible characteristics, what happens if they:

- Step under a bus.
- Take up a position with a competitor.
- Go to live in another country.

But if no individual can combine all these qualities, a team of individuals certainly could, for the following reasons:

- It is not the individual but the team that is instrumental in sustaining and enduring management success.
- A team can **renew** and regenerate itself through new recruitment as individual team members leave.
- A team can also build up a store of shared and collectively owned experiences, information and judgement which can be passed on to new team members.
- Many people are **more successful** working within a team or partnership than working alone.
- Team **synergy** generates more output than the sum of the individual inputs.
- The team can offer a wide range of technical support.
- A team can offer multi-tasking where team members can work on different parts of the project at the same time, which speeds up the design or production process (fast tracking).

4. Team Applications

Project teams are set-up for many applications, consider the following;

- A R&D scientific team is set-up to explore new product designs.
- A feasibility study team is set-up to consider the feasibility of the company pursuing certain projects and opportunities.
- A project management team is set-up to manage a project. Project teams often work through a matrix structure which is overlaid on the functional organisation structure.
- Quality circles are production teams with membership from all sections of the production line. Their objective is to solve production problems, raise productivity and reduce quality problems.

- Technology is enabling the formation of virtual teams. Using the Internet virtual teams can network from remote locations. Team members may rarely meet face-to-face, although they may see each other on a video link.
- Associations form committee teams and special interest groups.
- Companies form task forces to solve problems.
- Companies form maintenance teams to keep their equipment operational.

5. Team Size

The appropriate team size depends on a number of factors:

- How many people are required to perform the work for the project and spread the load.
- What variety of technical expertise is required by the project. If the team is too small it might not have the knowledge base and skill depth to meet the needs of the project.
- What is the appropriate level of conflict in a team? Mathematically, the odds of conflict increase with the number of people in the team.
- Large teams tend to be unwieldy and unable to reach agreement, or collect everyone's contribution. If decisions are made by majority vote, an uneven number could prevent 'ties' (although some members could abstain).
- Too large and the team might find communication and agreement difficult, the team could subdivide into cliques.
- The team needs a balance of personalities.

The ideal team size depends very much on its application. Teams tend to grow in size until some magic number is reached - then they subdivide. The experts suggest this is between five and ten people. Sporting teams provide us with some guidelines, consider a rugby team for example, which consists of fifteen players. This number is slightly higher than recommended, and sure enough there is subdivision into a pack of eight forwards and seven backs.

6. Why Teams Win

Research by Belbin at Henley Management College showed that some or all of the following characteristics are present in a successful team:

- The team leader has an appropriate management style for the project, and is not challenged by other team members.
- There is a chairman type person who encourages all the team members to contribute.
- At least one member of the team generates innovative ideas and spots marketable opportunities, as a means to solve problems and identify new products and new markets.
- There is a spread of mental abilities.

- There is a spread of personalities which gives the team a balanced appearance.
- There is a collaborative approach with constructive and non-disruptive behaviour which includes showing sensitivity, grasping other team members perspectives, being attentive, showing interest, showing a positive attitude and positive reinforcement.

The person in the chair or team leader will be successful if they gain and earn respect from the other team members. Generally the chairman does not need to dominate the proceedings but should know how to pull matters together and integrate the team. In practice Belbin found the leader always worked closely with the talented members of the team.

Innovation: Innovation and creativity to solve problems and respond to change are essential for continuing project success. Ideas can be generated in many ways from people both inside and outside the team.

Flexibility: In flexible teams the team members play the role or support the role that is in demand or overloaded at the time. Successful teams exhibit flexibility where members are able to move around in the team to find the best match between people and jobs. They also realise that if they do not have a balanced distribution of team roles they have to appoint members to play those missing roles.

Belbin (*Management Teams*) said that; '*... the essence of a team is that its members form a co-operative association through a division of labour that best reflects the contribution that each can make towards the common objectives.*'

7. Why Teams Fail

Belbin found that the single factor evident in all unsuccessful teams was low mental ability. If this is compared with the innovation and creativity of winning teams, then it implies that low mental ability teams were not able to:

- Take advantage of **opportunities**
- Are poor at **problem-solving**
- Are unable to **change** with the times

Other factors include:

- Unbalanced team roles - the team members cannot work together
- Apollo (clever) teams - there are too many ideas, too much ongoing destructive arguing, leading to conflict and poor decision-making.

Negative Selection: The failure of companies to produce teams which have an adequate proportion of managers with good mental ability must surely not be due to any conscious search for such people, but rather the unintended by-product of negative selection. Negative selection refers to the recruitment process designed to filter out the type of people the company really needs. Consider the company which is looking for an experienced manager to reverse their present decline, but will not increase the current salary package offered. This low salary will unintentionally exclude the quality manager the company needs.

8. Team Development Phases

Project teams pass through a number of distinctive development phases or stages. It is important to be aware of these phases so that you can guide your team through the stages, particularly the conflict phase to the productive phase.

Forming	The team members form a team, there is a sense of anticipation and commitment. Their motivation is high, but their effectiveness is moderate because they are unsure of each other and the purpose of the project.
Storming	Disagreement and conflict over task and ways of working as a team. Clash of personalities.
Norming	Consolidation differences are accepted and agree to work together.
Performing	Effective teamwork - work well and interact together as a team.
Maturing	Getting old gracefully, more interested in maintaining situation, rather than trying out new ideas.
Declining	Market has changed, team has no new products. The team are really over the hill, just hanging in there waiting for their pension.

Table 21.1: Team Development Phases

Table 21.1 shows that each development phase has different influences on the team members, however, the norming phase warrants special mention as this is where the real team work starts. The differences are accepted and the team members agree to work together as a team. The team establish order and cohesion, and the leader helps clarify team roles, norms and values. The topic of conversation tends to be concern about:
- When and how should the team work together?
- Problem-solving (brainstorming).
- How should the team make decisions? (Refer to the decision-making continuum, figure 22.1.)
- What type of individual behaviour is appropriate in the team?
- What level of work should everyone be involved with?
- What degree of openness, trust and confidence is desirable?

9. Team Building

Bringing a number of people together to perform a task does not necessarily mean they will work as a team even if they have complementary skills. They not only need leadership to give them direction, to stop them running around like headless chickens, but they also need team building to encourage them to want to work together.

Team building in its widest meaning incorporates a wide range of functions from bringing a team together (selection), integrating the team to work effectively together (team building), guiding the team to achieve success (coaching and mentoring), to succession planning as players leave and new members join the team.

If we look at the military approach to team work, before they send a platoon into action they will have trained together and be working effectively as a team. Musicians practice endlessly to be note perfect and in harmony, and sports teams train for fitness and practice different combinations and tactics. In industry, however, team building often happens after the project has started and takes its chances that the players will work together as a team. Is your company prepared to take that risk ? Consider the following:

- Team building should not be seen as a one-off event. For example, going on a team building course then getting back to work on Monday as if nothing has happened – team building should be a continuous process.
- Team building heightens a team awareness of each other's responsibilities, enhances a shared understanding of the project's objectives and goals, and helps to align the efforts of the various team members.
- Try and eliminate adversarial, fear-based relationships among the stakeholders. Team building strengthens trust and co-operation, improves communication, and ensures shared understanding and alignment of project objectives, roles and responsibilities, performance expectation, company culture and OBS structure, creating a win-win environment. When individuals understand how to work with each other better, get things done, and use less scarce resources, it enhances individual commitment and results in improved scope definition, cost and schedule performance.
- As a project is planned and controlled, so team work should also be planned and controlled with feedback provided as an ongoing basis - this will help to lead to constructive interaction and productive working relationships.

Outdoor Team Building: The traditional management training model is to teach management theory and knowledge through lectures, reading, discussions, examples and assignments. Business schools use case studies to add a further dimension to test conceptual thinking, problem-solving and decision-making. But unfortunately all these training methods fail to create a real dynamic situation as there is no live interaction.

This is where outdoor management team building courses comes to the rescue - by using outdoor pursuits as the training vehicle to set interactive management tasks. This way a real dynamic and unpredictable environment can be created where the management team building theory can be put into practice under varying levels of difficulty, and where feedback to the delegates on their performance will be immediate. This way the delegates learn how to manage people and make their mistakes on a training course rather than at work where mistakes could be more expensive.

10. Role of the Project Manager

The project manager's position evolved in the 1950s as the *single point of responsibility* to co-ordinate multi-disciplined projects and make the best use of the company's resources. The role of the project manager is influenced by the size of the project - on a small project for example, the project manager may be expected to be a technical expert as well. Consider the following points in favour of the project manager being a **technical expert:**

- Companies prefer their managers to be technical experts in the field of the project, as it enables the managers to confirm technical decisions themselves. This view is supported by the fact that most project management positions advertised require the managers to be technically competent in field of the project.
- If the project manager knows and understands the technical issues of the project they will be in a better position to apply judgement and forecast problems.
- Team selection can be based on both human compatibility and technical ability. The technical ability and demonstratable skills of the project managers can be verified directly.
- They can be effectively involved up-front during the feasibility study, estimating and quotation stage of the project.
- They will be able to gain respect from the team by demonstrating not only good management but also technical expertise (see *Herzberg's* motivation and hygiene factors in the *Project Leadership* chapter).

Now for the other side of the argument in favour of the project manager being a **generalist** in the field of the project:

- As a manager moves up the corporate ladder they will be concerned more with people, costs and co-ordinating multi-disciplines and less with technical issues.
- It may not be desirable to have the technical expert leading the team, as they could suppress innovation from the other team members, particularly in their area of expertise.
- Effective project management requires many non-technical skills such as human resource management, team building, financial accounting, negotiation, integration and co-ordination.

It would seem from commercial feedback that initially to embark on a career in project management you need experience in the field of the project, but once established you will slowly become more of a generalist in project management.

Key Points:

- Project teams are characterised by positive interaction.
- The ability to generate innovative ideas is essential for problem-solving and the success of the project.
- Employers prefer the project manager to have technical ability in the field of the project.

Case Study and Exercises:

Project teams work together to achieve common goals. Through interaction they strive to enhance their creativity, innovation, problem-solving, decision-making, morale and team performance. As team leader of a motor racing team you are responsible for designing and building the team. There are many challenges building a team - your presentation should consider the following:

1. Team selection techniques.

2. Ideal team size before subdivision.

3. Why teams win, why teams fail.

4. Team development phases.

5. Does the team leader need to be a technical expert?

22

Project Leadership

Learning Outcomes

After reading this chapter, you should be able to;

Understand how leadership styles relate to decision making

Understand motivation theory

Understand how to respond to interpersonal conflict

For project managers to be effective and successful they must not only demonstrate efficient administrative skills and technical know how, but must also practice an appropriate style of leadership. The leadership style used can profoundly impact employee morale and productivity, so that the success of a project may be directly dependent on good leadership. The APM bok says; '... *leadership is about setting goals and objectives and generating enthusiasm and motivation amongst the project team, and stakeholders, to work towards those objectives*.'

1. Leadership Styles

Leadership styles can be related to how the project manager and the team make decisions; consider the autocratic to democratic continuum. The leadership style used by the manager may depend on the type of decisions required, the pressures prevalent at the time and the type of people they are working with. The continuum of leadership styles relating to decision-making may be conveniently subdivided into a number of categories as shown in figure 22.1:

The six stages from autocratic to democratic leadership are:

1. **Autocratic (isolated decision):** The project manager solves the problem or makes the decision independently of the team, using information available at the time - there is no communication with the team members.
2. **Autocratic (informed decision):** The project manager obtains the necessary information from the team members then decides on the solution to the problem independently.
3. **Consultative Autocratic (discuss with individuals):** The project manager shares the problem with the team members individually, gathering their ideas and suggestions - then the project manager makes the decision independently.
4. **Consultative Autocratic (discuss with team):** The project manager shares the problem with the team members as a group - then the project manager makes the decision independently.
5. **Democratic:** The project manager shares the problem with the team members - then together they make the decision as a group - majority vote.
6. **Laissez-faire:** The project manager gives the problem to the team and lets them make the decision themselves - this is a policy of non-interference.

Even though the project manager may make the final decision, how the project manager sells the decision to the team is important. There is a big difference between telling someone what to do and using persuasive argument. The following questions are a guide to selecting the appropriate leadership style.

- Is one decision likely to be better than another? If not, go for number 1.
- Does the leader know enough to make the decision independently? If not avoid number 1.
- Is the problem clear and structured? If not use numbers 4 or 5.
- Must the team members accept the decision? If not then numbers 1 and 2 are possibilities, if they do then use numbers 4 or 5.
- Will the team members accept the manager's decision? If not then number 5 is preferable.
- Do the team members share the project manager's goals for the organisation? If not then number 5 is risky.
- Are the team members likely to conflict with each other? If yes then number 4 is better than 5.

Figure 22.1: Decision-Making Continuum

| 1 | 2 | 3 | 4 | 5 | 6 |

Boss makes the decision   Team makes the decision

The project manager may use all of the above methods on a project as the circumstances dictate. The concept of shared leadership is fundamental for project management and effective team building because it requires participation and involvement of all the team members. The project manager must delegate some authority to the team and in so doing the project manager will become more of a team member and the team members will assume more of a leadership role. This encourages the team members to participate in problem-solving and decision-making and accept the responsibility for the project achieving its goals. This will not only enhance the team's commitment, but also give the team a strong feeling of ownership.

2. Action-Centred Leadership

Action-centred leadership was originally developed by **John Adair** for leadership training at Sandhurst Military Academy. It is now widely applied to the commercial environment. John Adair has published a number of books on leadership and team work. Action-centred leadership focuses on the three basic project needs:

- Individual's needs
- Team's needs
- Task's needs.

These needs are presented as intersecting circles to indicate the separate needs and mutually overlapping needs. *Action-centred leadership* neatly combines the **motivation** theories for the individual's needs with the **team building** theories for the team's needs and the **project planning and control techniques** for the task's needs.

Individual's Needs: The individual's needs should be considered first, because if the individual's basic needs are not being satisfied then that person is unlikely to be able to contribute effectively to the team or task. A person with a serious problem at home, for example, will be mentally preoccupied. Only when the individual's problems have been resolved can they apply themselves effectively through the team to perform the task.

Team's Needs: For the team to be effective the individual team members must work together and interact as a team under a *single point of responsibility*, the team leader or the project manager.

Task's Needs: With both the individual's needs and the team's needs addressed, the project team is now in a position to effectively apply themselves to address the task's needs. The task's needs are to deliver the project's objectives; scope, time, cost and quality through an effective planning and control system that includes integrating the project process, communication, organisation structures and risk management.

At the end of the day the success of the project may be determined by the team's ability to effectively solve problems and be committed to their decisions.

Figure 22.2: Action Centred Leadership

3. Motivation

The term motivation is often misunderstood and misused in the managerial context. Motivation is an inner force that causes or induces someone to be inspired to do something. However, what inspires one person may not inspire another. And what inspires an individual in one set of circumstances may not inspire the individual in another. The manager's task is to influence the work situation in such a way as to encourage the individuals to inspire and motivate themselves to achieve the project's goals. When we assess a person's ability to complete a job successfully it can be subdivided into ability and commitment.

Performance = Ability x Commitment

Ability: Ability describes the personal qualities and competency a person brings to the job. These are qualities of skill (welding or programming for example) that enable a person to perform a task, and give them the capacity to cope with the demands of the job. A person's level of calibre is associated with their innate ability and the amount of training and experience they have acquired.

Commitment: The performance of an individual, however, also depends on their willingness and drive to complete the task, in other words, their commitment. Unlike ability, commitment is not a fixed commodity, it changes in response to conditions and situations the individual encounters.

To this extent, the manager must use an appropriate style of leadership to control the working environment in such a manner that the workforce will be committed to the task and so inspire and motivate themselves to achieve the objectives of the project. Therefore to achieve maximum output from the workforce the manager must address both ability and commitment.

4. Maslow's Hierarchy of Needs

Maslow's experiments in a Californian electronics factory, promoted theory Z, which outlined that workers needed secure structures and a sense of direction to maintain high standards and goals. The corner stone of motivation theory is Maslow's *hierarchy of needs*, which was first published in 1954. Maslow made the assumption that people work in order to satisfy various needs. Maslow stated that motivation is an unconscious attempt on behalf of the individual to satisfy certain inner needs. He expressed this in the form of a hierarchy.

The hierarchy illustrates a priority of needs (see figure 22.3). Maslow indicated that one is always striving to achieve the higher order needs, but this can only be achieved once the lower order needs have been satisfied.

Physiological Needs: This refers to the needs of the body to survive and self-preservation - the most fundamental need of all. If you were to be deprived of air to breath or food to eat, you would become totally preoccupied trying to acquire these lower order needs in preference to any other need. People who are addicted to drugs may adopt antisocial behaviour to satisfy these needs (stealing). However, once these needs have been fulfilled offering them more of what they wanted would have no motivational value.

Security and Safety Needs: This refers not only to the obvious immediate concerns for the continuity of job, income and protection from accident and physical danger, but also concerns fear of disapproval, comments against your personality and character, risk of failure and unfair criticism, which may be seen as psychologically damaging. When you have reached a level of financial security that satisfies, you will only want to ensure that you stay at that financial level. When the security needs are reasonably well satisfied you are unlikely to be motivated towards activities aimed at increasing security still further.

We generally prefer a safe, predictable environment to one plagued by unforeseen events. This protective desire may prompt us to be concerned with insurance and with jobs that offer security. Working on projects is a moot point - what are the persons feelings as the project moves to completion and their contract is terminated? If there is not another project in the pipeline then this security need will prevail. Security needs do not dominate our lives except in times of emergency or danger.

Social and Love Needs: This refers to the need to associate with other people, our need to be accepted by others and belong to a team or group. Sharing our lives with others is important to most of us, and we generally react quickly to the possibility that this need will be denied. We satisfy our love needs through our family and close

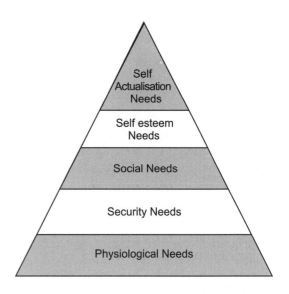

Figure 22.3: Maslow's Hierarchy of Needs

friends. We desire the approval and acceptance of our fellow workers and the many groups of people we associate with and with whom we tend to identify ourselves. We alter our behaviour and even our standards in order to be accepted by our chosen friends and groups. The lonely hearts clubs of this world owe their existence to this powerful need to give and share friendship and love.

Self-Esteem Needs: This refers to a person's **ego** needs, which drives the person to feel wanted and important within their own working group. This need for recognition, respect, prestige and status is a higher order need. This need goes beyond the more passive need to belong to ..... or to be loved by....... - to a more active desire for recognition and self-respect. Self-esteem needs involves self-evaluation, the desire for reputation or prestige, recognition, attention, importance or appreciation. In our culture self-esteem needs are particularly important. Satisfaction of self-esteem needs leads to self-confidence and a feeling of personal worth.

Self-esteem needs are often accompanied by many frustrations and personal conflicts, since people desire not only recognition and attention by their chosen groups but also the self-respect and status that their moral, social, and religious standards call for. When the chosen group calls for behaviour that conflicts with a person's standards, that person must make heroic choices in order to remain well adjusted. People play many roles in order to satisfy some of the different groups and team cultures to which they belong.

Self-Actualisation Needs: This refers to a person's own self-fulfilment and self-realisation - our desire to reach the height of our personal abilities and talents. In Maslow's words, *"What a man can be, he must be."* This category of need includes creativity, achievement, competence and productivity. This is the highest of all the needs. This need becomes increasingly important as the previous needs are satisfied. Maslow described self-actualised people as having the following characteristics:

- A more efficient perception of reality.
- Increased acceptance of self, of others and of nature.
- Spontaneity, simplicity and naturalness.
- Problem-centred rather than ego-centred.
- Increased detachment and desire for privacy.
- Ability to be independent of their physical and social environment.
- Freshness of appreciation and richness of emotional reaction.
- Higher frequency of '*peak*' mystic, or transcendent experiences.
- Increased identification with and feeling of mankind.
- Deeper, more profound interpersonal relationships.
- A more democratic character structure.
- Strongly ethical - able to distinguish clearly between means and ends.
- A natural, spontaneous creativity.

The rank and practical importance of these needs depends on the degree to which each is satisfied, because this degree of satisfaction is constantly changing. Maslow believed people have a need to grow and develop (self-actualise). By using and developing their capacities people begin to self-actualise, they experience satisfaction and enjoyment. Self-actualisation is the highest need - as this need is satisfied it is replaced with new areas or targets to achieve, causing a continuous process. Self-actualisation, therefore, differs from the other needs because it can never be satisfied!

The hierarchy of needs has an important impact on management thinking because it provides a powerful instrument for predicting the outcome of responses by individuals within the organisation. In organisations this self-actualisation need can exhibit a high desire for promotion. Large companies provide career opportunities through career development and training, this can satisfy a need of self-development and improve promotion prospects. Self-actualisation seems to be an intrinsic desire and not directly related to rewards of money.

Motivation Cycle: The motivation cycle outlines the dynamic and changeable nature of motivation. When a need becomes unsatisfied it creates within the individual a kind of tension, which in turn creates a driving force or impetus towards certain actions or behaviour. This behaviour will be aimed at satisfying the need and when the need is satisfied the tension is relieved, but now the cycle starts all over again with respect to another need.

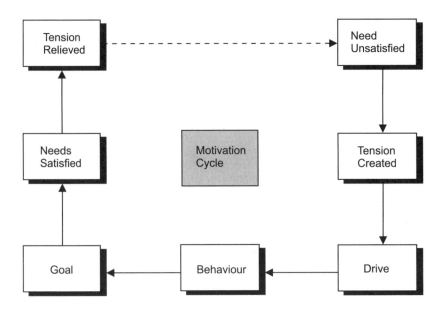

Figure 22.4: Motivation Cycle (from unsatisfied need to tension relieved)

5. Herzberg's Motivation and Hygiene Factors

Frederick Herzberg, a consultant for AT&T, preached "*Job enrichment and individual development*". Herzberg's theory was designed to improve our understanding of working people, what factors determine job satisfaction and what determines job dissatisfaction. Herzberg found these were separate independent factors operating at the same time. Here the term motivation indicates factors that increase your commitment to the job, while hygiene factors will cause a sense of grievance leading to your job dissatisfaction and hence a reduction of motivation and commitment.

A hygiene factor can be likened to a sewer, when it fails it becomes extremely important to people in the vicinity that it should be repaired as quickly as possible!!!! However, once repaired the sewer now loses importance to those people concerned, and improving its efficiency still further is of little interest.

Herzberg presented his motivation and hygiene factors in figure 22.5 where the horizontal axis indicates the frequency with which the factor was reported as causing high morale or causing a sense of grievance. The factors are listed vertically, sorted by high morale, while the depth of each box indicates how long the feeling lasted.

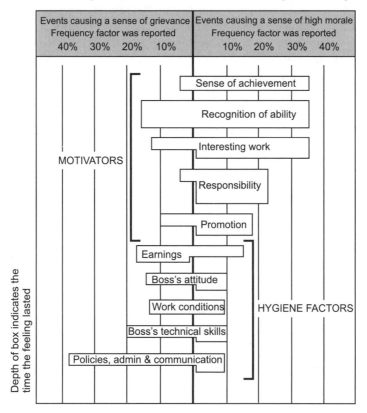

Figure 22.5: Herzberg's Motivation and Hygiene Factors

The analysis indicates some interesting findings:
- Earnings, although a motivator for a short period of time were mostly reported as a hygiene factor. This means that even if the employees are paid above average salary, they will only be motivated for a short period of time, until their new salary becomes their norm. If, however, they are paid less than their colleagues they will quickly become dissatisfied.
- Once the working conditions are at an acceptable level, improving them further will not necessarily stimulate additional effort or commitment.
- On the positive side there can be no substitute for factors like opportunity to gain a sense of achievement, recognition of ability, more interesting work, greater responsibility and opportunities for promotion.

The motivation theories outlined have the benefit of being mutually supportive. Herzberg's motivators for example, relate closely with Maslow's hierarchy of needs.

6. Conflict

All projects are subjected to some degree of interpersonal conflict, so it is important for the project manager to recognise the *symptoms* of group conflict and disruptive behaviour and develop a plan to minimise their negative impact on the team and project objectives. Some of the symptoms are:

- Poor communication laterally and vertically - decisions taken on incomplete information. Two levels in the same company are moving in different directions on the same problem.
- Inter-group hostility and jealousy expressed as; "*They never tell us anything*" or "*They expect us to know by intuition*".
- Interpersonal friction affects the relationships between individuals where it can deteriorate to icy formality or argument. Project problems seem to focus on people and personalities.
- Escalation of arbitration by senior management.
- Proliferation of rules and regulations - it becomes more and more difficult to do anything without riding roughshod over somebody's regulations.
- Low morale expressed as frustration and inefficiency.

Control of Conflict: When conflict symptoms and behaviours of concern have been identified the individuals should discuss them promptly and openly. If there are conflicts that cannot be addressed by rearranging the ecology to create an amenable working environment, then consider the following:

- **Arbitration:** Conduct arbitration at a low level. This solution is useful when the conflict is apparent and specific, but not very useful in episodic or continual conflict. Try and agree on an arbitrator at the outset of the project, because later when there is conflict, the parties will each nominate a person sympathetic to their own view.

- **Co-ordination Device:** A position is created in the company between the conflicting parties. This eliminates the contact and so eliminates the conflict. There are, however, additional administration costs for the company. This device is not an effective solution for episodic or occasional conflict, but useful where the conflicting pressures are continuous.
- **Negotiation:** An interesting variation on confrontation is an approach called role negotiation, where conflicting parties negotiate and trade items of behaviour, e.g. *"I will stop doing X if you stop doing Y"*. This method goes a long way to reduce the pains of conflict, particularly between individuals, although it may leave the underlying problem untouched.
- **Separation:** If interaction increases the depth of the sentiments then separation should cool them down. This solution will work if the true cause of the conflict is two incompatible individuals, incompatible in personality, or more often with relative status inappropriate to the situation. To separate the individuals, transferring one to another department may be a successful strategy. This will at least allow both parties to be productive in their different areas.
- **Withdrawal and Neglect:** Retreating from an actual or potential conflict situation - this is not a solution in itself unless it is trivial, but it could provide a cooling off period while a better solution is found.
- **Smoothing:** Smoothing emphasises the use of agreement rather than focusing on the differences of opinion. Smoothing allows the work to continue and can smooth ruffled feelings and defuse the situation, but is only a temporary solution.
- **Rules and Regulations:** Striving to compile rules, regulations and procedures by negotiation and agreement - this approach is useful when the conflict is recurrent and predictable, but should not be regarded as a permanent solution.
- **Compromising:** Is the search for solutions to bring some degree of satisfaction to both conflicting parties.
- **Confrontation:** A technique much favoured by those who believe in openness. This strategy will be effective, if the issue can be clearly defined and is not a symptom of more underlying differences. Confrontation and inter-group meetings can greatly increase understanding of people's views, but they cannot be a complete substitute from the ecological point of view.
- **Forcing:** Is the act of pushing one's point of view at the potential expense of another person's point of view.
- **Problem-Solving:** Is used to treat conflict as a technical problem to be solved by reasoned argument and examining the alternatives.

Permanent solutions are generally only reached by compromise, confrontation or problem-solving. Research by Thamhain and Wilemon suggest that forcing and withdrawal appears to increase conflict with functional support departments, while confrontation, compromise and smoothing tends to reduce conflict.

7. Delegation

Skilful delegation is the key to effective project management. Through delegation the project manager can improve project team efficiency, develop employee ability and contribute to the growth of the company.

Feedback from commerce and industry suggests, however, that delegation is not a widely practised technique and that project managers are held back by performing trifling tasks themselves. Project managers become overworked, overtaxed, and at the same time miss the opportunity to encourage initiative and motivate growth among their employees. Delegation has three basic elements:

- Assign a function, duty or task to an employee.
- Allocate sufficient authority so that the employee can command the resources necessary to accomplish the assignment.
- Gain commitment from the employee for the satisfactory completion of the task.

The employee must understand that they will be held accountable for the work delegated, but bear in mind that under performance may indicate that further training of the employee is required. It should always be remembered that delegating work will not reduce the project manager's ultimate responsibility and accountability for the task - this is not transferable. However, although it is unreasonable to imply that the project manager should be responsible for the actions of a team worker, it does mean the project manager is responsible for setting up the system to ensure that the team worker can do the job correctly.

Method of Delegation: The following list is a managerial guide to delegate a task and authority to a subordinate.

- Accept the need to delegate.
- Develop a detailed plan for delegation.
- Obtain the supervisor's approval for your delegation plan.
- Establish a climate of mutual confidence and trust (this will not happen over night).
- Select the function, duties and tasks to be delegated and assigned.
- Establish clear lines of authority and responsibility and ensure that they are understood by all.
- Adopt a constructive attitude, demonstrate patience when a subordinate makes a mistake.
- Monitor performance and provide frequent feedback.
- Reward effective delegation.

The crunch comes when the subordinate makes a poor decision, how do you react? Try not to reverse the decision without discussing it with them first, otherwise they are unlikely to be motivated to make another decision - they will rather refer decisions to you instead - and now you are back to square one.

Key Points:

- The decision-making continuum outlines how teams make decisions.
- Herzberg's motivation and hygiene factors outline what factors motivate team members to perform, while also identifying what causes a sense of grievance.
- As the work load increases the project manager must delegate or risk becoming bogged down performing trivial tasks.

Case Study and Exercises:

Is there a difference between a leader and a manager??? The Economist says *'A leader challenges the status quo; a manager accepts it. A manager's prime role is to prevent the complexity of a modern company degenerating into chaos. Managers take details - like financial planning, quality, stock levels, staffing and market research - and bring order, consistency and control to them. To managers, systems and structure are all. Because the abilities needed to lead and manage are so different, an aptitude for both is rarely in one larger-than-life individual. But because their kind are hard to find, companies cannot rely on locating a born leader-manager. Instead, firms may find it easier to build 'leadership teams', combining the talents of their best leaders with those of their top managers. This does not mean simply lumping them all together on the company board and crossing corporate fingers - there must be a conscious effort to get leaders and managers to influence each other.'*

Are you a leader or a manager??? Give your answer with respect to the following:

1. Decision making.
2. Action centred leadership.
3. Motivation.
4. Conflict resolution.
5. Delegation.

"Delegation doesn't always explode in your face"

Appendix 1 will develop the *critical path method* and *network diagram*. Please note the solution is detailed for the beginner - if this is understood I suggest you move on to appendix 2 where this worked example is developed further:

Preceding Activity	Succeeding Activity
Start	100
100	200
100	300
100	400
200	500
300	600
400	700
500	800
600	800
700	800
800	Finish

Activity	Duration
100	2
200	3
300	6
400	2
500	5
600	7
700	3
800	1

Table 1: Logic Table and Activity Data

Figure 1: Activity Box

ES = Early Start   EF = Early Finish
000 = Activity Number
F   = Float   DUR = Duration
LS = Late Start   LF = Late Finish

The logical relationship between the activities are shown as lines between the boxes, for example, from the logic table 1, activity 100 precedes the constraint while activity 200 succeeds the constraint. The lines are generally drawn horizontally or vertically, leaving or entering from the side of the box. The start of the project is from the left side of the page, moving right and downwards (figure 2).

Figure 2: Logic Relationship

Step 1: Draw the *network diagram*. From the logic table, look at the first four lines (table 2):

Table 2: Logic Table
(extract from table 1)

Preceding Activity	Succeeding Duration
Start	100
100	200
100	300
100	400

Activity 100 is drawn first, because this is the start activity, the other three activities (200, 300, 400) follow, finish-to-start (see figure 3).

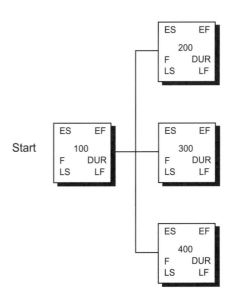

Figure 3: Network Diagram

Step 2: The next three lines from the logic table 1 are (table 3):

Preceding Activity	Succeeding Duration
200	500
300	600
400	700

Table 3: Logic Table
(extract from table 1)

This means that activity 500 follows 200, activity 600 follows 300 and activity 700 follows 400 (figure 4).

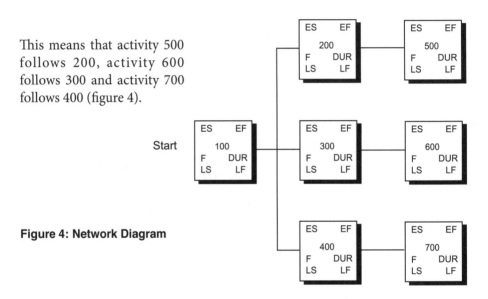

Figure 4: Network Diagram

Step 3: The last four lines of the logic table 1 are (table 4):

Preceding Activity	Succeeding Duration
500	800
600	800
700	800
800	Finish

Table 4: Logic Table
(extract from table 1)

This means activities 500, 600 and 700 must be completed before 800 can start and activity 800 is the last activity of the project (figure 5).

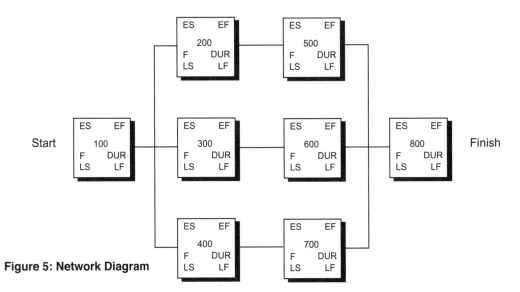

Figure 5: Network Diagram

The *network diagram* showing the logical relationships is now complete (figure 5). The *network diagram* on its own is an important presentation because it shows the sequence of work, besides the *critical path method* this is also a key input document for the *quality control plan*.

Step 4: The next step is to transfer the activity durations from the activity table (see table 1) to the activity boxes in the position marked **'dur'** (figure 6).

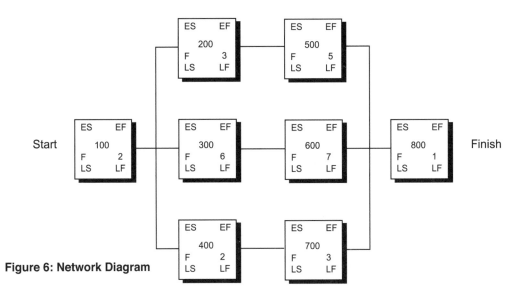

Figure 6: Network Diagram

Step 5: We now perform the forward pass to determine the *early start* (ES) and *early finish* (EF) of each activity. Activity 100 starts on day 1 or in calendar notation (say) 1st May. The activity has a duration of 2 days, so it will finish on day 2, or 2nd May. The equation is: EF = ES + duration - 1

Step 6: If the EF of activity 100 is 2nd May, then the ES of activities 200, 300 and 400 is the following day 3rd May. Calculate the EF for 200, 300 and 400 (figure 7).

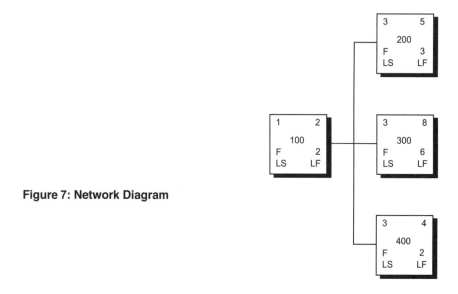

Figure 7: Network Diagram

Step 7: Calculate ES and EF for the activities 500, 600 and 700 (figure 8).

Figure 8: Network Diagram

Step 8: We now have an interesting situation, when there are many activities leading into one activity, select the highest EF value to give the ES for the following activity. This means activity 800 cannot start until all the preceding activities have finished (figure 9).

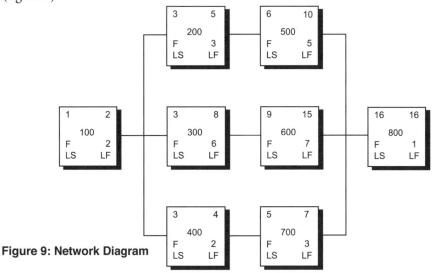

Figure 9: Network Diagram

Step 9: The EF of activity 800 is a keydate, as this indicates the earliest date it is possible to complete the project, in this case 16th May.

Step 10: We now perform a **backward pass** to determine the LS and LF of each activity. Starting with activity 800 set the LF to be the same as its EF (16th May), then work backwards to find the late start for each activity. The equation is:

LS = LF - duration + 1 (figure 10).

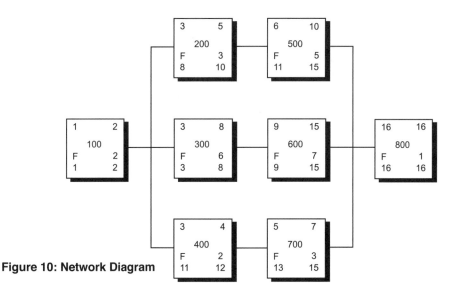

Figure 10: Network Diagram

Note: On the backward pass where there are many activities leading into one activity select the lowest number or date. This ensures that all the preceding activities have finished before the succeeding activities start.

Step 11: The next step is to calculate the activity float. Use the following equation:

Float = LS - ES

Float = 1 - 1 = 0 (for activity 100)

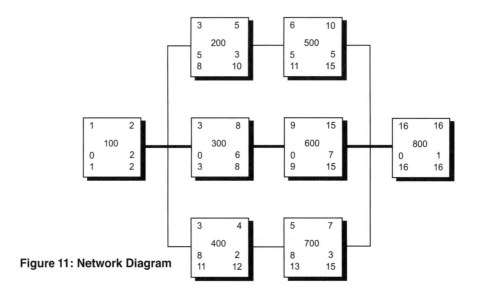

Figure 11: Network Diagram

Using this equation the float for all the activities can be calculated.

The critical path by definition links all the activities with zero float. It is important to identify the critical path, because if any of these activities are delayed the end date of the project will be extended. In this case the following activities have zero float; 100, 300, 600 and 800. It is normal practice to highlight the critical path in heavy print, double lines or red ink to make them standout.

Appendix 2

This worked example is a continuation from appendix 1 which developed the *network diagram*. Here the *critical path method* model will be developed further, to include; project acceleration (crashing resources), the expenditure S curve, the *cashflow statement* and the revised Gantt chart. To calculate the above, additional activity information is required together with data capture at timenow 4 and 8.

Activity Number	Normal Time	Resources Per Day	Total Normal Cost $	Crash Time	Total Crash Cost $	Additional Crash Cost Per Day
	A		B	C	D	[D-B]/[A-C]
100	2	2	$100	1	$200	$100
200	3	3	$150	2	$200	$50
300	6	3	$60	3	$120	$20
400	2	2	$100	2	$100	-
500	5	3	$50	4	$60	$10
600	7	2	$210	4	$255	$15
700	3	3	$90	2	$145	$55
800	1	2	$50	1	$50	-

Table 1: Activity Data (project acceleration)

Step 1: Appendix 1 analysed the network to give completion on day 16. Consider the situation where the client requests the contractor to advise the cost implication to complete the project in 10 days, or shorten the project by 6 days (see figure 1).

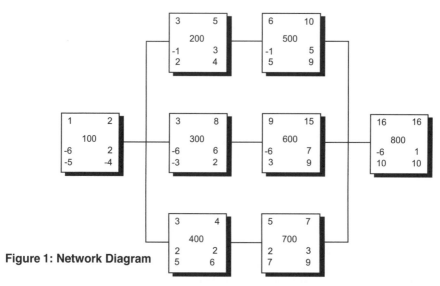

Figure 1: Network Diagram

The *network diagram* is first re-analysed by setting the LF of activity 800 to day 10, or 10th May and then performing a **backwards pass** to calculate the new LS, LF and float for all the activities. The negative float will indicate which activities need to be crashed and by how much. A priority list is then established (see table 2) with least cost to crash, first.

Activity	Cost to Crash	Priority
600	$15	1
300	$20	2
100	$100	3

Table 2: Priority List of Critical Activities

Crash by	Cost	(days x Activity no)
3 days	$45	(3 x 600)
4 days	$65	(3 x 600) + (1 x 300)
5 days	$85	(3 x 600) + (2 x 300)
6 days	$115	(3 x 600) + (3 x 300) + (1 x 500)

Table 3: Cost to Crash the Project by 3 to 6 days

After crashing an activity the network should be reprocessed to see if any other paths have gone critical. Note here how the network arm (200, 500) also goes critical when the target completion date is reduced to 10 days. For this example, the client decides not to crash the project.

Step 2: The information from the forward pass, backward pass and float calculations (see appendix 1) are usually presented in a tabular format (see table 4).

Activity Number	Duration (days)	Early Start	Early Finish	Late Start	Late Finish	Float (Days)
100	2	1 May	2 May	1 May	2 May	0
200	3	3 May	5 May	8 May	10 May	5
300	6	3 May	8 May	3 May	8 May	0
400	2	3 May	4 May	11 May	12 May	8
500	5	6 May	10 May	11 May	15 May	5
600	7	9 May	15 May	9 May	15 May	0
700	3	5 May	7 May	13 May	15 May	8
800	1	16 May	16 May	16 May	16 May	0

Table 4: Activity Data (transferred from appendix 1, figure 11, network diagram)

Step 3: The data can now be used to produce a graphical Gantt chart. For this example the Gantt chart will be ordered by activity number, however, in industry it is common to order by *early start* (ES) (see figure 2).

Figure 2: Early Start Gantt Chart (showing resources)

The Gantt chart is further enhanced by including the number of resources required per day which are summed daily to give the resource histogram. The resource histogram indicates the number of men required per day. For this example the company only has six men available, this means there will be an overload on days 3, 4, 5, 6 and 7th May (see figure 3).

Step 4: Resource overload is initially addressed by moving activities within their float. Try moving activities 400 and 700 to their LS (see figure 3).

Activity list	1	2	3	4	5	6	7	8	9	10	11	12	13	14	15	16
100	2	2														
200			3	3	3	-	-	-	-	- ◆						
300			3	3	3	3	3	3								
400 >>>			-	-	-	-	-	-	-	-	2	2 ◆				
500						3	3	3	3	3	-	-	-	-	- ◆	
600									2	2	2	2	2	2	2	
700 >>>					-	-	-	-	-	-	-	-	3	3	3 ◆	
800																2
Total	2	2	6	6	6	6	6	6	5	5	4	4	5	5	5	2

Figure 3: Gantt Chart and Resource Histogram (after moving 400 and 700)

Activity list		DAYS															
		1	2	3	4	5	6	7	8	9	10	11	12	13	14	15	16
100		2	2														
200				3	3	3	-	-	-	-	- ♦						
300				3	3	3	3	3	3								
400	>>>			-	-	-	2	2	-	-	-	-	- ♦				
500	>>>						-	-	3	3	3	3	3	-	-	- ♦	
600										2	2	2	2	2	2	2	
700	>>>						-	-	-	-	-	-	-	3	3	3 ♦	
800																	2
Total		2	2	6	6	6	5	5	6	5	5	5	5	5	5	5	2

Manpower Resource Histogram

Figure 4: Resource Histogram (A second way to smooth the resources is to move activity 400 to 6th May, 500 to 8th May and 700 to 13th May)

Activity list		DAYS															
		1	2	3	4	5	6	7	8	9	10	11	12	13	14	15	16
100		2	2														
200	>>>			-	-	-	-	-	3	3	3 ♦						
300				3	3	3	3	3	3								
400				2	2	-	-	-	-	-	-	-	- ♦				
500	>>>						-	-	-	-	-	3	3	3	3	3 ♦	
600										2	2	2	2	2	2	2	
700						3	3	3	-	-	-	-	-	-	-	- ♦	
800																	2
Total		2	2	5	5	6	6	6	6	5	5	5	5	5	5	5	2

Manpower Resource Histogram

Figure 5: Resource Histogram (A third way to smooth the resources would be to move activities 200 and 500 to their LS)

Mathematically there are many ways to smooth the resources as shown here. Care must be taken not to change the activity logic, for instance if activity 200 has moved, then activity 500 must also be moved because of their *finish-to-start* relationship (see *network diagram* figure 1).

Step 5: If the company resources were to be reduced further to 5 men, then moving activities within their float would not be sufficient, other methods need to be considered:

- **Split the activity** - this option is not always feasible or efficient.
- **Time-limited smoothing** - here the end date of the project is fixed, so where the resources are overloaded more men must be assigned.
- **Resource-limited smoothing** - here the maximum number of a resource is fixed, in this case it is 5 men. To achieve this lower resource level it will be necessary to move an activity on the critical path, thus extending the end date of the project.

Step 6: The next step is to consider the cashflow. This will be influenced by the timing of the costs, for this example the two extremes, ES and LS will be considered. The cost per day is assumed to be linear over the activity, the expenses are shown in the bars. The expenses are calculated per day by adding vertically, then accumulated from left to right (see figures 6 and 7).

Activity list	DAYS															
	1	2	3	4	5	6	7	8	9	10	11	12	13	14	15	16
100	50	50														
200			50	50	50	-	-	-	-	- ◆						
300			10	10	10	10	10	10								
400			50	50	-	-	-	-	-	-	-	- ◆				
500						10	10	10	10	10	-	-	-	-	-	◆
600									30	30	30	30	30	30	30	
700					30	30	30	-	-	-	-	-	-	-	◆	
800																50
Expenses per day	50	50	110	110	90	50	50	20	40	40	30	30	30	30	30	50
Accumulated expenses	50	100	210	320	410	460	510	530	570	610	640	670	700	730	760	810

Figure 6: Early Start Gantt Chart (showing expenses)

Activity list	DAYS															
	1	2	3	4	5	6	7	8	9	10	11	12	13	14	15	16
100	50	50														
200			-	-	-	-	-	50	50	50◆						
300			10	10	10	10	10	10								
400			-	-	-	-	-	-	-	-	50	50◆				
500						-	-	-	-	-	10	10	10	10	10◆	
600									30	30	30	30	30	30	30	
700								-	-	-	-	-	30	30	30◆	
800																50
Expenses per day	50	50	10	10	10	10	10	60	80	80	90	90	70	70	70	50
Accumulated expenses	50	100	110	120	130	140	150	210	290	370	460	550	620	690	760	810

Figure 7: Late Start Gantt Chart (showing expenses)

The two expense curves can now be plotted cost against time. The expense curve, also called *budgeted cost for work scheduled* (BCWS) is the link between the CPM and the budget (see figure 8).

This double curve between ES and LS is often called the **banana curve** because of its shape. The important feature here is to appreciate the affect scheduling has on the cashflow.

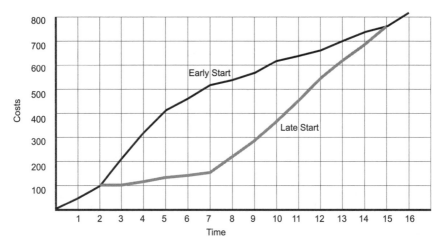

Figure 8: BCWS (S Curve of early start and late start expenses)

Step 7: This step will show how the *cashflow statement* is linked with the *scheduled Gantt chart*. Using the following information a *cashflow statement* will be developed for every period (for this example make every four time units or days equal to one period), also assume you are considering the cashflow from the contractor's perspective.

- For period 1 the brought forward amount is zero.
- Income is calculated at cost plus 30% as they occur on the ES Gantt chart.
- The client takes 1 period to pay and a completion bonus of $200 will be paid with the final invoice (see table 5).

Time Units	0-4	5-8	9-12	13-16	17-20
Periods	1	2	3	4	5
Costs	$320	$210	$140	$140	
Income (times 1.3)		$416	$273	$182	$182
Bonus					$200

Table 5: Cashflow (income)

- Cost of sales:

  [1] Overheads are $50 per period

  [2] Activity costs from the ES Gantt chart (assume costs are split 50:50 between labour and materials). The labour costs are paid in the period they occur (see table 6).

Time Units	0-4	5-8	9-12	13-16	17-20
Periods	1	2	3	4	5
Total Costs	$320	$210	$140	$140	
Labour Coats	$160	$105	$70	$70	

Table 6: Cashflow (Labour costs)

  [3] The material supplier gives 1 period to pay, therefore the cashflow is moved forward 1 period (see table 7).

Time Units	0-4	5-8	9-12	13-16	17-20
Periods	1	2	3	4	5
Total Costs	$320	$210	$140	$140	$0
Material Coats	$0	$160	$105	$70	$70

Table 7: Cashflow (Material costs)

  [4] If the closing statement is negative the funds can be borrowed @ 10% per period, these bank charges are then levied in the following period. Round up 0.5 and above if necessary (see table 8).

Time Units	0-4	5-8	9-12	13-16	17-20
Brought forward	$0	($210)	($130)	($95)	($113)
Income	$0	$416	$273	$185	$182
Completion Bonus	-	-	-	-	$320
Total available [A]	**$0**	**$206**	**$143**	**$87**	**$269**
Overheads	$50	$50	$50	$50	$0
Labour	$160	$105	$70	$70	$0
Material	$0	$160	$105	$70	$70
Interest	$0	$21	$13	$10	$11
Total Payment [B]	**$210**	**$336**	**$238**	**$200**	**$81**
Closing Amount [A-B]	**($210)**	**($130)**	**($95)**	**($113)**	**($188)**

Table 8: Cashflow Statement

From the *cashflow statement* it is obvious that the project will require up-front financing, but will, however, go positive during the last period.

Step 8: The above calculations form the main part of the **baseline plan**, once this information is available the project can be executed. Using the data capture at timenow 4 the revised Gantt chart can be drawn in conjunction with the *network diagram*, see appendix 1.

Activity Number	Actual Start	Actual Finish	Percentage Complete	Remaining Duration
100	1 May	2 May	100%	-
200	2 May	4 May	100%	-
300	3 May	-	-	5
400	4 May	-	50%	-

Table 9: Data Capture at Timenow 4

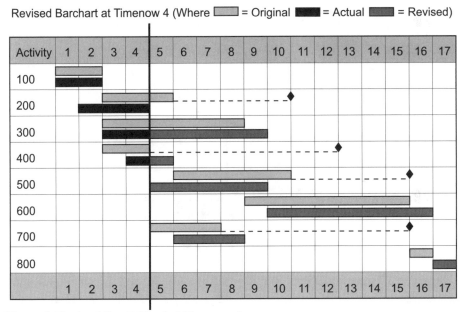

Revised Barchart at Timenow 4 (Where ☐ = Original ■ = Actual ▨ = Revised)

Figure 9: Revised Gantt Chart at Timenow 4

Timenow 4: The analysis at timenow 4 shows that activity 100 has started and finished as planned, but 200 started and finished 1 day early. Because 200 and 500 have a *finish-to-start* relationship, 500 should be able to start 1 day early assuming resources are available. Activity 300 started on time but is going to be finished 1 day late, this will have a knock-on effect and delay 600 and 800 by 1 day. Activity 400 started 1 day late and is estimated to finish 1 day late, this will delay 700 by 1 day. Finally the last activity 800 will be delayed 1 day because 600 is forecast to finish 1 day late.

Activity Number	Actual Start	Actual Finish	Percentage Complete	Remaining Duration
100	1 May	2 May	100%	-
200	2 May	4 May	100%	-
300	3 May	7 May	100%	-
400	4 May	6 May	100%	-
500	5 May	-	-	1
600	6 May	-	-	5
700	7 May	-	50%	-
800	-	-	-	-

Table 10: Data Capture at Timenow 8

Figure 10: Revised Gantt Chart at Timenow 8

Timenow 8: The analysis shows activities 300 and 400 are now finished, 500 and 600 have a remaining duration of 1 and 5 days respectively, 700 is 50% complete which can be mathematically transposed to a remaining duration of 1.5 or round up to 2 days. Because 600 is forecast to finish early, 800 can also finish early on day 14, if the resources are available.

Appendix 3

Appendix 3 will develop financial selection models from the **Project Selection** chapter. Consider the purchasing of a machine for $25,000 with the following cashflow (see table 1):

Cash Flow Timing (Years)	Project Cash Flow ($)
0	($25,000)
1	$5,000
2	$7,000
3	$13,000
4	$16,000

Table 1: Cashflow

The solutions will be presented under the following headings:
- Payback period
- Return on investment
- Net present value (NPV) at 15%
- Internal rate of return (IRR)

Payback Period: If the project starts with a capital outlay of $25,000, the payback period is the time to recover this initial outlay from the cashflow. In this case it will take 3 years (see table 2).

Cash Flow Timing (Years)	Project Cash Flow ($)	Cash Flow Balance ($)
0	($25,000)	($25,000)
1	$5,000	($20,000)
2	$7,000	($13,000)
3	$13,000	$0

Table 2: CashFlow

Return on Investment: The return on investment is determined from the following expression:

Annual profit = $\dfrac{\text{Total gain - Total outlay}}{\text{Number of years invested}}$

The total gain is the same as the total cashflow during the life of the project;

$5,000 + $7,000 + $13,000 + $16,000 = $41,000.

The total outlay is the same as the initial investment = ($25,000). The number of years of the investment is 4 years.

Annual profit = $\dfrac{\$41,000 - \$25,000}{4}$

$= $4000

The annual return on investment is the annual profit expressed as a percentage of the initial investment.

Annual return on investment = $\dfrac{\$4,000}{\$25,000}$ x $\dfrac{100}{1}$ = 16%

Net Present Value (NPV): Using the proforma below, transfer the discount factor at 15% from the discount table (see **Project Selection** chapter), then multiply the cashflow by the discount factor and sum the present values.

Cash Flow Timing (Years)	Discount Factor (15%)	Project Cash Flow	Present Value
0		($25,000)	
1		$5,000	
2		$7,000	
3		$13,000	
4		$16,000	
		NPV	

Table 3: Net Present Value (NPV)

Cash Flow Timing (Years)	Discount Factor (15%)	Project Cash Flow	Present Value
0	1.000	($25,000)	($25,000)
1	0.8696	$5,000	$4,348
2	0.7561	$7,000	$5,293
3	0.6575	$13,000	$8,548
4	0.5718	$16,000	$9,149
		NPV	$2,338

Table 4: NPV Solution

Internal Rate of Return (IRR): The IRR value is the same as the discount factor when the NPV is zero. The IRR figure is found by varying the discount factor until the NPV is zero. The first guess is often a stab in the dark, but it will indicate which way to go. If the NPV is positive increase the discount factor and if the NPV is negative decrease the discount factor.

Cash Flow Timing (Years)	Discount Factor (16%)	Project Cash Flow	Present Value
0	1.000	($25,000)	($25,000)
1	0.8621	$5,000	$4,311
2	0.7432	$7,000	$5,202
3	0.6407	$13,000	$8,329
4	0.5523	$16,000	$8,837
		NPV	$1,679

Table 5: NPV DF 16%

Cash Flow Timing (Years)	Discount Factor (17%)	Project Cash Flow	Present Value
0	1.000	($25,000)	($25,000)
1	0.8547	$5,000	$4,274
2	0.7305	$7,000	$5,114
3	0.6244	$13,000	$8,117
4	0.5337	$16,000	$8,539
		NPV	$1,044

Table 6: NPV DF 17%

Cash Flow Timing (Years)	Discount Factor (18%)	Project Cash Flow	Present Value
0	1.000	($25,000)	($25,000)
1	0.8475	$5,000	$4,348
2	0.7182	$7,000	$5,027
3	0.6086	$13,000	$7,912
4	0.5158	$16,000	$8,253
		NPV	$430

Table 7: NPV DF 18%

Cash Flow Timing (Years)	Discount Factor (19%)	Project Cash Flow	Present Value
0	1.000	($25,000)	($25,000)
1	0.8403	$5,000	$4,202
2	0.7062	$7,000	$4,943
3	0.5934	$13,000	$7,714
4	0.4987	$16,000	$7,979
		NPV	($162)

Table 8: NPV DF 19%

Solution: The discount factor is increased in 1% steps until the NPV value goes negative. The IRR, therefore, lies between 18% and 19%.

This appendix shows how to use a number of project management techniques to plan and control a house building project. From the scope of work and information given, perform the following *earned value* calculations:

- Draw a three level WBS and analyse the CPM
- Draw an ES Gantt chart and resource histogram
- Track the project at timenow 4 and 8

Project Information: The scope of work includes the construction of a house, the outbuildings and landscaping the garden. The main house can be sub-divided into the principle trades: civil, carpenters/plumbers and electricians/painters. The outbuildings consist of a garage and a greenhouse, whilst the landscaping includes the grounds and the fencing. The civil work can be further sub-divided into: foundations, walls and roof. The carpenters and plumbers also includes the doors/windows and built in cupboards (bic's). The electricians and painters also includes the internal finishes.

Activity	Description	Duration	Resources	Costs (BAC)
100	Garage	3	2	$9,000
200	Greenhouse	2	2	$2,000
300	Foundations	1	3	$1,000
400	Walls	3	4	$12,000
500	Roofs	5	2	$10,000
600	Doors	3	2	$6,000
700	Plumbing	2	2	$4,000
800	Bic's	3	1	$6,000
900	Wiring	4	1	$8,000
1000	Finishes	2	2	$4,000
1100	Painting	2	6	$6,000
1200	Driveway	2	3	$8,000
1300	Garden	4	2	$8,000
1400	Fence	4	2	$4,000
			Total	**$88,000**

Table 1: Activity Table

Preceding Activity	Succeeding Activity
Start	300
Start	1200
300	400
1200	400
1200	100
1200	1400
400	700
400	600
400	500
700	1000
600	900

Preceding Activity	Succeeding Activity
800	900
500	800
100	200
200	1100
1000	1100
900	1100
800	1100
1400	1300
1100	Finish
1300	Finish

Table 2: Logic Table (house project)

Figure 1: WBS work packages and CPM activities (house project)

Note: The numbering system for the WBS work packages and the activities are different. This will allow both numbering systems to operate linked and autonomously. One or more activities can be linked to a work package, this gives the planner more flexibility when developing the network logic.

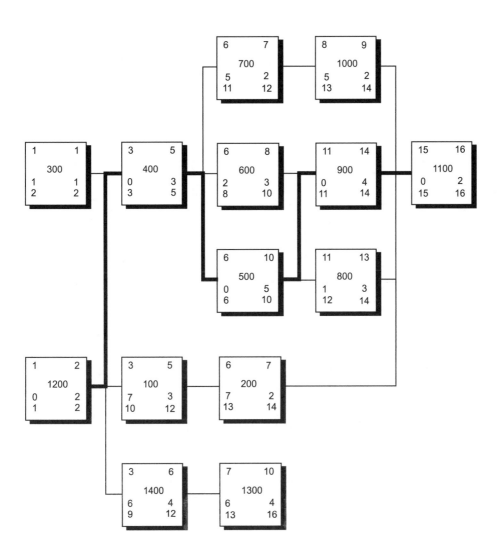

Figure 2: Network Diagram (house project)

Activity Table: The activity table collates the data from the *network diagram* (see figure 2) and presents it in a tabular format.

Activity Number	Description	Early Start	Early Finish	Late Start	Late Finish	Float (Days)
100	Garage	3 May	5 May	10 May	12 May	7
200	Greenhouse	6 May	7 May	13 May	14 May	7
300	Foundations	1 May	1 May	2 May	2 May	1
400	Walls	3 May	5 May	3 May	5 May	0
500	Roof	6 May	10 May	6 May	10 May	0
600	Doors	6 May	8 May	8 May	10 May	2
700	Plumbing	6 May	7 May	11 May	12 May	5
800	Bic's	11 May	13 May	12 May	14 May	1
900	Electrical	11 May	14 May	11 May	14 May	0
1000	Fittings	8 May	9 May	13 May	14 May	5
1100	Painting	15 May	16 May	15 May	16 May	0
1200	Road	1 May	2 May	1 May	2 May	0
1300	Garden	7 May	10 May	13 May	16 May	6
1400	Fence	3 May	6 May	9 May	12 May	6

Table 3: Activity Data (house project)

Early Start Gantt Chart and Resource Histogram: The values from the activity data table (table 3) are transferred to the early start Gantt chart (figure 3). The numbers in the Gantt chart are the resources per day transferred from table 1. These values are added vertically to give the total daily resource requirement and is shown in the resource histogram (figure 3). The daily resource totals are then accumulated to give the running total which gives the characteristic S curve presentation (figure 4). Although this curve is for resources (because the figures were available) a similar curve can be drawn for costs. This curve (figure 4) is generally known as the budgeted cost for work scheduled (BCWS).

Activity	1	2	3	4	5	6	7	8	9	10	11	12	13	14	15	16
100			2	2	2	-	-	-	-	-	-	◆				
200						2	2	-	-	-	-	-	-	◆		
300	3	-	◆													
400			4	4	4											
500						2	2	2	2	2						
600						2	2	2	-	-	◆					
700						2	2	-	-	-	-	◆				
800											1	1	1	◆		
900											1	1	1	1		
1000								2	2	-	-	-	-	◆		
1100															6	6
1200	3	3														
1300						2	2	2	2	-	-	-	-	-	-	◆
1400			2	2	2	2	-	-	-	-	-	◆				
Daily	6	3	8	8	8	10	10	8	6	4	2	2	2	1	6	6
Accum	6	9	17	25	33	43	53	61	67	71	73	75	77	78	84	90

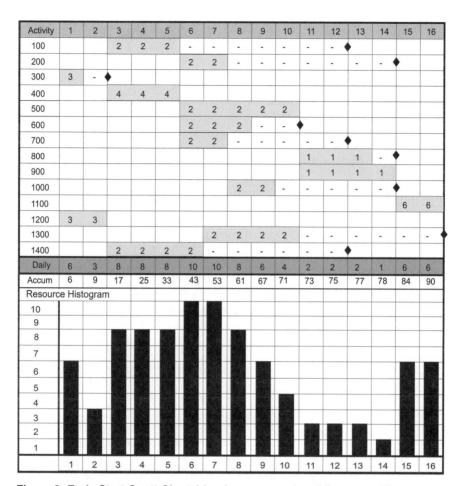

Figure 3: Early Start Gantt Chart (showing resources) **and Resource Histogram**
(showing the total daily resource and the accumulated running total)

Figure 4: BCWS (accumulated resources against time -
assume accumulated costs flow the same curve)

The *resource histogram* (figure 3) indicates the resource requirement per day. For the purpose of this exercise the available resources are assumed to be sufficient.

Expenditure Gantt Chart and Expense Curves: The expenditure Gantt chart assumes a linear cashflow over the activities. The accumulation of the daily expenses will provide the basis for cost control. The BCWS is the integration of cost and time which forms the baseline plan to track the project's performance against (figure 4).

Earned Value	BCWP = PC * BAC
Schedule variance	SV = BCWP - BCWS
Schedule variance %	SV% = SV / BCWS
Cost variance	CV = BCWP - ACWP
Cost variance %	CV% = CV / BCWP
Estimate at completion	EAC = (ACWP / BCWP) * BAC

Table 4: Earned Value Equations (these equations will be used in the earned value analysis)

Data Capture at Timenow 4: The project has now started and the progress information is presented in the following format (table 5).

Activity Number	Actual Costs	Actual Start	Actual Finish	Percentage Complete	Remaining Duration
100	$8,000	3 May	-	67%	-
300	$0	1 May	2 May	100%	-
400	$3,500	4 May	-	33%	-
1200	$7,000	2 May	3 May	100%	-
1300	$1,000	-	-	-	-
1400	$0	4 May	-	25%	-

Table 5: Data Capture at Timenow 4

Activity	BAC	BCWS	PC	BCWP	ACWP	SV	SV%	CV	CV%	EAC
100	$9,000		67%		$8,000					
200	$2,000		0%		$0					
300	$1,000		100%		$0					
400	$12,000		33%		$3,500					
500	$10,000		0%		$0					
600	$6,000		0%		$0					
700	$4,000		0%		$0					
800	$6,000		0%		$0					
900	$8,000		0%		$0					
1000	$4,000		0%		$0					
1100	$6,000		0%		$0					
1200	$8,000		100%		$7,000					
1300	$8,000		0%		$1,000					
1400	$4,000		25%		$0					
Totals	**$88,000**				**$19,500**					

Table 6: Earned Value proforma

Earned Value at Timenow 4: The earned value table provides a simple format to compare the baseline plan with the progress. The partly completed proforma can be completed as a self-test.

Activity	BAC	BCWS	PC	BCWP	ACWP	SV	SV%	CV	CV%	EAC
100	$9,000	$6,000	67%	$6,000	$8,000	$0	0%	($2,000)	(33.3%)	$12,000
200	$2,000	$0	0%	$0	$0	$0	0%	$0	0%	$2,000
300	$1,000	$1,000	100%	$1,000	$0	$0	0%	$1,000	100%	$1,000
400	$12,000	$8,000	33%	$4,000	$3,500	($4,000)	(50%)	$500	(12.5%)	$10,500
500	$10,000	$0	0%	$0	$0	$0	0%	$0	0%	$10,000
600	$6,000	$0	0%	$0	$0	$0	0%	$0	0%	$6,000
700	$4,000	$0	0%	$0	$0	$0	0%	$0	0%	$4,000
800	$6,000	$0	0%	$0	$0	$0	0%	$0	0%	$6,000
900	$8,000	$0	0%	$0	$0	$0	0%	$0	0%	$8,000
1000	$4,000	$0	0%	$0	$0	$0	0%	$0	0%	$4,000
1100	$6,000	$0	0%	$0	$0	$0	0%	$0	0%	$6,000
1200	$8,000	$8,000	100%	$8,000	$7,000	$0	0%	$1,000	(12.5%)	$7,000
1300	$8,000	$0	0%	$0	$1,000	$0	0%	($1,000)	(100%)	$8,000
1400	$4,000	$2,000	25%	$1,000	$0	($1000)	(50%)	$1,000	100%	$4,000
Totals	**$88,000**	**$25,000**	**22.7%**	**$20,000**	**$19,500**	**($5,000)**	**(20%)**	**$500**	**2.5%**	**$88,500**

Table 7: Earned Value at Timenow 4

Revised Gantt Chart at Timenow 4: The revised Gantt chart and the earned value table, contain complementary information. When calculating the revised Gantt chart it is important to follow the activity logic through to completion (see network diagram figure 2).

Figure 5: Revised Gantt Chart at Timenow 4

Project Analysis at Timenow 4: The variance figures indicate that overall the project is late, but slightly under budget. The figures may be distorted, however, because activity 1300 costs have been reported, although there appears to be no progress. Similarly activity 300, progress is reported, but no costs. These are flags highlighting data that is conflicting and therefore needs to be checked.

Activity 400 is on the critical path and is 1 day late. The knock-on effect can be seen on the revised Gantt chart. If this activity were crashed by 1 day this would bring the schedule back on course. The activity is under budget so there should be funds to cover any additional expenditure.

Activity Number	Actual Costs	Actual Start	Actual Finish	Percentage Complete	Remaining Duration
100	$11,000	3 May	6 May	100%	-
200	$2,000	7 May	8 May	100%	-
300	$2,000	1 May	2 May	100%	-
400	$11,500	4 May	6 May	100%	-
500	$7,000	7 May	(crash)	50%	2
600	$4,000	7 May	-	66.6%	-
700	$2,500	8 May	-	50%	-
800	$0	-	-	-	-
900	$0	-	-	-	-
1000	$1,500	8 May	-	50%	-
1100	$0	-	-	-	-
1200	$7,000	2 May	3 May	100%	-
1300	$3000	8 May	-	25%	-
1400	$3,500	4 May	7 May	100%	-

Table 8: Data Capture at Timenow 8 (the project has now progressed to timenow 8)

Activity	BAC	BCWS	PC	BCWP	ACWP	SV	SV%	CV	CV%	EAC
100	$9,000	$9,000	100%	$9,000	$11,000	$0	0%	($2,000)	(22.2%)	$11,000
200	$2,000	$2,000	100%	$2,000	$2,000	$0	0%	$0	0%	$2,000
300	$1,000	$1,000	100%	$1,000	$2,000	$0	0%	($1,000)	(100%)	$2,000
400	$12,000	$12,000	100%	$12,000	$11,500	$0	0%	$500	(4.2%)	$11,500
500	$10,000	$6,000	50%	$5,000	$7,000	($1,000)	(16.6%)	($2,000)	(40%)	$14,000
600	$6,000	$6,000	66.6%	$4,000	$4,000	($2,000)	(33.3%)	$0	0%	$6,000
700	$4,000	$4,000	50%	$2,000	$2,500	($2,000)	(50%)	($500)	(25%)	$5,000
800	$6,000	$0	0%	$0	$0	$0	0%	$0	0%	$6,000
900	$8,000	$0	0%	$0	$0	$0	0%	$0	0%	$8,000
1000	$4,000	$2,000	50%	$2,000	$1,500	$0	0%	$500	25%	$3,000
1100	$6,000	$0	0%	$0	$0	$0	0%	$0	0%	$6,000
1200	$8,000	$8,000	100%	$8,000	$7,000	$0	0%	$1,000	(12.5%)	$7,000
1300	$8,000	$4,000	25%	$2,000	$3,000	($2,000)	(50%)	($1,000)	(50%)	$12,000
1400	$4,000	$4,000	100%	$4,000	$3,500	$0	0%	$500	12.5%	$13,500
Totals	$88,000	$58,000	58%	$51,000	$55,500	($7,000)	(12%)	($4,000)	(7.8%)	$97,000

Table 9: Earned Value at Timenow 8

Figure 6: Revised Gantt Chart at Timenow 8

Project Analysis at Timenow 8: From the schedule and cost variances, overall the project is still late, but now the budget is over spent. The trends indicate SV% improving from (20%) to (12%), but CV% deteriorating from 2.5% to (7.8%). This is flag to check productivity on activities 100, 500, 700 and 1300. They are either under performing, the estimate was too optimistic, or there are special circumstances.

Although the SV is negative the revised Gantt chart indicates that the project will finish on time. The discrepancy is caused by activities with float running late. The negative cost variance indicates a need to apply control on activities 500, 700 and 1300, to bring the project in on budget.

Abbreviations

ACWP: Actual Cost of Work Performed
AOA: Activity-on-Arrow
AON: Activity-on-Node
APM: Association of Project Managers
AV: Actual Value
BAC: Budget at Completion
BCWP: Budgeted Cost of Work Performed
BCWS: Budgeted Cost of Work Scheduled
BOK: Body of Knowledge
BOM: Bill of Materials
BOOT: Build Own Operate Transfer
BOT: Build Operate Transfer
CIF: Cost Insurance Freight
COD: Cash on Delivery
CPI: Cost Price Index
CPM: Critical Path Method
CV: Cost Variance
DCF: Discounted Cashflow
DDP: Delivered Duty Paid
DoD: Dept of Defence
EAC: Estimate-at-Competition
EV: Earned Value
FF: Finish-to-Finish
FIFO: First In First Out
FOB: Free on Board
FRI: Forecast Rate of Invoicing
FS: Finish-to-Start
IPMA: International Project Management Association
IRR: Internal Rate of Return
JIT: Just-in-Time
LIFO: Last In First Out

MBE: Management by Exception
MBO: Management by Objectives
MRP: Material Requirement Planning
NCR: Non Conformance Report
NPV: Net Present Value
OBS: Organisation Breakdown Structure
PC: Percentage Complete
PDM: Precedence Diagram Method
PERT: Project Evaluation and Review Technique
PMBOK: Project Management Body of Knowledge
PMI: Project Management Institute
PMP: Project Management Professional
PV: Planned Value
QCP: Quality Control Plan
ROI: Return on Investment
ROT: Refurbish Operate Transfer
SF: Start-to-Finish
SPI: Schedule Performance Index
SS: Start-to-Start
SV: Schedule Variance
TQM: Total Quality Management
WBS: Work Breakdown Structure

Bibliography

Adair, John, *Action-Centred Leadership*, Pan, 1989
AS/NZS 4360:1995., *Risk Management*
Association of Project Managers (APM)., *Body of Knowledge (BOK)*

Begg, D., *Economics*, McGraw-Hill, 1997
Belbin, M., *Management Teams,* Butterworth-Heinemann, 1996
Benedetto, R., *Matrix Management Theory in Practice*, Kendall Hunt
Bentley, C., *Configuration Management Within Prince*, 1993
BS 5750 (1979), *Quality Management*
Burke, Rory, *Entrepreneurs Toolkit*, Burke Publishing, 2006
Burke, Rory, *Small Business, Entrepreneur,* Burke Publishing, 2006
Burleson, C., *Effective Meetings*, Wiley

Carnall, C., *Managing Change*, Prentice-Hall, 1990
Chapman, C., and **Ward**, Stephen, *Project Risk Management: Processes, Techniques and Insights*, Wiley, 1996
Charland, T., *Advanced Project Management Techniques Handbook*, 1990
Clark, C., *Brainstorming*, Wilshire
Cleland, D., *Project Management Field Guide*, Van Nostrand Reinhold, 1997
Crosby, P.B., *Quality is Free*, McGraw-Hill, 1987
Crosby, P.B., *Quality Without Tears*, McGraw-Hill, 1995

Davidson Frame, J., *The Project Office (Best Management Practices)*, Crisp, 1998
Dinsmore, P., *Human Factors in Project Management*, Amacom

Fewings, Peter, *Construction Project Management,* Taylor & Francis
Field, M., and **Keller,** L., *Project Management*, Thomson
Frank, M., *How to Run a Successful Meeting in Half the Time*, Corgi
Frigenti, Enzo, and **Comninos**, D., *The Practice of Project Management: a guide to the business - focused approach*, Kogan Page, 2002.

Gido, J., and **Clements**, J., *Successful Project Management*, South Western College Pub, 1999
Gray, C., and **Larson**, E., *Project Management (the Managerial Process)*, McGraw-Hill Irwin

Haynes, Marion, *Project Management (Fifty Minute Book)*, Elaine Fritz, 1997

Jones, Peter, *Handbook of Team Design: A Practitioner's Guide to Team Systems Development*, McGraw-Hill, 1997

Kerzner, H., *Project Management A Systems Approach to Planning, Scheduling and Controlling*, Van Nostrand Reinhold, 1997
Kimbler, D., and **William**, Ferrell, *TQM-Based Project Planning*, 1997

Lewis, James, *Project Planning, Scheduling & Control: A Hands-On Guide to Bringing Projects in on Time and on Budget*, McGraw-Hill, 1995
Lock, D., *Project Management*, Gower, 1996
Lockyer, Keith, *Production Management*, Financial Times Pitman, 1992
Lockyer, Keith, and **Gordon**, James, *Project Management and Project Network Techniques*, Financial Times Pitman, 1996
Lysons, C., *Purchasing*, Financial Times Pitman, 1998

Meredith, J., and **Samuel**, J., *Project Management A Managerial Approach*, Wiley, 1995
Morris, Peter, *The Anatomy of Projects*, Thomas Telford, 1997
Morris, Peter, *The Management of Projects*, Thomas Telford, 1994

Obeng, Eddie, *All Change: Project Manager's Secret Handbook*, Financial Times Management, 1996
O'Connell, Fergus, *How to Run Successful Projects II: The Silver Bullet*, Prentice Hall, 1996
Oosthuizen, Pieter, *Goodbye MBA*, International Thomson, 1998

Pennypacker, James, *Project Management Forms*, Cambridge University Press, 1997
Pokras, Sandy, *Rapid Team Deployment: Building High-Performance Project Teams (Fifty-Minute Series)*, 1995
Project Management Institute (PMI)., *A Guide to the Project Management Body of Knowledge (PMBOK)*, 1996

Raftery, John, *Risk Analysis in Project Management*, Routledge, 1993
Rosenau, M., *Successful Project Management*, Van Nostrand Reinhold, 1998

Schuyler, John, *Decision Analysis in Projects*, Cambridge University Press, 1996
Stuckenbruck, L., *The Implementation of Project Management: The Professional Handbook*, PMI

Turner, R., *Handbook of Project-Based Management*, McGraw-Hill, 1993

Walker, Anthony, *Project Management in Construction*, Blackwell Science, 1996
Westney, Richard, *Computerized Management of Multiple Small Projects*, Marcel Dekker
Wideman, *A Framework for Project and Program Management Integration*, PMBOK Handbook Series - volume 1, 1991

Van Der Waldt, Andre, *Project Management For Strategic Change and Upliftment*, International Thomson, 1998

Index

This bluewater trilogy by Rory and Sandra Burke includes a preparation guide, a travelogue and a checklist. Bluewater cruising has all the features of a complex project, requiring effective budgeting, procurement, scope management and time planning. Most importantly it requires effective risk management and disaster recovery for the safety of the crew and integrity of the yacht.

Managing Your Bluewater Cruise

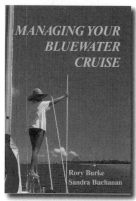

ISBN: 0-473-03822-6

352 pages, 200+ photographs, UK: £9.95

This preparation guide discusses a range of pertinent issues from establishing budgets and buying equipment to preventative maintenance and heavy weather sailing. The text works closely with the ORC category 1 requirements and includes many comments from other cruisers who are *'out there doing it'*. This book also outlines what training courses to attend before leaving, what gear to take, provisioning strategy and, equally important, how to stow it all. If you wish to bridge the gap between fantasy and reality then your bluewater cruise must be effectively managed.

Greenwich to the Dateline

ISBN: 0-620-16557-x

352 pages, 200+ photographs, UK: £9.95

This is a travelogue of our bluewater cruising adventure from the Greenwich Meridian to the International Dateline – sit back with a sundowner and be inspired to cruise to the Caribbean and Pacific islands. In this catalogue of rewarding experiences we describe how we converted our travelling dreams into a bluewater cruising reality.

Bluewater Checklist

ISBN: 0-9582 391-0-x

96 pages, UK: £4.95

Checklists provide an effective management tool to confirm everything is on board, and all tasks are completed. Why try to remember everything in your head when checklists never forget!!! This book provides a comprehensive portfolio of checklists covering every aspect of bluewater cruising. To ensure your bluewater cruise will be successful, it must be effectively managed. Checklists provide an excellent tool for this purpose - even NASA uses them!!!

This *Fashion Design Series* by *Sandra Burke* promotes fashion design skills and techniques which can be effectively applied in the world of fashion. In a competitive market it is important to produce designs that are not only stylish and pleasing to the eye, but also commercially viable.

Fashion Artist - *Drawing Techniques to Portfolio Presentation*
ISBN 0-9582 391-7-7, Sandra Burke

Fashion drawing is an essential part of the fashion designer's portfolio of skills, enabling them to develop ideas and visually communicate design concepts on paper. This book is set out as a self-learning programme to teach you how to draw fashion figures and clothing, and present them in a portfolio. The text is supported with explanatory drawings and photographs.

Fashion Computing – *Design Techniques and CAD*
ISBN 0-9582 391-3-4, Sandra Burke

This book introduces you to the computer drawing and design skills used by the fashion industry. Through visuals and easy steps, you learn creative fashion computing design techniques. It includes, flats/working drawings, illustrations, fabrics, presentation and the digital fashion portfolio. Specific software includes: Photoshop, Illustrator, CorelDRAW, Freehand, PowerPoint, Gerber and Lectra Systems.

Fashion Designer – *Design Techniques, Catwalk to Street*
ISBN 0-9582 391-2-6, Sandra Burke

This book will help you develop your portfolio of fashion design skills while guiding you through the fashion design process in today's fashion industry. It explains how to analyse and forecast fashion trends, interpret a design brief, choose fabrics and colour ways, develop designs, create design presentations and develop collections for specific target markets.

Fashion Entrepreneur
ISBN 0-9582 733-0-8, Sandra Burke

With your head buzzing with innovative and creative ideas – welcome to the Fashion Entrepreneurs' world of glamour, style and wealth. This book outlines the traits and techniques fashion designers use to spot opportunities and set up small businesses. These topics include: writing business plans, raising finance, sales and marketing, and the small business management skills required to run a fashion companies on a day-to-day basis.

Project Management - *Planning and Control Techniques (5ed)*
Rory Burke
ISBN 0-9582 733-1-6
384 pages

PM 5ed presents the latest planning and control techniques, particularly those used by the project management software and the body of knowledge (APM bok and PMI's PMBOK). This book has established itself internationally as the standard text for Project Management programs.

Introduction to Project Management
Rory Burke
ISBN: 0-9582 733-3-2
288 pages

This book is a broad based introduction to the field of Project Management which explains all the special planning and control techniques needed to manage projects successfully. This book is ideal for managers entering project management and team members in the project management office (PMO).

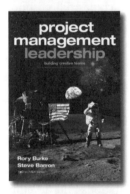

Project Management Leadership - *building creative teams*
Rory Burke and Steve Baron
ISBN 0-9582 733-5-9
384 pages

This book is a comprehensive guide outlining the essential leadership skills to manage the human side of managing projects. Key topics include: leadership styles, delegation, motivation, negotiation, conflict resolution, and team building.

Project Management Entrepreneur - *creating new ventures*
Rory Burke
ISBN 0-9582 733-2-4
384 pages

This is the first book to integrate the three management skills of Entrepreneurship, Project Management, and Small Business Management. Entrepreneur skills are required to spot opportunities, project management skills are required to implement the new venture and small business management skills are required to run the business on a day-to-day basis.

German translation of:

Project Management - *Planning and Control Techniques*
Rory Burke
ISBN: 3-8266-1443-7

Project management techniques are perfect for a country renowned for its precise time keeping and production quality.

Greek translation of:

Project Management - *Planning and Control Techniques*
Rory Burke
ISBN: 960-218-289-X

The 2004 Olympic Games clearly showed how project management techniques can be used to control an event to meet a fixed end date.

Chinese translation of:

Project Management - *Planning and Control Techniques*
Rory Burke
ISBN: 0-471-98762-X

With the boom in demand for Chinese manufacturing, so there is an associated boom in Chinese infrastructure projects and the need for project management techniques.

Cosmic MBA Series

Entrepreneurs Toolkit

Rory Burke
ISBN: 0-9582 391-4-2
160 pages

Entrepreneurs Toolkit is a comprehensive guide outlining the essential entrepreneur skills to spot a marketable opportunity, the essential business skills to start a new venture and the essential management skills to make-it-happen.

Small Business Entrepreneur

Rory Burke
ISBN: 0-9582 391-6-9
160 pages

Small Business Entrepreneur is a comprehensive guide outlining the essential management skills to run a small business on a day-to-day basis. This includes developing a business plan and sources of finance.

BBC interview

Rory Burke was educated at Wicklow and Oswestry. He has an MSc in Project Management (Henley) and degrees in Naval Architecture (Southampton) and Computer Aided Engineering (Coventry). After working internationally on marine and offshore projects, Rory set-up a publishing business to strike a work-life balance between sailing and writing. Rory is a visiting lecturer to universities in Britain, America, Canada, HK, New Zealand, Australia and South Africa.